the little

MW01089619

Quicken

For Windows 3.1 and Windows 95

BOOK

Lawrence J Magid and Louis G. Fortis

Illustrated by John Grimes

 Peachpit Press

The Little Quicken Book
Lawrence J. Magid and Louis G. Fortis

Peachpit Press
2414 Sixth Street
Berkeley, CA 94710
800/283-9444
510/548-4393
510/548-5991 (fax)

Find us on the World Wide Web at: **http://www.peachpit.com**

Peachpit Press is a division of Addison Wesley Longman

Copyright © 1996 Lawrence J. Magid and Louis G. Fortis
Illustrations copyright © 1996 John Grimes

Editor: Nolan Hester
Cover design: **TMA** Ted Mader Associates
Cover illustration: John Grimes
Interior design: David Van Ness
Copy editor: Liz Sizensky

Notice of Rights
All rights reserved. No part of this book may be reproduced or transmitted in
any form by any means, electronic, mechanical, photocopying, recording, or
otherwise, without the prior written permission of the publisher. For information on getting permission for reprints and excerpts, contact Trish Booth at
Peachpit Press.

Notice of Liability
The information in this book is distributed on an "As Is" basis, without warranty. While every precaution has been taken in the preparation of the book,
neither the author nor Peachpit Press shall have any liability to any person or
entity with respect to any loss or damage caused or alleged to be caused
directly or indirectly by the instructions contained in this book or by the computer software and hardware products described in it.

ISBN 1-56609-185-3

9 8 7 6 5 4 3 2 1

Printed and bound in the United States of America
♻ Printed on recycled paper

Acknowledgments

Writing a book is hardly ever a one-person task. To begin with, it requires the support of one's family. My family—Patti, Katherine, and William deserve plenty of credit for all they do for me on a daily basis. But there are also those who helped directly in the preparation of the manuscript. Jon Angel, a very talented writer, researcher, and editor, did an incredible job helping to shape and re-shape many of the chapters. Likewise for David Plotkin, a freelance writer and Quicken meister par excellance who helped me with the drafting of several chapters.

Nancy Olson, my office assistant, kept me on schedule throughout the process. The staff at Peachpit Press—especially editor Nolan Hester and founder Ted Nace—are great friends to any author who is fortunate enough to write for that fine company. Peachpit is also publisher of both the first and second editions of another of my books, *The Little PC Book.*

Intuit, the publisher of Quicken provided me with preliminary and final copies of the software at all stages of development and answers to all of my questions. Intuit, however, has no financial interest in this book nor do I have any financial interest in Intuit. I am impressed with Quicken as a product but I do not necessarily endorse it over others. This is a highly competitive field and there are other excellent products and companies in the financial management arena. Thanks to the staff of the Palo Alto, California, office of Union Bank for helping me set up a home banking account early in the game. They provided me with all the help I needed though, sadly, I had to fund the account with my own money.

I would also like to thank my brother, Sandy Magid, a San Rafael, California, certified public accountant and finance guru who gave me lots of advice about bookkeeping, taxes, and what to expect—and not expect—from a personal finance program.

Finally, thanks to my longtime friend and co-author Louis Fortis. An economist, former state legislator, and successful business person, Louis's practical advice and economic analysis helped elevate this book from a primer on Quicken to a manual on how to manage your financial affairs.

Lawrence J. Magid
Palo Alto, California
e-mail: Magid@latimes.com
web site: http://www.larrysworld.com

I would like to thank Judith Kelly who very patiently worked with me editing my work. I would also like thank my good friend Larry Magid, whom I've enjoyed working with on numerous projects over the past 20 years.

Louis G. Fortis
Madison, Wisconsin

Table of Contents

Part I/Understanding Quicken

Part 2/Unraveling the Money Mystery: A Quick Guide to Personal Finance

Understanding Quicken

one

How Quicken Changed My Life

Me Manage Money?

Anyone who knew me as a child will laugh when they discover that I've written a book on personal finances. My brother, Sandy, is the one who became a CPA. I was the kid who went off to Berkeley to raise hell and, later, get a doctorate in education. I spent most of my twenties more concerned with social issues and relationships than with my personal wealth.

Balance a checkbook? Who needs it? As long as there were checks still left in my checkbook, I assumed that there was money in the bank. Just kidding—but I certainly didn't spend much time worrying about money.

Yet I'm now qualified to write about personal finances because, over the years, I've managed to turn things around. It didn't take getting an MBA. It just took some harsh reality, a commitment to planning for the future, and a copy of Quicken for Windows.

Something started happening in 1981. I got married and, three years later, my first child, Katherine, was born. Suddenly, I needed life insurance, a college fund, and a home mortgage. I also came to the realization that I wasn't going to be young forever. Poverty and old age can be a brutal combination. It was time to start doing something about my personal finances.

Don't think I've become a financial information junkie. I'm not one of these people who keeps track of every penny he spends. If you're like me—financially responsible but not fanatical—then this book is for you.

Fortunately, something else happened in the early 1980s: personal computers. These miniaturized versions of computing devices, once available only to large corporations, banks, insurance companies, and big institutions, were now available to the masses. And I was one of the first to get one. I bought my first personal computer, an Apple II, in 1980, and replaced it in 1982 with my first IBM PC.

At that time, there were no personal financial management programs. But there was VisiCalc, an early spreadsheet program. I grabbed a copy of VisiCalc and started using it to keep track of my money. It was unsophisticated, compared to today's Quicken, but it did give me a vague idea of how much I had in the bank and where the money was going. Come to think of it, I wasn't all that sophisticated, either. There were times when I didn't want to know where I stood financially.

Don't think I've become a financial information junkie. I'm not one of these people who keeps track of every penny he spends. I can live without documenting that $1.25 I spent for a cup of coffee or the $1.50 for a frozen yogurt. I don't really need to know exactly how many quarters I gave my kids to spend at the video arcade, and it isn't even all that important to me to know exactly how much I spend on entertainment or non-business-related dining. Some people like to track all of these expenses, and I applaud that. But I'm not so exact. What I do want, however, is a rough idea of how much money and other assets I have, an exact accounting of what I owe and what is owed to me, and an exact accounting of my business and other tax-related expenses and income. Quicken lets me have all of that and more. If you're like me—financially responsible but not fanatical—then this book is for you. I'm not going to preach or insist that you adhere to any doctrine. Of course, if you want to become an information junkie, Quicken has all the tools you need, and this book will be as good a starting place as any. Be my guest.

Financial Empowerment

This isn't just a book about Quicken. It's about financial empowerment. My message may no longer be as radical as the picket signs I carried when I was a college student at Berkeley, but that old slogan, "Power to the People," certainly does apply when it comes to taking control of your finances. Quicken can empower you to become a master of your personal finances rather than a slave to your bank, your creditors, and all the other people who are more than happy to stick their hands in your pocket.

I'm not going to lie to you: Quicken hasn't turned me into a millionaire. It hasn't guaranteed me financial security or a prosperous retirement, and it hasn't actually made me any money. But it has helped me manage the money that I do have, and it's made it a lot easier for me to put money aside for the future. Thanks, in part, to Quicken, I have no short-term debt, a clean credit rating, a good start on a retirement account, and some money put aside for my children's education.

Quicken didn't make any of this happen by itself. My wife and I get some of the credit. But, as a personal financial management tool, Quicken has helped us make the necessary moves to protect our financial future and our current financial state of health. Brisk sales of my first Peachpit Press book, *The Little PC Book*, didn't hurt either.

You can learn all you want about Quicken, but, for my family, the secret is simple: We use Quicken to keep a running tally of how we're doing—sort of like a daily financial checkup. More importantly, we use it to move money where it will, ultimately, do us the most good—in savings and investment accounts. Like most Quicken owners, I use the product to pay my bills. But, in addition to paying the doctor, the mortgage, the cable TV company, and all the other necessities and luxuries of life, I use Quicken, each month and whenever some extra money comes along, to transfer money from my checking account into one of my savings or investment accounts. It's never very much money at any given time—but it's starting to add up.

Automatic Bill Paying

Another great thing about Quicken is the way it automates bill paying. My wife and I used to play Russian roulette with our credit card bills. We didn't want to pay them too early because we'd lose some of the interest the bank pays us for our money. But, if we waited too long, we ran the risk of missing the due date and having to pay a late fee and an extra interest charge, and, worst of all, risking a ding on our credit rating. We've never avoided our bills, but, when we bought a house 15 years ago, we noticed that there were a few "late payments" on our credit report. When we financed our new house last year, we had a squeaky clean report. It's not that we have any more money or are any more responsible, it's just that we use Quicken, and CheckFree, to "pay" our bills the day we get them. Does this mean we lose "float" on our money? Not at all. You can use Quicken to program CheckFree to pay a bill up to a year in advance. So, we might process the payment on one day but not have it sent and deducted from our account until the day it's due. I'll have lots more to say about this in Chapter 15.

Moving Money Is Easy

Quicken has a lot of neat features. My favorite, however, is electronic banking. Quicken 5 users can sign up with one of more than 20 banks for online banking and bill paying. Participating institutions include Chase Manhattan, Chemical Bank, Smith Barney, and American Express. You'll pay about 40 cents per transaction to bank electronically using your computer, modem, and Quicken 5.

I'm now using online banking to pay bills and check my balances and I'm hooked. I no longer have to write or even "print" my checks. I just enter the information into Quicken and let my modem send the information to my bank. Three or four days later the check, on an electronic funds transfer, arrives at its destination. I can also check balances and electronically reconcile my account. As a result I always know exactly what I have in my account.

Electronic banking is new to Quicken 5 but, for years, I was using CheckFree, a bill paying service that's still available to Quicken users. It, along with a service offered by Intuit (Quicken may be cheap, but Intuit has all sorts of other ways to get your money), allow you to pay bills electronically even if your bank doesn't offer online banking. The major difference between these services and electronic banking is that you can only use it to pay bills. You can't get your balance, reconcile your account automatically or transfer funds between accounts at your bank. You can, however, use CheckFree, Intuit's bill paying service or online banking to "write checks" to yourself. At least once a month I use the service to write a check to the brokerage that handles my mutual funds. Although I have a long way to go before I can retire or even pay my kids' college tuition, I am building equity one payment a time. I'm not saying you need an electronic banking service or CheckFree to fund your savings and investment accounts but anything that makes it easier means that you're more likely to move money in the right direction.

Keeping Track of Investments

I'm hardly a Wall Street tycoon but I do have some mutual funds and a handful of individual stocks. Each month I get tons of paper from the investment firms, telling me how much I've earned (or lost) and whether they've paid any dividends. That information can be mind-boggling, especially if you're dealing with more than one firm. Some months—I admit it—I just stick those forms in a drawer. Whenever I get the time, though, I meticulously enter them into Quicken so I can keep track of how I'm doing. Unfortunately, I haven't been doing all that well lately: As good as it is, Quicken can't select stocks for you or predict how they'll do.

Planning and Budgeting

Figuring out what to spend used to be easy. If I had money in my pocket, I could "afford" whatever I wanted. Now, life isn't that simple. Regardless of how much cash we have on hand, few of us can afford to spend as if there were no tomorrow. I can't claim that I always stay within my budget, but having a budget—even if I stray from it—is better than having no spending plan at all.

Keeping Track of Credit Card Spending

If you're the type of person who just isn't able to pay off your credit card bills each month, then you might want to avoid using plastic altogether. But, if you can make timely payments and avoid having to pay interest, credit cards can actually work in your favor. For one thing, every time you buy something with a credit card, you get a written record of the transaction.

Quicken gives you something even better. A number of banks and credit card companies now link their credit cards to Quicken. With this service you get two statements. One comes on paper and the other arrives via modem. I get my statements by modem, so, each month, all of my Visa and American Express transactions are automatically entered into my Quicken credit card register. This not only saves me time, but also guarantees that I won't fail to record any transactions. As a self-employed person, I find that extremely important. I use my Quicken credit card for all my business-related expenses and, thanks to the credit card statement's link to Quicken, I never have to worry about forgetting to record a tax-deductible expense. Because of the automatic way the data is entered, I capture expenses that I might not otherwise write down. Those little $5 and $10 expenses can add up, and, at the end of the year, they help lower the amount I owe to Uncle Sam. I'll have lots more to say about this in Chapter 18.

Keeping Track of Cash

As you'll see in Chapter 8, Quicken lets you set up lots of different types of accounts, including "cash" accounts. I'm not one of those people who keep track of every penny in their pockets, but I do like to keep track of all my assets and, for tax purposes, all my tax-deductible spending. Not everything I spend is by check or credit card. The taxi I take on business, the quarters I put into a pay phone for a business call, or that computer magazine I buy to help me with an article I'm writing are all tax-deductible expenses, so I record them in a Quicken cash account. At the end of the year, these cash transactions get included in my Quicken financial report and, therefore, help me reduce my tax liability.

What Quicken Isn't

Quicken can't solve all of your problems. It won't get you out of debt or put money into your pocket. It won't give you more sex appeal—though people who can control their money are more desirable as mates—and it won't assure you a college education for your children or a secure retirement. With or without Quicken, it's still up to you to save and spend wisely.

Quicken can help you estimate your federal taxes, but it won't do your tax return. You can, however, use Quicken data files with TaxCut, TurboTax, and other leading tax preparation programs. Or you can use Quicken to create a printed report to give to a professional tax preparer.

Now that you know my philosophy about Quicken for Windows, and what Quicken can do for you, I'll go over the basics of how you can use Quicken 5. In the next chapter, you'll learn how to install the Quicken software for either Windows 3.1 or Windows 95.

Getting Started

2

Different Packages for Different Folks

This book is about Quicken 5 for Windows, the latest version as of the publication date. The basic Quicken program is available only on floppy disks. Quicken Deluxe, which includes a number of additional features, comes either on floppies or on a CD-ROM. On floppies, the Deluxe version adds features such as Quicken Investor Insight, Quicken Home Inventory, and a Financial Address Book. On CD-ROM, it includes all the above plus two multimedia-based components, Finance 101 and Ask the Experts (featuring Jane Bryant Quinn and Marshall Loeb).

My installation instructions (see the "Installing Quicken" section on page 13) detail how to install either Quicken for Windows or Quicken Deluxe for Windows. The main part of this book covers the basic Quicken for Windows, but features specific to Quicken Deluxe for Windows are covered in Chapters 14 and 19.

If you have an earlier version of Quicken, some items discussed in this book may look or work differently, and certain features may be missing. Intuit has a habit of upgrading Quicken on an annual basis.

(You may find the resulting plethora of version numbers confusing, too: the Macintosh Quicken is now in Version 6, as is DOS Quicken.)

These upgrades have added features, smoothed out the rough edges, and generally improved the product. Of course, Intuit isn't doing this out of the goodness of its heart. You'll have to pay if you want to play with the new version (see the "Buying Quicken for Windows" section on page 10). Even if you still have an earlier version, however, you'll find this book useful; Quicken's concepts and basic mode of operation have remained helpfully unchanged.

Hardware Requirements

As software has become easier and more sophisticated, it has also grown more portly—just like many of us on the wrong side of 30. By today's standards, Quicken is by no means a glutton. However, an average installation will consume about 14MB of your hard disk space, or 36MB if you purchase Quicken Deluxe. This, then, is probably a good time to do some hard disk housekeeping, deleting or archiving files you no longer need—or buying an additional hard drive if you have to.

Intuit says that Quicken will run on a 386 system with 4MB of RAM, or 8MB for Quicken Deluxe. As with other Windows software, these claims should be viewed a little like the EPA fuel economy ratings. However, Quicken itself is not an inherently taxing program (except for Deluxe's multimedia functions); if you're satisfied with your computer's Windows performance now, you'll probably be content with it under Quicken, too.

Unlike many new Windows programs, Quicken is designed to work under Windows 3.x *and* Windows 95. Better still, it operates almost exactly the same in each environment. For the most part, I'm assuming that you have made, or will make, the move to Windows 95. The instructions on how to install Quicken illustrate the process for both Windows 3.1 and Windows 95. Later in the book, though, all the screens and descriptions you'll see derive from Windows 95. They should apply equally well to Windows 3.1, but your mileage may vary.

There's no law that says you have to buy the upgrade. If your needs are being met by your current version, you can just stay with what you have. (Quicken Version 4 runs fine under Windows 95.) Before buying an upgrade, it's best to check out the new features. The magazine index at your local library will uncover many reviews of the latest Quicken.

Buying Quicken for Windows

As with most other types of software, Quicken for Windows is available from quite a variety of sources, including:

- Computer software stores (Egghead, Babbages, etc.)
- Mail-order firms
- Intuit (direct purchase)

If you are a registered user of Quicken, you've probably already been notified about the upgrade. This notification includes the opportunity to order the upgrade directly from Intuit at a discounted price. With this discount, the price of the upgrade is competitive with computer stores, but you can still usually do a little better in the stores than by buying directly from Intuit. However, if you are in a big hurry to get your hands on the new software, you may get it more quickly if you take advantage of purchasing it directly from Intuit.

The local computer store may let you check out the newest version of Quicken. Many software and computer stores have Quicken already installed on one of their machines, and the salespeople may be able to demonstrate it for you. Additionally, most software stores will allow you to return Quicken for an exchange in the admittedly rare event that one or more of the installation disks is defective.

If you just want the lowest possible price for your copy of Quicken, mail order might be the way to go. In the pages of just about any computer periodical, you can find half a dozen firms that sell Quicken. There are some things to keep in mind when buying by mail order. First of all, there is necessarily a delay in receiving your software, since the mail-order firm has to process the order and ship the software to you. This delay can be as little as 1 to 2 days (but you will probably have to pay extra for overnight shipping, potentially wiping out any savings) to 10 to 12 days if the package is out of stock. Don't assume that the mail-order firm will let you know if Quicken is back-ordered!

Although most mail-order firms will replace a defective package, you must send the old package back to them at your expense and wait for the replacement package to arrive. If you need to start using

Quicken right away, this is probably not the way to go. Also, use a credit card when purchasing by mail order, as the credit card company will often step in to resolve disputes.

Be Sure You Have the Latest Version

When purchasing Quicken, make sure you're getting Version 5 by checking the box at the software store or discussing the matter with the telephone representative at the mail-order firm. Although it is unlikely that you will get an earlier version, a few firms do sell heavily discounted "old-version" software packages. It would be easy for you to snap up what seems like a bargain, only to be disappointed when you check the fine print.

Before You Install

Before you can use Quicken for Windows, you must install it on your hard drive. This step is necessary even if you have purchased a CD-ROM version of the program, since it can't run directly from that drive. Installing Quicken for Windows copies the necessary files onto your hard drive, optionally creates a Start Menu entry or Program Manager group, and modifies certain other files on your hard drive to allow Quicken for Windows to run properly.

Backing Up Your Current Files

If you have been using a previous version of Quicken (either Windows or DOS), back up your existing Quicken data files prior to installing the new version of Quicken. This is always a good safety measure, despite the fact that Intuit's installation program does not deliberately overwrite any of your old data.

If you have been using a previous version of Quicken back up your existing Quicken data files prior to installing the new version.

With Quicken 5, backing up is particularly important because this program version uses a new file format. When you give it permission, it will convert your data into a format that only Quicken 5 can read. In the rather unlikely event that you want to switch back to Quicken 4—perhaps because you think Version 5 is too slow on your machine—you'll want to have a copy of your data in the old format.

Quicken stores your data in multiple disk files, making it difficult to back them up manually. Fortunately, its File menu has a Backup command you can use to copy everything into a safekeeping subdirectory of your choice. Use it before you exit Quicken 4 for the last time.

Some virus protection programs may interfere with the Quicken installation program, so turn off any virus protection programs. In fact, it's always good practice to shut down other Windows programs (Word, Excel, and the like) when you install a new application. This frees up memory, prevents any competition for computing resources, and allows the installation program to update files that may be shared with other programs.

Prior to installing Quicken for Windows, it is a good idea to back up your AUTOEXEC.BAT file, as Quicken for Windows will modify this file if you choose to run the Billminder program when you start up your computer. Billminder (covered in Chapter 9) automatically reminds you when bills are due.

Note: *If you are installing Quicken 5 under Windows 95, you can skip the following steps and go directly to the relevant section on page 19 or 22.*

To back up your AUTOEXEC.BAT file, use the following steps:

From MS-DOS
1. Get to the DOS prompt. If you are in Windows, you can either exit completely, or click on the MS-DOS icon in the Main group of Program Manager.

2. Ensure that you are at the root directory of your "boot-up" drive. For most people, this is their C drive. To reach the root directory of your C drive from the DOS prompt, type **C:** at the DOS prompt to switch to the C drive, then type **CD** to switch to the root directory. If your boot drive is not your C drive, substitute the drive letter of your boot drive.

3. Type the command **COPY AUTOEXEC.BAT AUTOEXEC.BAK**. This copies the AUTOEXEC.BAT file to a file named AUTOEXEC.BAK. If you later need to restore the file, you can type **COPY AUTOEXEC.BAK AUTOEXEC.BAT**.

Note: Changes to your AUTOEXEC.BAT file do not take effect until you reboot your computer. Thus, if you need to copy your AUTOEXEC.BAK file back to the AUTOEXEC.BAT file as detailed in Step 3 above, you must reboot your computer to enable the changes to take effect.

From the Windows File Manager

1. Click on the File Manager icon in the Program Manager.

2. When File Manager comes up, click on the top line of the display (C:\).

3. Go to the File Manager's View menu and select Tree and Directory as well as Sort by Name.

4. Scroll through the list of files and directories until you see AUTOEXEC.BAT. Click it once to highlight it.

5. Select Copy from the File Manager's File Menu and enter AUTOEXEC.BAT. Select OK and you will have a copy of the file.

Installing Quicken

Installing Quicken or Quicken Deluxe using Windows 3.1 From Floppy Disks

To install Quicken or Quicken Deluxe for Windows from floppy disks, use the following steps:

1. If Windows is not already running, start Windows by typing **WIN** at the DOS command prompt.

2. Insert the Quicken for Windows Install Disk 1 in your computer's floppy disk drive (either drive A or drive B).

3. If Program Manager is not already open on the desktop, double-click on the Program Manager icon. The Program Manager will open and display a window in which there are program group icons.

4. From the Program Manager's File menu, choose Run. The Run dialog box will open on the screen.

5. Click the Command Line text box in the Run dialog box. Then type **a:setup** (if you placed the Install Disk 1 in drive A) or **b:setup** (if you placed the Install Disk 1 in drive B).

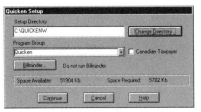

The Quicken for Windows Setup screen helps you install the program.

6. Click OK to begin the installation process. The Run dialog box will close and the Quicken Setup screen will appear. If you are installing just Quicken for Windows, the screen will look like the one at left. The rest of the installation instructions in this section assume you are installing Quicken for Windows. If you are installing Quicken *Deluxe* for Windows, see the next section, "Installing Quicken Deluxe using Windows 3.1."

    Note: If you are satisfied with all the selections in the Quicken for Windows Setup, just click Continue to install the program. You don't need to use any of the instructions in the rest of this section.

The Select Destination Directory dialog box enables you to change the directory and drive where you are going to install Quicken for Windows.

7. The default drive and directory destination to install Quicken for Windows is displayed in the upper-left-hand corner of the Quicken Setup dialog box. To change the destination, click on the Change Directory button. The Select Destination Directory dialog box will open to set the drive and directory on which you want to install Quicken for Windows. If you wish to create a new directory, you can do so simply by typing in its name and path manually, as I have done in the screen you see. Click OK when you are done selecting a drive and directory, and you'll be returned to the previous screen.

8. The default program group in Program Manager for Quicken is displayed below the label "Program Group." You have the option to either create a new program group for Quicken in Program Manager, or add the Quicken icon to an existing program group. To change the program group where Quicken will appear, either accept the default name, enter a new one, or click on the down arrow to select one of your existing groups.

This window enables you to choose the name of a new program group or place Quicken's icon into an existing program group.

9. Billminder is one of Quicken's automatic ways to remind you about upcoming bills. You may run Billminder either when you first boot your computer, when you run Windows, or only when you run Quicken. The Billminder selection is displayed next to the button labeled "<u>B</u>illminder." To change the Billminder selection, click on the Billminder button or type Alt B. A window will appear. Click the option you want, then click OK.

> **Note:** *You can change the Billminder option later, but you will need to manually edit your AUTOEXEC.BAT file (to run Billminder automatically at boot-up) or your WIN.INI file (to run Billminder when you run Windows).*

This window enables you to choose the Billminder option you want.

10. If you live in Canada, click on the Canadian Taxpayer checkbox.

11. Click the Continue button to proceed to the next screen.

12. Quicken Deluxe now comes with an Internet Access package consisting of a customized version of Netscape Navigator and the Eudora Lite electronic mail program. You can access Intuit's area on the World Wide Web free of charge, thanks to a special arrangement with the nationwide Internet Service Provider Concentric Network Corporation. If

the setup program detects that you already have a copy of Netscape Navigator on your computer—two copies cannot coexist reliably on one machine—it warns you and avoids adding this component. You'll still get the free Web access via your existing browser.

This window informs you that your existing copy of Netscape Navigator will be used for communications.

13. If you do not have Netscape Navigator, Quicken will ask whether you want to

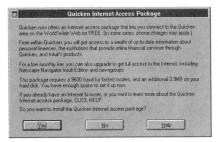

This window asks you if you want to install
Quicken's Internet Access package.

install the Internet Access package.

Note: If you don't install the Quicken Internet Access package now, you can do so later by rerunning the Quicken setup program.

14. Click on the Continue button (or type Alt N) to complete the installation process. Follow the instructions on the screen to switch disks when prompted. When you see the message that you installed Quicken successfully, click OK.

15. If you installed the Quicken Internet Access package, the program may ask you to restart your computer in order to load new drivers. However, if you do not plan to use this feature right away, you can tell Quicken that you will restart your computer later.

16. If your computer has a modem—and it is turned on—Quicken Deluxe asks if you would like to register the program electronically. If you answer yes, you can fill out an onscreen form via a special toll-free number. If you answer no, installation will proceed normally, but you'll have to fill out and mail in the Quicken registration card.

17. Remove the floppy disks and store them in a safe place.

18. To start using Quicken, double-click on the Quicken 5 for Windows icon.

Installing Quicken Deluxe using Windows 3.1 From the CD-ROM

Quicken Deluxe for Windows comes either on floppies or on a CD-ROM. Installing Quicken Deluxe for Windows is similar to installing Quicken, except you have more optional features.

To install Quicken Deluxe for Windows via CD-ROM, use the following steps.

1. Follow Steps 1 through 6 in the previous section, "Installing Quicken or Quicken Deluxe using Windows 3.1 from Floppy Disks." In Step 5,

The Quicken Deluxe Setup window offers extra options.

above, enter the drive letter that references your CD-ROM drive. After you complete Step 6, the main Quicken Deluxe setup window will appear.

2. The default drive and directory destination to install Quicken Deluxe for Windows is displayed in the upper-left-hand corner of the Quicken Deluxe Setup dialog box. To change the destination, click on the Change Directory button. The Select Destination Directory dialog box will open. Use the Directories list (Alt D) to set the drive and directory on which you want to install Quicken Deluxe. If you wish to create a new directory, you can do so by typing in its name and path manually. Click OK when you are done selecting a drive and directory, and you'll be returned to the previous screen.

3. The default program group in Program Manager for Quicken Deluxe is displayed in the drop-down list labeled "Program Groups." You have the option to either create a new program group for Quicken Deluxe in Program Manager, or add the Quicken icon to an existing program group. To change the program group where Quicken Deluxe will appear, edit the default "Quicken" program group name. To add Quicken Deluxe for Windows to an existing program group, drop down the list of existing program groups and select one by clicking on it.

The setup window lets you create a new program group for Quicken Deluxe or place it in an existing group.

4. Highlight the programs you want to install in the upper-left corner of the Program Group Setup Window. If you don't want to install the application, make sure its name is not highlighted in color. The Select All button lets you choose everything at once, and the Select None button clears the list so you can add

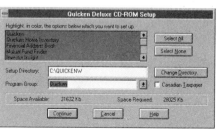

You can install just the basic Quicken program, or select many optional components.

programs one at a time. At the bottom of the application list, the Quicken install window indicates the amount of free space you'll need on your hard drive for the installation .

5. If you live in Canada, click on the Canadian Taxpayer box.

6. Click the Continue button (or type Alt N) to complete the installation process.

7. Quicken Deluxe now comes with an Internet Access package consisting of a customized version of Netscape Navigator and the Eudora Lite electronic mail program. You can access Intuit's site on the World Wide Web free of charge, thanks to a special arrangement with the nationwide Internet Service Provider Concentric Network Corporation. If the setup program detects that you already have a copy of Netscape Navigator on your computer—two copies cannot coexist reliably on one machine—it warns you and avoids adding this component. You'll still get the free Web access via your existing browser.

8. If you do not have Netscape Navigator, Quicken will ask whether you want to install the Internet Access package.

9. If your computer has a modem—and it is turned on— Quicken Deluxe now asks if you would like to register the program electronically via a special toll-free number. If you answer yes, you can fill out an onscreen form. If you answer no, installation will proceed normally, but you'll have to fill out and mail in the Quicken registration card.

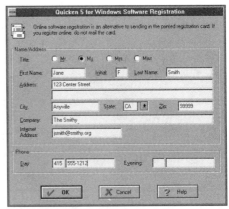

Quicken's Software Registration form lets you register your software electronically.

10. Quicken Deluxe now installs the runtime version of Microsoft's Video for Windows, which will update any existing Microsoft Video files you may have.

11. In order to use all the features of Quicken Deluxe, you need to exit and restart Windows—either by accepting this option on the program's dialog boxes, or by doing it yourself when you have completed other tasks.

The setup program for Microsoft's Video for Windows runs automatically after Quicken Deluxe has been set up.

12. To start using Quicken Deluxe, double-click on the Quicken 5 for Windows icon.

Installing Quicken using Windows 95 From Floppy Disks

To install Quicken for Windows from floppy disks, use the following steps:

1. If Windows is not already running, start Windows by typing **WIN** at the DOS command prompt.

2. Insert the Quicken for Windows Install Disk 1 in your computer's floppy disk drive (either drive A or drive B).

3. Open the Windows 95 Control Panel by clicking on the Start button, then, while holding the left mouse button down, selecting Settings→Control Panel. Release the mouse button when Control Panel is highlighted and the panel will open.

4. From the Control Panel, double-click on the Add/Remove Programs icon.

You add programs to Windows 95 using the Add/Remove Programs icon in the Control Panel.

5. A tabbed dialog box will appear. Make sure the Install/Uninstall tab is seen at the top left, then click on the Install button.

6. The next screen prompts you to insert the floppy disk in the drive. You've already done that, so just click on the Next button. Windows 95 then searches for the Quicken setup program and asks

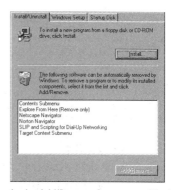

you to confirm its location. Click on Finish to tell Windows to continue.

In the Add/Remove Programs tabbed dialog box, just click on the Install button.

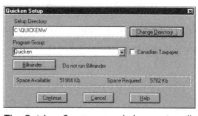

Windows 95 automatically finds the Quicken setup program, whether it be on a floppy disk or a CD-ROM.

7. Click OK to begin the installation process, and the Quicken Setup window will eventually appear. If you are installing just Quicken for Windows, the screen looks like the one in the figure "Quicken Setup" screen, below. The rest of the install instructions in this section assume you are installing

Quicken for Windows. If you are installing Quicken Deluxe for Windows, see the next section, "Installing Quicken Deluxe using Windows 95."

Note: *If you are satisfied with all the selections in the Quicken Install window, just click Continue (or type Alt N) to install the program. You don't need to use any of the instructions in the rest of this section.*

The Quicken Setup screen helps you install the program.

8. The default drive and directory destination to install Quicken for Windows is displayed in the upper-left-hand corner of the Quicken Setup dialog box. To change the destination, click on the Change Directory button. The Select Destination Directory dialog box will open. Use the Directories list (Alt D) to set the drive and directory on which you want to install Quicken for Windows. If you wish to create a new directory, you can do

The Select Destination Directory dialog box enables you to change the directory and drive where you are going to install Quicken for Windows.

so simply by typing in its name and path manually, as I have done in the screen you see. Click OK when you are done selecting a drive and directory, and you'll be returned to the previous screen.

9. Billminder is one of Quicken's automatic ways to remind you about upcoming bills. You may run Billminder either when you first boot your computer, when you run Windows, or only when you run Quicken. The Billminder selection is displayed next to the button labeled "Billminder." To change the Billminder selection, click on the Billminder button (or type Alt B). A window will appear to enable you to choose Billminder options. Click the option you want, then click on OK.

This window enables you to choose the Billminder option you want.

10. If you live in Canada, click on the Canadian Taxpayer checkbox.

11. Click the Continue button (or type Alt N) to proceed to the next screen.

12. Quicken now comes with an Internet Access package consisting of a customized version of Netscape Navigator and the Eudora Lite electronic mail program. You can access Intuit's area on the World Wide Web free of charge, thanks to a special arrangement with the nationwide Internet Service Provider Concentric Network Corporation. If the setup program detects that you already have a copy of Netscape Navigator on your computer—two copies cannot coexist reliably on one machine—it warns you and avoids adding this component. You'll still get the free Web access via your existing browser.

13. If you do not have Netscape Navigator, Quicken will ask whether you want to install the Quicken Internet Access package.

14. Click the Yes button to complete the installation process. Follow the instructions on the screen to switch disks when prompted. When you see the message that you installed Quicken successfully, click OK.

This window asks you if you want to install Quicken's Internet Access package.

15. If your computer has a modem—and it is turned on—Quicken now asks if you would like to register the program electronically. If you answer yes, you can fill out an onscreen form via a special toll-free number. If you answer no, installation will proceed normally, but you'll have to fill out and mail in the Quicken registration card.

16. Remove the floppy disks and store them in a safe place.

17. The Quicken setup program places Quicken in the Windows 95 Start Menu. You can run the program either by opening the Start Menu, or by clicking on the Quicken 5 for Windows icon in the \StartMenu\Programs\Quicken folder.

The Quicken setup program leaves this window open so you can run the program immediately by clicking on its icon.

Installing Quicken Deluxe using Windows 95 From the CD-ROM

Installing Quicken Deluxe for Windows is similar to installing Quicken, except you have more optional features and, if you purchased the CD-ROM, you don't have to swap floppy disks.

To install Quicken Deluxe for Windows from the CD-ROM, use the following steps.

1. Follow Steps 1 through 7 in the previous section, "Installing Quicken for Windows from Floppy Disks." In Step 5, Windows 95 will automatically locate the Quicken Deluxe setup program on your CD-ROM drive. After you complete Step 6, the main Quicken Deluxe CD-ROM Setup window appears.

The Quicken Deluxe CD-ROM Setup window offers extra options.

2. The default drive and directory destination to install Quicken Deluxe for Windows is displayed in the upper-left-hand corner of the Quicken Setup dialog box. To change the destination, click on the Change Directory button. The Select Destination Directory dialog box will open. Use the Directories list

(Alt D) to set the drive and directory on which you want to install Quicken Deluxe. If you wish to create a new directory, you can do so by typing in its name and path manually. Click OK when you are done selecting a drive and directory, and you'll be returned to the previous screen.

The Select Destination Directory dialog box enables you to change the directory and drive where you are going to install Quicken Deluxe for Windows.

3. Highlight the programs you want to install in the upper-left corner of the Setup window. If you don't want to install the application, make sure its name is not highlighted in color. The Select All button lets you choose everything at once, and the Select None button clears the list so you can add programs one at a time. At the bottom of the application list, the Quicken Deluxe Install window indicates the amount of free space you need on your hard drive for installation.

4. If you live in Canada, click on the Canadian Taxpayer box.

5. Click the Continue button (or type Alt N) to complete the installation process.

6. Quicken Deluxe now comes with an Internet Access package consisting of a customized version of Netscape Navigator and the Eudora Lite electronic mail program. You can access Intuit's area on the World Wide Web free of charge, thanks to a special arrangement with the nationwide Internet Service Provider Concentric Network Corporation. If the setup program detects that you already have a copy of Netscape Navigator on your computer—two copies cannot coexist reliably on one machine—it warns you and avoids adding this component. You'll still get the free Web access via your existing browser.

7. If you do not have Netscape Navigator, Quicken Deluxe will ask whether you want to install the Quicken Internet Access package.

8. If your computer has a modem—and it is turned on—Quicken Deluxe now asks if you would like to register the program electronically via a special toll-free number. If you answer yes, you can fill out an onscreen form. If you answer no, installation will proceed normally, but you'll have to fill out and mail in the Quicken registration card.

9. To use all the Quicken Deluxe features, you need to exit and restart Windows—either by accepting this option on the program's dialog boxes, or by doing it yourself when you have completed other tasks.

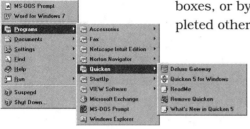

10. To start using Quicken Deluxe, double-click on the Quicken 5 for Windows icon, or click on the Start button and select the Programs→Quicken menu path.

The setup program enters Quicken into Windows 95's Start Menu.

Why Register Quicken?

"Registering" your software lets Intuit, makers of Quicken, know who you are, your address, and some information about you. There are two reasons to register. One is so you can get more junk mail. You go on a list so Intuit can send you offers for discounts on Intuit products such as preprinted checks. Another reason is so you can be notified about upgrades for Quicken and, just in case, warned about software defects ("bugs").

Summary

All it takes to install Quicken or Quicken Deluxe is to insert the disks or CD-ROMs and follow the directions. With Quicken Deluxe, you can also install other utilities that will help you track your finances and possessions. And . . . don't forget to register your software.

Beware of Auto-Save! Quicken automatically saves your data as you work, which is normally a good thing, but if you make a mistake as you work that mistake is automatically saved to the file. That's yet another reason why you should make regular backups of your Quicken files.

Working with Quicken

PENALTY SIGNALS FOR
FINANCIAL MISMANAGEMENT

ROUGHING
THE WALLET

IN OVER
YOUR HEAD

FAILURE
TO SAVE

LACK OF
SMARTS

FILING FOR
CHAPTER II
(BANKRUPTCY)

LOST SHIRT,
NO RESERVES

CHOKING ON
MONTHLY
PAYMENTS

BAD
RECORD
KEEPING

Once you have successfully installed Quicken for Windows, you are ready to start managing your finances. Fortunately, Quicken provides a cornucopia of help and guidance to keep you on the right track.

In addition to the menu commands that are standard for all Windows applications, Quicken for Windows has icon bars and "quick tabs" that provide access to commonly used commands. It also has online help (available from the <u>H</u>elp menu or by typing Alt+H), an onscreen manual (also accessed via the <u>H</u>elp menu or by typing Alt+H), Quick Tours (brief lessons that explain how to use Quicken's features), and "Qcards" (cards that provide information about many actions as you perform them).

But wait—that's not all. Quicken Deluxe adds audio to the Qcards, which it renames "Guide Cards." These let you choose a combination of spoken and written information that helps you learn best. Quicken Deluxe also offers "Video Quick Tours," in which a Quicken employee appears on your screen to guide you through an important or complex aspect of the program.

After all of the above, you might be expecting some free Ginsu knives, too. Fear not: Though Quicken's new user interface sounds flashy and distracting, it's actually very straightforward. You'll wind up doing just as I do, performing most of your work from the "HomeBase," a simple graphical menu that helps you switch between Quicken's various functions.

Starting Quicken for the First Time

What happens when you start Quicken depends on whether you're a first-time user or an old-timer. To start the program, do this:

1. If you have Quicken, just locate the Quicken program group or Start Menu entry and then double-click on Quicken 5 for Windows. Then skip to Step 4 below.

2. If you have Quicken Deluxe, use the same procedure but click on the Quicken Deluxe Gateway icon or menu listing. The Quicken Deluxe Gateway window visually shows you all of Quicken Deluxe's functions. In addition, a "personal profile" icon is an important feature. Intuit recommends you click here and enter some basic personal information, such as marital status, age, and annual income. Then click Save.

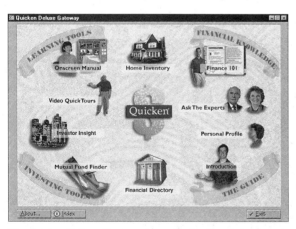

The Quicken Deluxe Gateway shows you Quicken Deluxe's special functions and lets you enter personal information.

Note: *Quicken uses this personal information to customize some of the answers you receive from Ask the Experts and other Quicken features.*

3. Next, click on the big Quicken "dollar sign" logo at the center of the menu.

4. If you've used Quicken previously, your data files will be converted and are ready for use. Skip to Step 12 below.

5. If you haven't used Quicken before, you'll see a New User Setup screen. (In Quicken Deluxe, an audio Guide Card control panel will appear at the lower left, though it's not shown in the figure at top right.)

The New User Setup screen leads you through setting up a checking account.

6. You'll want to have the name of your checking account and, preferably, some balance information. Click on the Next button and you'll see a screen like one at right. Enter a generic name for the checking account you wish to start tracking, then click on Next again.

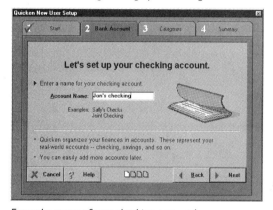

Enter the name of your checking account here.

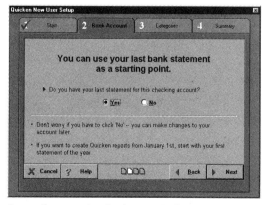

Do you have your last bank statement?

7. Quicken will now ask if you have your last bank statement for this account. If you do not, it enters a balance of $0.00, which you can change later. Being the eager-to-get-organized person you are, you'll probably be able to answer "yes" and then click on Next to continue.

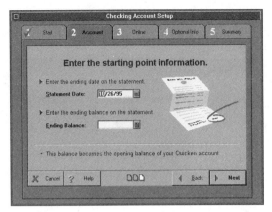

Entering your last bank statement balance.

8. Enter the ending statement balance, which will become the opening balance of your Quicken account as in the figure above.

9. Quicken will now confirm that it has set up an account register for you (see the figure at right).

Quicken has set up an account register for you.

10. Now Quicken will set up some "categories" for you. The prime difference between your new electronic checkbook register and your old-fashioned paper one, categories are what will help you figure out where your money goes. In the next three menus (see the figures at right and at the top of the next page), Quicken explains categories, then asks whether you want them set up for a business as well as a

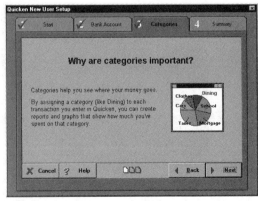

An explanatory screen shows you why categories are important.

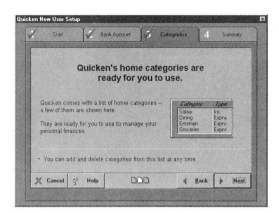

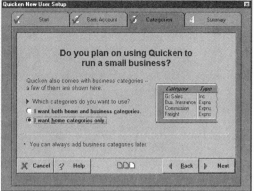

Quicken comes with a set of home categories built in. However, you can change them later.

This screen lets you add business categories.

home. No matter what you do, you'll be able to add and delete categories later to your heart's content. Click on the Next button when you're through with each screen, or click on the Back button if you want to go back and review your work.

11. A final screen will let you double-check your work (see the figure below left). After you click on the Next button, you will be offered the chance to go on one or more of Quicken's Quick Tours (see the figure below right). By all means do so now, if you want to. When you finish your tour, you'll wind up at Quicken's HomeBase (see Step 12).

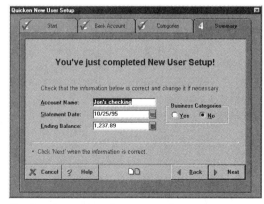

One last chance to confirm your entries . . .

. . . and the opportunity to take a Quick Tour, or just go right to HomeBase.

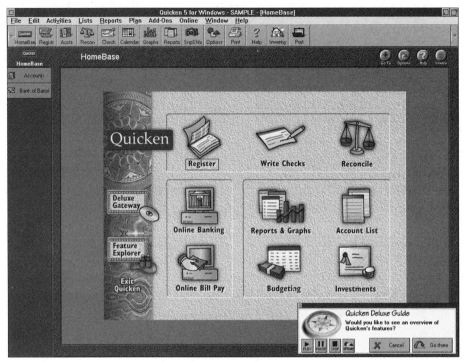

HomeBase.

12. The HomeBase gives an easy-to-read overview of Quicken's basic functions. If you have Quicken Deluxe, you'll also see a box at the lower right offering to give you an overview of Quicken's features. The Quicken HomeBase button in the upper left corner of the screen is always visible, so you can easily return here at any time.

Choosing Menu Commands

As with most Windows programs, Quicken for Windows sports a menu bar across the top of the screen. To select an item from a menu, simply click on the menu name to cause the item list to drop down. Then, click on the item you want.

You may also make selections from most menus by using the keyboard. This process will require you to memorize some keystrokes but, once you've memorized them, it's sometimes faster than using a mouse. It just depends on what you prefer. Using the keyboard, you

can make a menu list drop down by pressing the
Alt key and the underlined letter in the menu
name. For example, to drop down the list of items
for the Edit menu, press Alt and type the letter
"E," because "E" is underlined.

Once the menu list has dropped down, you
can select an item from the menu by pressing the
key for the underlined letter for that item. For
example, you can select the Copy Transaction
item from the Edit menu by first pressing Alt+E
to drop down the Edit menu list, then pressing
the "Y" key (see the figure at right).

*Choosing a menu item using
the keyboard interface.*

Many items in the menus can be activated directly by holding down
either the shift key or the Ctrl key and pressing another key. For example, you can activate the New Transaction command from the Edit menu

by pressing Ctrl+N. The key combination is displayed alongside the command name in the menu
list as in the figure at right. As you select the
menu commands, you can familiarize yourself
with the equivalent keyboard commands. Note
that Quicken uses Shift+Del for Cut and Shift+Ins

*You may activate a menu item by pressing
the key combination listed alongside the
item in the menus. For example, type
Ctrl+N to enter a new transaction.*

for Insert. This differs from many Windows programs; however, it may
be changed in the Options dialog box accessible from HomeBase.

Using HomeBase to Navigate Quicken

The HomeBase is a special type of menu that uses space and icons to
make its various functions clearer. It doesn't look like a regular Windows menu, but it's designed to let you click on a button to reach
Quicken's main features. Tasks are split into topics—selecting a new
topic or a task within a topic requires only a mouse click.

To access the HomeBase control panel, select HomeBase from the
Activities menu or click on the HomeBase icon in the upper left corner
of the screen. As you can see, the HomeBase window is divided into
three general areas. The top three icons, representing Register, Write
Checks, and Reconcile, are oriented toward day-to-day activities.
Online banking and bill paying have their own area in the lower left

corner. And the money management area in the lower right part of the screen covers long-term activities such as budgeting, investing, reporting, and tracking multiple accounts.

Here is a rundown of what each topic button covers:

- The Register, Write Checks, and Reconcile topics enable you to use the current register, financial calendar, or account list. A register works like the check register you use with a checkbook, except there are registers for all types of accounts—including credit cards, cash, and investments. You can also write checks and reconcile your account.

- The Reports and Graphs topic includes reports for itemized categories, income and expense reports, and lists of other available reports and graphs.

- The Budgeting topic allows you to access such functions as budgeting, financial planning, forecasting, tax planning, and setting up a savings goal.

- The Investments topic lets you create an Investment account or an entire portfolio, update your portfolio prices, report on the value of your portfolio, and obtain an investment graph.

- The Online Banking and Online Bill Pay topics let you download data directly from your financial institution. You can also set up electronic bill paying here.

- The Deluxe Gateway topic, if present, calls up Quicken Deluxe-specific features such as Finance 101, Ask the Experts, Video Quick Tours, Mutual Fund Finder, Home Inventory, and more (see the figure "Deluxe Gateway Topic").

You can modify many options by clicking on the Options icon in the upper right corner of the HomeBase window. The HomeBase Options window will appear, and you may change such settings as the date format, the colors used in the register, the default date range used in reports, and much more.

The Deluxe Gateway topic pops up a list of otherwise-hidden programs on the HomeBase screen.

Using Icons

By clicking on the icon button in the upper right corner of the Home-Base screen, you can turn on Quicken's icon bar, which displays icons across the top of the screen for the most commonly used operations and makes it even easier to use Quicken.

Quicken's Options window, available via a button in HomeBase.

You may modify the icons in the Iconbar by clicking on HomeBase's Options button, which will bring up the window shown at left. Clicking on the Iconbar button will bring up a second window (shown at right) where you can customize the Iconbar by clicking on the buttons you want to either add or delete. If the icon you want is not visible on the screen, you can click on the arrows at either end of the Iconbar until the icon you want scrolls into view.

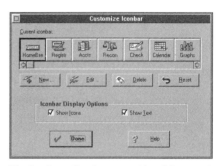

The Iconbar editor lets you add or delete entries in the Iconbar. Use the arrows to see the complete list of entries.

Quicken's Iconbar lets you select commonly used actions by clicking on an icon. For the default Iconbar, the icons are:

The HomeBse icon: Activates the HomeBase window. As detailed above, this window makes it easier to use Quicken by enabling you to select topics and pick common activities from those topics.

The Registr icon: Activates the window for a register. If you have more than one account, Quicken will display icons for commonly used registers at the bottom of the screen, and the Registr icon will activate the highlighted register. If you don't have register icons at the bottom of the screen, then the Registr icon opens the window for the last register you used. Working with registers is covered in Chapter 4.

The Accts icon: Opens the list of available accounts. You'll set up a separate account for each checking account, credit card, and investment, as well as for cash, assets, and liabilities. You may edit, delete, and create new accounts using this window. Setting up accounts is covered in Chapters 4 and 8.

The Recon icon: Enables you to reconcile an account (compare your records to the bank's records). If you have set up Quicken to display icons for commonly used registers at the bottom of the screen, this icon opens the Reconcile window for the highlighted register. If you don't have register icons at the bottom of the screen, then the Recon icon opens the Reconcile window for the last register you used. Reconciling your accounts is covered in Chapter 7.

The Check icon: Once you open an account, this icon opens the Write Checks window to enable you to write checks against a checking account. If you have set up Quicken to display icons for commonly used registers at the bottom of the screen, this icon activates the Write Checks window for the highlighted register. If you don't have register icons at the bottom of the screen, then the Check icon opens the Write Checks window for the last register you used. Writing checks is covered in Chapter 6.

The Calendar icon: Opens Quicken's Financial Calendar. From the Financial Calendar, you can schedule transactions, add notes to a date, and review the transactions you have made by date. Using the Financial Calendar is covered in Chapter 9.

The Graphs icon: Brings up the Create Graph window, which enables you to create Income and Expense, Budget Variance, Net Worth, and Investment graphs.

The Reports icon: When you have created your accounts, this icon will display the Create Report window, which enables you to choose the type of report you want, select a time period, and even customize the report. Setting up and running reports is covered in Chapter 11.

The SnpShts icon: Provides a "snapshot"—a summary of your account activity that displays six panels of summary graphs and reports.

The Options icon: Brings up the Options window. This window includes buttons for customizing various parts of Quicken, including Checks, Registers, Reports, Reminders, the icon bar, and general options.

The Print icon: Enables you to print the contents of any selected register. You can set the time period, report title, simple formatting options, and whether to print transaction splits.

The Help icon: Brings up Quicken's online Help feature, as discussed in the section "Getting Onscreen Help" later in this chapter. More information on getting help is featured in Chapter 16.

The Inventry icon: Brings up Quicken Deluxe's Home Inventory screen, which guides you, room by room, through creating an itemized list of your home's contents.

The Port icon: Opens Quicken Deluxe's Portfolio view, in which you can record your investment transactions. You can use the Portfolio view to show the current market value, return on investment, price changes, and other data.

Using QuickTours

If you are like most people, having to work your way through a big manual (or even this book) before starting to use Quicken probably doesn't excite you too much. To make it easier to get started, Quicken provides "Quick-Tours" plus, in Quicken Deluxe, "Video QuickTours."

To start any of these, pull down the Help menu. In addition to the features mentioned above, this menu also provides access to a Windows tutorial and gives you a way to load sample data.

The QuickTours discuss most of Quicken's operations through a series of onscreen slides. Each slide displays

| Quicken Help   F1 |
| How To Use Help |
| QuickTours... |
| Video QuickTours... |
| Quicken Tips... |
| Windows Tutorial... |
| Deluxe Index... |
| Onscreen Manual... |
| Ask the Experts... |
| Finance 101... |
| Load Sample Data |
| Guide Card Settings... |
| About Quicken... |

The Help menu provides access to QuickTours and a bevy of other features.

This list of QuickTours lets you select one using your mouse or the tab key.

actual Quicken windows along with text that explains how to use a particular feature. To start a tour, select Quick-Tours from the Help menu and you'll see the menu of topics as in the figure at left.

If you have Quicken Deluxe, you can start a Video QuickTour by selecting Video Quick-Tours from the Help menu and then choosing one of seven video tours (shown below). These tours display actual Quicken screens and enliven them using audio and animated figures.

As you progress through these tutorials, you will learn enough to get started using Quicken. Of course, they don't cover everything, but that's why you have this book and the Quicken documentation (which, in Quicken Deluxe, is mostly replaced by the online manual).

You can exit a Quicken tour at any time by pressing the Escape (Esc) key, which is usually located in the upper left corner of your keyboard.

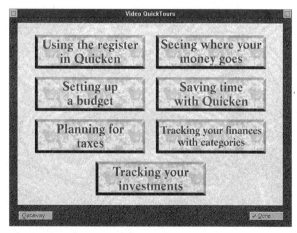

Quicken Deluxe users can choose from seven different video tours.

Using Qcards/Guide Cards

If you don't know how to perform a task, wouldn't it be helpful to have a guide walk you through the operation step by step? Quicken offers this in the form of "Qcards," or, as Quicken Deluxe terms them, "Guide Cards." Now, you won't have to pull out the manual when you are stuck. Instead, just make sure that Qcards are available by using the Qcard Settings or Guide Card Settings item in the Help menu.

Note: Qcards can be annoying once you learn a feature. To turn them off, select All cards off from the Help menu so that the check mark goes away. You may also disable any Qcard or Guide Card for the current window by clicking on the close box in the upper left corner.

The Guide Card Settings menu in Quicken Deluxe lets you turn cards off, or use text only, text with audio, or audio only.

When Qcards/Guide Cards are enabled, they appear on the screen with instructions on how to proceed with your work. For example, if you are in a checking account register, with the cursor on the date field, the Qcard instructs you on how to fill in a date and how to move to the next task you need to perform. As you move through the fields in the register, the Qcard instructions change, telling you how to proceed to the next step. You can access the online help from the Help button at the bottom right corner of the Qcard.

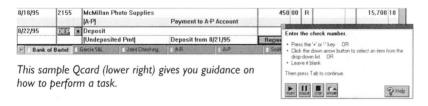

This sample Qcard (lower right) gives you guidance on how to perform a task.

Getting Onscreen Help

Like most other Windows applications, Quicken provides online help. To access the online help feature, select Quicken Help from the Help menu. This opens the Help window and displays information ("context-sensitive help") that is tailored to your current task. For example, if you have an account register open, the Help window displays information about using the Account Register window.

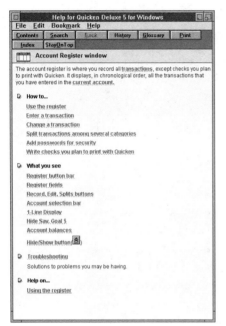

Quicken's online help provides context-sensitive information.

Text in a Help window is typically displayed in two colors. Black text provides information. Text that is displayed in green ("hypertext") indicates that additional information is available. For example, if you click on the word "transactions" in the Account Register window Help screen, a small box appears that gives you a brief definition of what a "transaction" is. This additional window stays on the screen until you click the mouse again.

Some of the hypertext displays additional information in the Help window, replacing the original information you were viewing. For example, if you click on "Write checks you plan to print with Quicken," a small window pops up displaying a variety of topics on writing checks. If you select "Write Checks," the original "Account Register window" help information is replaced by the "Write Checks" information (see the figure at right). You can continue using the hypertext to explore the online help system, and, at any time, you can return to the previous help information by clicking on the Back button.

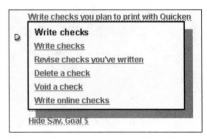

Hypertext help can pop up additional information

You can also get a list of the Help windows you have explored during your help session by clicking on the History button. From the History window, you can return to any Help window by double-clicking on its name. You can also view the entire contents of the online help system by clicking on the Contents button. This can be helpful when you need help on a topic that is not the topic Quicken initially opens in the Help window. In the Contents window, you can use the hypertext to select the Help topic you want to explore.

You can search for a particular word or phrase in the online help system to get help on that topic. To execute a search:

1. Click on the Search button. The Search window will open (see the figure "Search window").

2. Type the word or phrase in the text box at the top of the window, or select a word or phrase from the scrolling list.

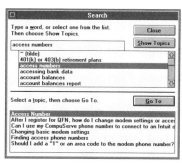

3. Click on the Show Topics button to display any related topics in the list at the bottom of the Search window.

4. Select the topic you want to view, and click on the Go To button.

The Search window in Quicken's online help system enables you to get help on a particular topic.

Summary

Quicken provides a variety of ways to help you get started easily, including menus, the Iconbar, HomeBase, QuickTours and Video QuickTours. It also provides an enormous amount of assistance through its online help system and the Qcards/Guide Cards.

Setting Up an Account and Entering Data

4

LOOKS LIKE OUR
RECEPTION WENT
SIX PERCENT OVER
BUDGET.

NO PROBLEM. WE LOP
A COUPLE OF DAYS OFF
OUR HONEYMOON AND
STILL MAKE OUR NUMBERS.

You can't (legally) write a check unless you have a checking account, and you wouldn't dare try to use a credit card unless you had an account for it. Well, Quicken is just as strict. Before you can do any useful work in Quicken, you need to set up accounts to store the data you enter.

Of course, if you've already used an earlier version of Quicken, you've already got at least one account. If you are new to Quicken, but you worked through the New User Setup procedure outlined in Chapter 3, you have an account, too—albeit a very simple one.

Quicken lets you set up several different types of accounts, including checking, savings, cash, credit card, money market, asset, liability, and investment accounts. Most people never use all of these—and they probably should. That's really what this chapter is all about: Once you feel confident and well-versed in the concepts behind creating one type of account, you're likely to take advantage of the others.

The accounts all work similarly, except for the investment accounts. This chapter covers how to set up a checking account and use an account register. Setting up other types of accounts is covered in Chapter 8.

After you set up an account, you can start entering your data into the account "register." Each Quicken account has a register associated with it. Putting information in an account register works much like entering data in your paper check register—only it's a lot smarter. The Quicken account register does the math for you, and it automatically transfers payments from one account to another when appropriate. Use your checking account to pay a credit card bill and—presto—the data is automatically entered in both the checking and credit card registers.

Of course, the register also stores information about the deposits you make and the money you spend. I don't mean to be preachy, but it's important to stay current on entering data into the register so that you get accurate balances, reports, and graphs. Unless, of course, you're like a friend I knew in college: If he had any checks left in his checkbook, he just assumed that he had money in his account. Nice try.

Creating an Account

You create an account in Quicken using the Create Account window. There are three ways to open the Create New Account window:

1. Select Create New Account from the Activities menu.

2. Open HomeBase (select the HomeBse icon in the icon bar, choose the HomeBase Quick Tab at the left of the screen, or choose HomeBase from the Activities menu), click on the Account List icon, and select New at the top of the Account List window.

3. Open the Account List window (select the Accts icon in the icon bar or choose the Accounts Quick Tab at the left of the screen), and click on the New button.

The Create New Account window enables you to create a new account for your use.

From the Create New Account window, select the type of account you want to create by clicking on the button for that account type. For this example, click on the Checking button. The Create Checking Account window opens.

Click on the Next button, fill in the account name (maximum of 15 letters) and description (maximum of 20 letters), and click on the Next button. Quicken now asks you whether you have the last statement for this checking account.

If you answer "Yes," Quicken asks you to fill in the amount that was in the account as of a certain date. If you answer "No," Quicken starts the account with today's date and a balance of zero.

Note: *Be sure that your PC has the correct date set. You can do that within Windows 95 by clicking on the Start Menu, then selecting Control Panel from the Settings menu and clicking on the Date/Time icon.*

As you'll see in Chapter 9, you may need to enter information about your opening balance and outstanding checks in the register if you want to be able to reconcile Quicken with your bank's records. After you have selected either Yes or No, click on the Next button. If you answered "Yes," Quicken requests the closing statement date and the statement balance.

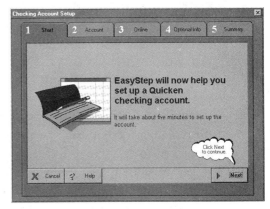

The Create Checking Account window begins the process of gathering the information Quicken needs to create your new checking account.

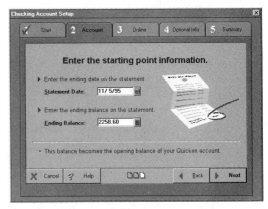

Enter the statement date and balance of your last bank statement for this new account.

Entering the Statement Date and Using the Quicken Calendar

You may either type in the statement date, or click on the miniature icon to the right of the date box to open a miniature calendar. From this calendar, you may select a date by clicking on the date you want, move to the previous month by clicking on the Backward (█) button, or move to the next month by clicking on the Forward (█) button. You may fill in the closing balance by typing in the amount, or click on the button alongside the Ending Balance text to open a calculator. You may enter the amount by clicking on the calculator buttons with the mouse pointer. When you are done entering the number, click on the █ Enter █ button.

Click on the Next button again to continue. Quicken will ask if you have signed up to use an online service with this account. If you want to set up an online service, please refer to Chapter 15. Otherwise, accept the default "No" answer by clicking on the Next button again or selecting Tab #4 at the top of the window.

Note: *Here and in the examples that follow, the keyboard shortcut for the Next button consists of simply hitting Enter.*

Quicken offers you an opportunity to enter additional account information. If you wish to do so, click on Yes. A screen will appear that permits you to note the financial institution, account number, contact, phone number, checking interest rate (if any), and other comments. Whether or not you chose to add additional account information, clicking on the Next button again takes you to the Summary screen.

Here you need only double-check the account name, balance, and date you have entered. Then hit the Enter key and click on Next again. You will now be given one more chance to enable online banking or online bill paying (see Chapter 15). You can also choose to return to the Additional Information screen.

In addition, clicking on the Tax Information button lets you specify if the account contains any tax-deferred funds (IRA, 401(k), etc.). If it does, you should use the drop-down menus at the right of the Transfers In and Transfers Out boxes. These allow you to associate the relevant tax schedules with transfers into or out of the account.

Click on Done to create your new checking account. If you created the account from the Account List window, the window remains open and the new account is listed in it. If you created the account from

HomeBase or the Activities menu, the new checking account register opens on the screen for you to work with.

Note: You may not be able to see your new account in the Account List window. This will occur if you have created an account type that is not the same as the type currently displayed in the Account List window. For example, if you create a new checking account, but the Account List window is displaying Credit accounts, you won't see the new account appear in the list. To see the new account, select the tab for the new account (for example, the Bank tab for checking accounts) or the All Types tab.

Using the Account List

Quicken's Account List organizes your list of accounts. To open the Account List window, click on the Accts button in the icon bar, or select Accounts from the List menu. The Account List displays a list of all your accounts, grouped by the type of account. To select a different account type, simply click on the tab at the top of the list to display that page in the Account List. Quite a bit of information is displayed about the accounts, including the name, description, number of transactions, and balance. A small picture of a check (with a check mark) in the Chks column at the far right indicates that there are unprinted checks in that account.

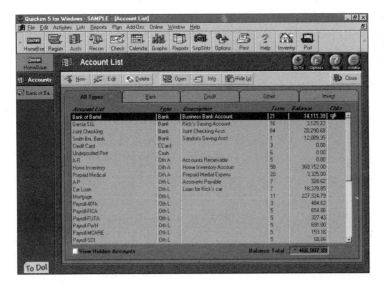

Quicken's Account List enables you to work directly with all your accounts.

You may work with your accounts directly from the Account List. You have the following options from the Account List window:

- To create a new account, click on the <u>N</u>ew button to open the Create New Account window. Fill in the information as detailed above.

You must confirm that you want to delete an account.

- To delete an account, select the account from the list and click on the <u>D</u>elete button. Quicken opens the Deleting Account window. Before Quicken will get rid of the account, you must confirm that you want to delete it by typing "Yes."

- To edit the description and other attributes of an existing account, select the account you want to work with, then click on the Edit button. The Edit Account window will open. You may adjust the account name and description from this window by clicking on the Account tab. You may also click on the Optional Info tab (#4) to open the Additional Information window. In this window, you may add the bank name, account number, name and phone number for a contact person, comments, and the current interest rate. Returning to the Edit Account window, you may select the Summary tab and then click on the <u>T</u>ax button to open the Tax Schedule window. In this window, you may indicate that an account is tax-deferred (for example, an IRA, Keogh, or 401(k) plan). You may also select the tax form to show

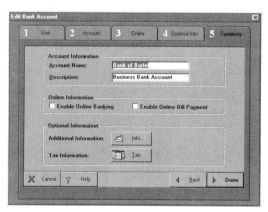

The Edit Account window enables you to change basic information about an account . . .

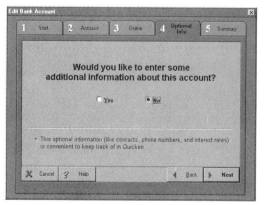

change information about the bank and contact person . . .

transfers in and out of this account. As
mentioned above, the tax forms need to
be selected from the drop-down list to
the right of the Transfers In and Transfers Out boxes.

. . . or change your tax-deferred information.

- To open a particular account register,
select the account and click on the Open button, or simply double-click on the account name in the Account List window.

Exploring the Register Window

The Register window is where you enter, edit, and delete the information for an account. This window has many properties in common with
the windows in other Windows programs, but it also has unique features that make it eas-
ier to get at your data.

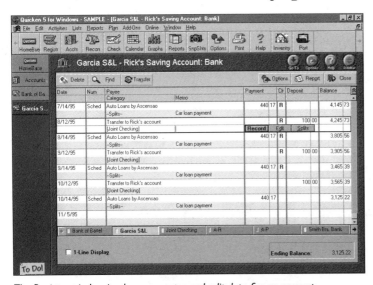

The Register window is where you enter and edit data for an account.

To the left of the
register itself, you see
Quicken 5's new Quick
Tabs feature. By click-
ing on one of these
tabs, you can switch
between multiple open
accounts, HomeBase,
or other areas of the
program. They're a
convenient feature if
you have a 15-inch or
17-inch monitor with
Super VGA resolution.

If you have a standard VGA screen, however, you may find that the
Quick Tabs make the register too hard to read. If that's the case, click
on the "Shrink" button at the right side of the menu bar. It's just below
the button that would close the Quicken window completely, and it
looks like this: 🗗

Quicken will ask you if you want to turn Quick Tabs off. If you
say "Yes," the program switches to the Windows 3.1-style Multiple

Document Interface. This means that any of the open accounts or registers may be resized or minimized as if they were separate software programs. Minimized, they appear as a secondary task bar (if you're running Windows 95) or as icons on the Quicken desktop (if you're running Windows 3.1).

Standard Windows Properties

In the upper right corner of the Register window are the Minimize, Maximize, and Close buttons. Clicking on the Minimize button (in Windows 95, this has a line at the bottom of it) reduces the Register window to a bar at the bottom of the Quicken window. The register is not closed, but is simply stored out of your way. To reopen the Register window after you have minimized it, either double-click on the icon, or click on the icon once, then select Restore or Maximize from the pop-up menu that

appears. The Restore command reopens the Register window to the size and position that it was before you minimized it. The Maximize command reopens the Register window to its largest size, filling the entire Quicken window.

The Maximize button (it has a window icon with the dark bar uppermost) expands the Register window to its largest size, filling the entire Quicken

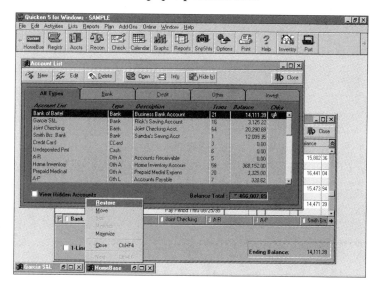

Minimized registers are not closed but are stored out of your way as subsidiary task bars.

window. When the Register window is maximized, the Minimize and Maximize buttons disappear and are replaced by a single Restore button. The Restore button (which is what I called the "Shrink" button above) displays a pair of windows, one on top of the other. Clicking on the Restore button changes the window back to the size that it was before you maximized it.

You may close a Register window by double-clicking on the Control button in the upper left corner of the window (decorated with a Windows logo), or by clicking once on the Control button and selecting Close. You may also minimize, maximize, or restore a Register window by clicking once on the Control button, and then selecting Restore, Minimize, or Maximize from the pop-up menu.

If you have turned off Quick Tabs, you may move a Register window by clicking on the window title bar and dragging the window to the new location. And, of course, you can view register entries that don't fit on the screen by using the standard window scroll bar on the right side of the window. As you drag the scroll bar, Quicken displays a box (called the "QuickScroll box") containing the date and check number (if appropriate) of the transaction that will be at the top of the register window if you release the mouse button.

The QuickScroll box displays details of the transaction that will appear at the top of the Register window.

The Button Bar

Across the top of the Register window is a button bar, which makes common register operations easily available. It contains buttons for deleting and finding transactions, transferring money from one account to another, setting the register options, running a QuickReport, and closing the Register window. All these operations will be covered later in this chapter. The button bar takes up quite a bit of room in the Register window, so you have the option of turning it on and off. If the button bar is visible, you may turn it off by clicking on the Hide button bar button. This button has a pair of upward-pointing chevrons stacked on top of one another. It's located just above the scroll bar on the right side of the window. If the button bar is not visible, you may display it by clicking on the pair of downward-pointing chevrons that appear in the same location.

The Account List Line

Just below the data-entry area is a line of buttons, one for each of your accounts. You may scroll this Account List line back and forth by clicking on the arrows at the left and right ends of the line. The button that represents the currently open Register window is displayed in bold type. You may open any other account register by clicking on the appropriate button in the Account List line. You can rearrange the buttons on the Account List line. To do so:

1. Click on the account button you want to move.

2. Holding the mouse button down, drag the account button to its new location on the line. If you drag the button off the right or left side of the Register window, the Account List Line will scroll automatically in that direction.

3. When you have placed the account button where you want it, release the mouse button.

The Data Area

You use the main portion of the Register window to enter your transaction data. By default, the register displays two lines of data for each transaction. In a checking account, you can enter the date, check number, payee, the payment or deposit amount, the category, and a memo. There is also a column (marked "Clr") to indicate whether the transaction has been reconciled against the bank statement. You can enter data in this column, although Quicken will do it for you when and if you reconcile your account with your bank's records (see Chapter 7). The Register window also displays a running account balance. You cannot modify the account balance manually—Quicken calculates it for you.

If you wish, you can condense the information in the register to a single line so that Quicken will display more transactions in the Register window. To display only a single line for each transaction, click on the 1 Line Display checkbox near the bottom of the Register window. In single-line mode, the Register window displays the date, check number, payee, category, payment or deposit amount, Clr column, and the balance. The memo field isn't displayed in single-line mode, so you can't

Keystrokes in the Register Window

You can use certain keystrokes to move instantly to the various sections of the data area of the Register window. These keystrokes are summarized below:

Keystroke	Moves you to this part of the register
Up Arrow	Same field in the previous transaction
Down Arrow	Same field in the next transaction
Tab	Next field
Shift+Tab	Previous field
Home	Beginning of the field
End	End of the field
Ctrl+Home	First transaction in the account
Home+Home	First field in the transaction
Ctrl+End	Last transaction in the account
End+End	Last field in the transaction
Ctrl+Page Up	First transaction in the current month
Ctrl+Page Down	Last transaction in the current month
Page Up	Up one screen
Page Down	Down one screen

see memos about transactions or record memos for transactions you enter from within the register.

Note: At any time, you may switch back to the default two-line mode, and add memo information to transactions that were entered in single-line mode. In addition, you can enter the memo field if you write checks from the Write Checks window (Ctrl +W or press the Write Checks icon).

The Balance Amounts

Quicken maintains the current balance for the account in the lower right corner of the window. The "Ending Balance" is calculated using all the transactions in the register. If you have recorded post-dated transactions (transactions with a date later than today), the "Current Balance" amount displays the balance in the account as of today.

Note: If you have post-dated transactions, Quicken displays a bold line in the register between the transactions dated on or before today, and transactions dated after today.

Entering Data in the Register

The register lets you enter any transaction that affects your account—whether it's a check you write by hand, an ATM (Automatic Teller Machine) transaction, a deposit, an account fee, an interest payment, a service charge, or an electronic fund transfer. I prefer writing checks using the Write Checks window, which pops up if you press Ctrl+W or click on the Write Checks icon in the toolbar. Entering the data in either the Write Checks window or the register does the same thing, but the Write Checks window looks like a real check. Kind of like the old days.

Nevertheless, I'm going to explain how to enter data in the check register because it's a good idea to know how to use the register. Even if you don't write your checks there, you'll still be using the register for lots of other things.

Note: *If you plan to print checks with Quicken or use electronic banking of any kind (see Chapters 6 and 15), you should definitely enter the checks using the Write Checks window, not the Register window. Rest assured that when you use the Write Checks window, Quicken will automatically add the check to the register.*

What You See Depends on What You're Doing

Exactly what you see on the screen as you enter data in the Register window depends on the choices you have made in the Register Options window (see "Setting Register Options," later in this chapter). As we discuss how you enter data in each field of a transaction, we will note areas where the register options affect the techniques you use for data input.

Entering the Date

To enter the date, move the mouse pointer to the Date column and click to select it. You may type the date into the Date column, or use the pop-up calendar to enter a date. If you have chosen to display buttons on QuickFill fields (see "Setting Register Options," later in this chapter), you can click on the Calendar button in the Date field to display the pop-up calendar. Alternatively, you can click on the Date field with the right mouse button to display the pop-up calendar.

The pop-up calendar helps you enter a date into a register transaction.

To select a date from the currently displayed month, click on the date you want. You may move to the previous month by clicking on the Backward (⟨«⟩) button or to the next month by clicking on the Forward (⟨»⟩) button.

Entering the Check Number

You use the column labeled "Num" to enter information about the check number. You can type up to five characters, or select from the available list. Depending on your register options, the list will either pop up automatically when you select the Num field or you can display the list by clicking with your right mouse button on the Num field.

Keystroke Shortcuts for Entering Dates

You may use certain keystroke shortcuts to enter a date in the Date field.

Keystroke	Causes this date to be used
t	Today
+	Next day
–	Previous day
m	Beginning of the month
h	End of the month
y	Beginning of the year
r	End of the year

Also depending on your register options, Quicken may automatically fill in the rest of your Num entry after you type the first character or two.

Note: Quicken does not limit you to typing just digits for the five characters of a check number. You may type any five characters.

Num Pop-Up List Options

Option	What it means
ATM	A transaction that takes place using an Automatic Teller Machine (for example, cash withdrawal).
Next Check #	Quicken scans the current account to find the last check number you used, then provides the next check number in the Num field.
Transfer	Identifies a transfer to or from another account.
Deposit	A deposit (adding funds) to this account.
Send	Indicates transactions that are waiting to be transmitted to a bank or CheckFree electronically (see Chapter 15). Used automatically by Quicken.
EFT	Indicates transactions that have been transmitted electronically to a bank or to CheckFree. Used automatically by Quicken.
Fixed	Indicates fixed payments made electronically. Used automatically by Quicken.
Print	Indicates checks you write using the Write Checks window that have not yet been printed by Quicken. See Chapter 6 for more information.

You may select New from the Num pop-up list to add a new five-character value to the list. If you select New, Quicken will open the Add new Num/Ref dialog box. Type in the new value and click OK.

Entering the Payee

You may either type in the name of the payee, or select the payee from a list of memorized transactions (transactions you have asked Quicken to "remember"—see "Memorizing Transactions," later in this chapter). Depending on the way you have set your register options, the Payee list will either pop up automatically when you select the Payee field, or you may display the list by clicking on the Arrow button (if it is visible) or clicking with the right mouse button on the Payee field. Choose the payee you want from the list by clicking on its name.

Several of the register options affect how Quicken handles your Payee entry. If you have set up the automatic completion of fields, then Quicken will fill in the name of the first payee in a memorized transaction that matches your entry. For example, if you type "B," Quicken will fill in the rest of the name of the first payee that begins with "B." As you continue to type, Quicken continues to try and match your entry to a payee in a memorized transaction. If your payee is not in the memorized transaction list, you can just ignore Quicken's entries and continue typing the full name of the payee. However, if the payee *is* on the memorized transaction list, you can just press Tab when Quicken correctly matches the payee's name.

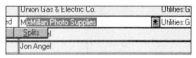

Quicken attempts to match your payee to one it already has memorized.

Note: *Sometimes Quicken makes a false assumption. Imagine you were writing a check to United Van Lines but you had earlier memorized United Airlines as a payee. Quicken will automatically enter United Airlines as soon as you type the "U." If you had earlier memorized United Van Lines, you can just keep on typing until its name is entered or you can select the arrow for the drop-down list and then choose the name from the list. If you haven't earlier memorized that payee, you just keep on typing. Quicken will accept what you type for the transaction and will also memorize the new payee for future use—if you've set the memorization option.*

Another register option that affects how Quicken handles your Payee entry is the Automatic Recall of Transactions. If you have this option turned on and Quicken is able to match your entered payee to a payee in a memorized transaction, Quicken will fill in the rest of the fields (including Category, Amount, and Memo) from the memorized transaction. Of course, you can edit any of these fields before recording the transaction.

Entering the Category

You may enter the transaction's category by either typing it in or selecting it from a list of transactions. Depending on your register option settings, this list will either appear automatically, or you can display it by clicking on the arrow button (if it is visible) or clicking with your right mouse button on the Category field. As detailed in Chapter 5, you can create a new category (and subcategory, if desired) by typing a new name in the Category field. If Quicken doesn't recognize the category name, it will prompt you for the additional information it needs to create the new category. If the transaction must be split into multiple categories, see the next section, "Splitting a Category."

    Note: *If you have set up the automatic completion of fields through the register options, Quicken will try to match your Category field entry to an existing category as you type in the name. When the correct category name appears in the Category field, you can press the Tab key to accept the category and move to the next field.*

    You can also enter another account name to indicate that money is being transferred to that account. This would come in handy if you were writing a check to pay a credit card account.

Splitting a Category

You may need to assign more than a single category to a transaction. For example, you may use a check to a department store to purchase office supplies, clothing, and jewelry. Another example is a single bank deposit that includes your paycheck, an expense reimbursement from your employer, a birthday gift, and maybe your $1,000,000 sweepstakes check from Ed McMahon. In both examples, you would want to show these as single transactions so that your records match the store's or the bank's records. The bank, for example, will show only a single deposit in your account statement. However, you may need to split the transaction into multiple categories, especially if some of the items are tax-related and some are not.

To split a single transaction into multiple categories, use the following steps:

1. Enter the transaction as you would normally, except for the Category field.

2. Enter the amount of the transaction in either the Payment or the Deposit field. If you don't know the total amount, leave the Amount field blank. Quicken will total the amount and display it in the Splits Total field as you enter each split transaction.

3. Click on the <u>S</u>plits button. Quicken will open the Splits window and will enter any amount information on the first line.

4. Enter a category on the first line of the Splits window. If you wish, you can also enter a memo.

Quicken's Splits window enables you to split the categories for single transactions.

5. Enter the amount for the category on the first line. Simply type over the amount that Quicken displays if it is different from the amount you want to allocate to this category.

Quicken will subtract the amount you enter from the total amount you entered before opening the Splits window. The remainder will be displayed in the amount field on the next line.

Note: *Instead of entering an amount, you can enter a percentage of the total amount. For example, if you type 40% in the Amount column, Quicken enters 40% of the total amount on that line. This feature is extremely useful if you have a home business, for example, and allocate expenses for utilities and insurance according to your home office's square footage. The feature works only if you entered an amount in the register before opening the Splits window.*

6. Continue to add categories and amounts on the lines in the Splits window until you have categorized the entire transaction. You can have up to 30 lines in one split transaction.

You may delete a category line in the Splits window by selecting the line and clicking the <u>D</u>elete button. You may also insert a line by clicking on the line above where you want the new line to appear, and clicking on the Inse<u>r</u>t button.

Note: *To quickly remove all entries in the Splits window, click on the* <u>C</u>*lear All button.*

7. Click OK to close the Splits window.

If you didn't enter an amount in the register (in the Payment or Deposit field) before opening the Splits window, Quicken will ask if the total amount should be recorded as a payment or as a deposit. Select either Payment or Deposit and click OK.

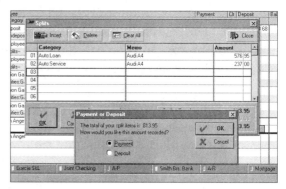

If you didn't specify an amount before opening the Splits window, choose Payment or Deposit.

8. Click the Record button at the bottom of the Register window to record the split transaction.

Adjusting the Amount of a Split-Category Transaction

If you enter an amount for a Payment or Deposit in the Register window before opening the Splits window, you may find that you need to adjust the amount of the transaction later. There are several ways to adjust the total transaction amount:

- If you discover that you have recorded all your categories in the Splits window but there is still an unaccounted-for balance on the last line of the Splits window, you can click on the Adj <u>T</u>ot button in the Splits window. Clicking on this button adjusts the Splits Total to match the categories you have entered. When you click on <u>O</u>K, Quicken adjusts the Payment or Deposit to match the Splits Total. You can also use the Adj <u>T</u>ot button to reopen the Splits window for a transaction to adjust the amounts, or to add or remove category lines.

- If you complete filling in the Splits window, click on OK, and there is an unaccounted-for amount on the last line of the Splits window, Quicken will display the Split Adjustment window. You may choose either to adjust the total or to create an uncategorized split item to balance the transaction.
- If you adjust the Payment or Deposit amount in the register for a transaction with split categories, Quicken will open the Split Adjustment window when you record the change.

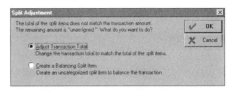

If your Split total doesn't agree with the amount you entered in the register, make a choice here to adjust the split.

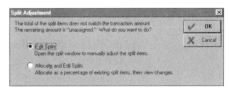

If you change the amount of a split-category transaction, the Split Adjustment window appears.

You have two choices in splitting adjustments:
- Edit Splits: This option opens the Splits window so you can manually correct the amount. The Remainder line in the Splits window indicates the amount that is unaccounted for in the category lines.
- Allocate and Edit Splits: This option takes the unaccounted-for amount and allocates it to the existing category lines by the percentage of the existing lines—essentially spreading the unaccounted-for amount among the categories. It then opens the Splits window to enable you to make any adjustments you need.

Entering the Payment or Deposit Amount

You may enter the payment or deposit amount by clicking in the Payment or Deposit column and typing in the amount. You may also click on the Calculator button (if it is visible) or click with your right mouse button in the Payment or Deposit field to display the Calculator dialog box.

Entering the Memo

The Memo field enables you to enter additional information about a transaction. Type in the information you want, up to 32 characters.

The Calculator dialog box helps you enter numbers.

Working with Transactions

You can use the buttons in the button bar to edit or delete a transaction, find a specific transaction or date, copy or paste entire transactions, memorize a transaction, or enter a transfer of funds from one account to another.

Editing Transactions

To edit transactions, you make choices from the Edit menu. The choices are:

- New Transaction: Moves you to the last line in the current register and highlights the date field, ready for you to enter a new transaction.
- Delete Transaction: Deletes the currently selected transaction, after confirming that you really want to delete it.

  Note: You may also use the Delete button to perform this action.
- Insert Transaction: Inserts a new transaction into the register ahead of a selected transaction. However, once you place a date on the new transaction and record it, Quicken will rearrange the register to place the new transaction in the correct position.
- Void Transaction: Voids the currently selected transaction. Voiding a transaction doesn't delete it; instead, it adds the word "Void" to the Payee line, shows the transaction as cleared, and removes the amount of the transaction from the register and splits.
- Copy Transaction: Places a copy of the entire transaction (including date, number, payee, category, amount, and memo) on the clipboard. This is different from using the Copy item in the Edit menu, which copies only the selected text in a field.
- Paste Transaction: Pastes the copied transaction into the register. This only works if you have previously used Copy Transaction to copy a transaction.
- Memorize Transaction: Adds the currently selected transaction to the list of memorized transactions (see "Memorizing Transactions," later in this chapter). If the memorized transaction list already contains a transaction with the same payee, Quicken will ask you whether you want to replace the current payee in the memorized transaction list, add another memorized transaction with the same payee, or cancel memorizing the transaction.

- Go to Transfer: Certain transactions have matching transactions in other registers. For example, if you transfer money from your checking account to your savings account, there will be a debit transaction in your checking account, and a credit transaction in your savings account. This is also true for transactions such as writing a check to pay a credit card bill. The Go to Transfer menu item jumps to the transaction in another account that matches the currently selected transaction. You can initiate the jump either directly from the register, or by selecting an item in the Splits window that has a matching transaction.

- Go to A Specific Date: Quickly takes you to the first transaction that was entered on the date you specify. This command is only available on the Edit pop-up menu (accessible by pressing Alt+D anywhere within the register).

The Quicken Go to A Specific Date window helps you locate a particular transaction.

Entering a Transfer

Quicken permits you to transfer money between your account registers. You might wish to transfer money to your checking account from

You may transfer money between accounts in Quicken.

your savings account, or to pay a credit card bill by transferring funds (and writing a check or sending an electronic payment) from your credit card account to your checking account.

To initiate a transfer, click on the Transfer button. Quicken will open the Transfer Money Between Accounts window.

Fill in the data in the Transfer Money Between Accounts window:

1. Type in a Description if you don't like the default.

2. Enter a dollar figure either by typing it in or by using the Calculator dialog box.

3. Enter the Date either by typing it in or by using the Calendar dialog box to select a date.

4. Select the account from which you are going to transfer the money from the drop-down <u>T</u>ransfer Money From list. The default account is the currently selected register.

5. Select the account to which you are going to transfer the money from the drop-down T<u>o</u> list.

6. Click on OK to complete the transfer of funds. Quicken will display the name of the account that is receiving the transfer in the Category field (surrounded by square brackets). Quicken also will create a parallel transaction in the other account, and

The Transfer starts out in the "Garcia Savings and Loan" account and indicates that the funds are received by the "Bank of Bartel" account . . .

. . . and here is the matching transaction in the "Bank of Bartel" account.

indicate the name of the originating account in the Category field of the parallel transaction.

Editing a Transfer

When you edit a transaction that includes a transfer, the matching transaction created by the transfer also changes:

- If you delete the transaction, Quicken deletes the matching transaction in the other account.
- If you change the date or amount of the transaction, that information changes in the matching transaction. However, if you change any information other than the date or amount (for example, payee, check number, memo, cleared status, etc.) that information does *not* change in the matching transaction.

    Note: *You may jump to the matching transaction to make matching entries by selecting <u>G</u>o to Transfer from the E<u>d</u>it pop-up menu or the <u>E</u>dit drop-down menu.*

- If a transfer was made in a split transaction, you can change it only from the originating transaction (in the Split window). You cannot change it from the account that received the matching transaction.

Finding a Transaction

You can find specific transactions in the register using the Find command, even if you don't know the contents of all the fields in the transaction. To find a transaction, use the following steps:

1. Select <u>F</u>ind from the <u>E</u>dit menu, click on the F<u>i</u>nd button in the register button bar, or type Ctrl+F. Quicken will open the Quicken Find window.

The Quicken Find window helps you find specific transactions.

2. Type some or all of the text, or the exact amount you want in the F<u>i</u>nd field. The text can be upper- or lower-case, and may contain letters and numbers. You may also use special characters (called "wildcards") that match unspecified characters (see the "Wildcards for the Quicken Find Window" sidebar below).

3. Optionally, select a field name from the <u>S</u>earch drop-down list. You may choose to search for the text or amount in all fields, or select just a single field to search in. The fields available in the <u>S</u>earch drop-down list depend on the type of register you have open.

4. Optionally, choose a search criterion from the Ma<u>t</u>ch If drop-down list. You may choose to find any transaction that contains the text (default), exactly matches the text (same as using "=" in the text string), or starts with or ends with the text. You may also search for entries (normally numeric) that are greater than, greater than or equal to, less than, or less than or equal to the entered value.

Wildcards for the Quicken Find Window

Symbol	Matches
=	An exact match (includes only transactions that match exactly what you type).
.. (two periods)	A match that contains unspecified characters wherever you type ".." For example, "Un.." would find United Airlines, United Van Lines, or Universal Studios.
?	A match with one unspecified character (for example, "C?T" could match Cat, Cut, Cot, etc.).
~ (tilde)	Excludes all transactions that match the text you typed.

Note: *Wildcards can be combined. For example, the combination of ~.. would search for fields that are blank, while ..tax.. would search for any fields that contain the word "tax" anywhere in the text.*

5. If you wish to search backward through the register, make sure there is a check mark in the Search Ba_ck_wards checkbox. Otherwise, Quicken will start with the currently selected transaction and search toward the end of the register; however, when it reaches the end, it will ask if you wish to search from the beginning so you don't have to worry about not finding any items.

6. Click either Fi_n_d or _F_ind All. The Fi_n_d button finds the first matching transaction in the register. Each time you click on the Fi_n_d button, Quicken will search for the next matching transaction. If Quicken reaches the end of the register (or the beginning, if searching backward), it will ask whether you want to continue the search from the beginning (or end, if searching backward) of the register. Click on Yes or No to continue the search.

> **Note:** _If you wish to edit the found transaction, you must click on the Register window, which may hide the Quicken Find window. If you need to use the Quicken Find window again, select Quicken Find from the_ _W_indow _menu._

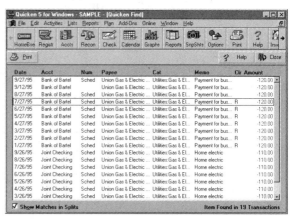

The Find All command produces a report of all matching transactions.

The _F_ind All button searches through all your registers to find the matching transactions and produces a report that summarizes them. You can jump to one of the transactions by double-clicking on it. You may also print a list of the found transactions by clicking on the _P_rint button.

> **Note:** _The Find All command is different from the QuickReport feature, which is covered later in this chapter._

Finding and Replacing Items

Quicken enables you to find and replace specific information in a register. This can be handy if a specific piece of information that you record commonly changes. To find information and replace it:

1. Choose Find/Replace from the Edit menu. Quicken opens the Find and Replace window.

2. Type some or all of the text, or the exact amount you want in the Find field. The text can be upper- or lowercase, and may contain letters and numbers. You may also use special characters (called "wildcards") that match unspecified characters (see "Wildcards for the Quicken Find Window" on page 61).

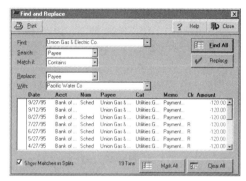

Use Find and Replace to find all matching transactions and replace a field value.

3. Optionally, select a field name from the Search drop-down list. You may choose to search for the text or amount in all fields, or select just a single field to search in. The fields available in the Search drop-down list depend on the type of register you have open.

4. Optionally, choose a search criterion from the Match If drop-down list.

5. Click on the Find All button. Quicken assembles a list of matching transactions in the Find and Replace window.

6. Select the field in which you want to replace the information from the Replace drop-down list. You may select only a single field for replacing information, even if your search was for "All Fields" from the Search list.

7. Type the information you want to use to replace the information in the Find field.

8. Select the transactions for which you want to replace the contents from the list of matching transactions at the bottom of the Find and Replace window. You may select all the transactions by clicking on the Mark All button. You can deselect all transactions by clicking on the Clear All button.

9. Click on the Replace button to replace all the selected transactions.

Caution: Be very careful before using Find and Replace as it is easy to make some rather drastic changes.

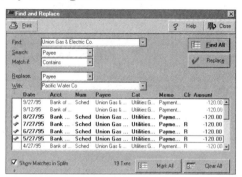

Select all the transactions you want to replace from the Find and Replace window.

Memorized Transactions

A "memorized transaction" is a transaction that Quicken "remembers." With a memorized transaction, you can enter the details of the transaction just once, then recall the transaction whenever you need to enter it. For example, you might wish to memorize payments that you make periodically for the same amount—such as your mortgage or car payment. When you recall a memorized transaction to enter it in an account register, you can edit any of the data in the transaction before you record the payment or deposit. Thus, memorized transactions are useful for payments for which the amount varies (such as a phone bill) but the rest of the information remains the same.

Note: Before you can set up a transaction group (for fast entry of multiple transactions), you must memorize all the transactions you want to include in the group. See Chapter 9 for more information on transaction groups.

Memorizing Transactions

You can memorize a transaction with split categories and even memorize the split percentages instead of the actual amounts. If you memorize the percentages, Quicken will split the overall amount you enter by the memorized percentages.

Note: You can assign an icon in the Quicken toolbar to a memorized transaction. Clicking on the icon will then automatically open the appropriate register, insert the memorized transaction, and wait for you to click the Record button.

There are two ways to memorize a transaction: directly from the register and by using the Memorized Transaction list. To memorize a transaction from the register, use the following steps:

1. Enter the transaction in the register, or select an existing transaction.

2. From the Edit menu, select Memorize Transaction, or press Ctrl+M. Quicken tells you that the transaction is about to be memorized.

3. Click OK. Quicken memorizes all the information in the selected transaction except for the date and any check number. If a memorized transaction already exists with the current payee, Quicken warns you and asks whether you want to Replace the existing transaction, Add another transaction with the same payee, or Cancel the memorization.

To memorize a transaction from the Memorized Transaction List, use the following steps:

1. Choose Memorized Transaction from the Lists menu. Quicken will open the Memorized Transaction List.

2. Click on the New button. Quicken opens the Create Memorized Transaction window.

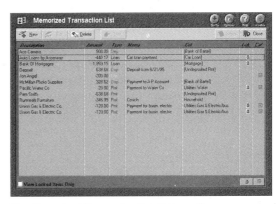

The Memorized Transaction List displays all your memorized transactions.

3. Fill in the Type, using the drop-down menu. For checks you are going to print from Quicken, choose the Print Check type. Select Payment if this is a check you intend to write manually, or if it is some other type of withdrawal (for example, an ATM withdrawal). Select Deposit if this transaction adds money to your account. Select Online Pmt if you will be paying this through CheckFree.

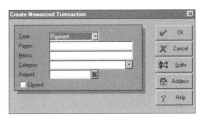

Use this window to create a new memorized transaction from the Memorized Transaction List.

4. Fill in the Payee, Memo, Category, and (optionally) the Amount fields.

Suggestion: It can sometimes be a mistake to have an amount in a memorized transaction. Let's say you pay a $300 phone bill one month and memorize the transaction. The next month's bill may be only $50 but, if you're not careful, you may accidentally pay $300 because that's what is memorized. An option is to not type in any amount (or type "00") and then press Ctrl+M. That memorizes everything except the amount (it sets it for 0), forcing you to enter a real amount every time you pay that vendor.

5. If you wish, you may split the category by clicking on the Splits button and entering the splits information in the Splits window (see "Splitting a Category," earlier in this chapter). If you enter percentages in the Splits window, Quicken will ask you whether you want to memorize the percentages, rather than the actual amount. If you memorize the percentages, any amount you enter in a future use of this transaction will be allocated per the memorized percentages.

6. If you wish, you may add an address to the transaction by clicking on the Address button to open the Printed Check Information window. This window is only available if the transaction is a check.

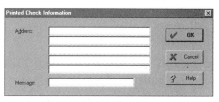

Use the Printed Check Information to add an address to a check you intend to print.

7. Click OK. Quicken will memorize all the information in the new transaction. If a memorized transaction already exists with the current payee, Quicken will warn you and ask whether you want to Replace the existing transaction, Add another transaction with the same payee, or Cancel the memorization.

Note: You can set Quicken to automatically memorize each transaction to a payee that isn't in the Memorized Transaction List already (see "Setting Register Options," later in this chapter). In order to keep your list of memorized transactions to a reasonable length, however, transactions that you make to a payee only once shouldn't be memorized.

Recalling Memorized Transactions

Once you have memorized a transaction, you may recall it directly from the register, from the Write Checks window, or from the Memorized

Transaction List. To recall a memorized transaction directly from the register, you must have both Automatic Completion of Fields and Automatic Recall of Transactions turned on in the register options (see "Setting Register Options," later in this chapter). To recall a memorized transaction:

1. Begin typing in the payee information for the transaction. As you type, Quicken will fill in matching payee names from the Memorized Transaction list.

2. When the payee name matches the one you want, simply press the Tab key to accept the payee. Quicken will then fill in the balance of the transaction from the Memorized Transaction List. Alternately, you can press the Down arrow to select the payee from the list. It will present the payees that match what you've already typed.

3. If necessary, edit the information in the transaction. One of the most common items that must be changed is the amount of the transaction. Quicken will highlight the amount by default.

4. Click on Record to enter the new transaction.

To recall a transaction from the Memorized Transaction List:

1. Scroll to the bottom of the register to select a new transaction.

2. Select Memorized Transaction from the Lists menu. Quicken opens the Memorized Transaction List.

3. Double-click on the transaction, or select it and click the Use button to enter the transaction in the register.

4. If necessary, edit the information in the transaction. One of the most common items that must be changed is the amount of the transaction. Quicken will highlight the amount by default.

5. Click Record to enter the new transaction.

Working with the Memorized Transaction List

In addition to the New and Use buttons (discussed earlier), you may use the following tools to work with memorized transactions in the Memorized Transaction List:

- The Edit button opens the Edit Memorized Transaction window so that you may make changes to the transaction. All the options from the Create Memorized Transaction window are available.
- The Delete button deletes the selected memorized transaction after first confirming that you want to do that.
- The Report button provides a QuickReport of all transactions that involve the selected payee. To create a QuickReport, select the payee you are interested in, and click on Report. Quicken will provide a Payee Report. If you double-click on any line in the report, Quicken will open the appropriate register and highlight the transaction in that register. If you don't see the Report button

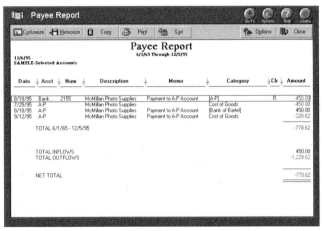

Quicken's Payee Report quickly summarizes all transactions for a given payee.

The chevron symbol in the upper right corner of the register toggles the buttons on and off.

and other buttons on the top of the register, click on the chevron symbol in the upper right corner of the register. Clicking on that symbol toggles the buttons on and off.

- The Lck (Lock) column indicates the lock status of the memorized transaction. When a memorized transaction is locked, any changes you make to subsequent occurrences of the transaction (such as changing the amount) when adding the transaction to a register don't affect the memorized transaction. If the transaction is not locked, any changes you make to the transaction when adding it to a register change the memorized transaction. Thus, the next time you add the memorized transaction to a register, it will reflect those changes. To change the lock status of a transaction, select the transaction and click the small lock symbol in the lower right corner of the Memorized Transaction List window.

> **Note:** *Transactions you memorize manually are locked by default.*

- The Cal column displays the calendar status of a transaction. Quicken has a Financial Calendar (see Chapter 9) that displays transactions by date. Alongside the calendar is a column of memorized transactions. You can drag any of these transactions onto the calendar to schedule an occurrence of the transaction. If the calendar status of a memorized transaction is "on" (the small calendar shows in the column), Quicken displays the transaction in the Financial Calendar list. To cut down on the number of transactions displayed in the Financial Calendar list, turn off the calendar status. To toggle (turn on or off) the calendar status of a memorized transaction, select the transaction and click on the Calendar button in the lower right corner of the Memorized Transaction List window.

> **Caution:** *The QuickReport only covers payees that are exactly as typed. If you have both fixed and variable payments to the payee it will not report both. In that case you need to customize the report to be sure it covers all payees that begin with the characters listed. See the wildcard discussion earlier in this chapter.*

Setting Register Options

You can set the register options in Quicken to customize the way the register looks and works. To change the register options, click on the Options button in the register button bar. If you do not have the button bar turned on, you can select Options from the Edit menu and then click on the Register button.

Quicken opens the Register Options window. This window displays three sets of options: Display, Miscellaneous, and QuickFill, split into three panels. To switch panels, simply click on the tab for the panel you want.

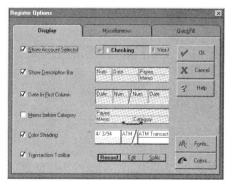

The Register Options window enables you to customize how the register looks and works.

The Display Options

The Display options are summarized in the sidebar "Register Display Options." An option is selected when a checkbox is displayed alongside its name.

Use the Choose Register Font window to change the font Quicken uses in the register.

You can change the fonts that Quicken uses in the register by clicking on the Fonts button in the Display panel. Quicken opens the Choose Register Font window. Choose the font from the list of available fonts. Choose the size from the Size list or type in a size. Click on Bold to use a bold font in the register. You may click on Reset to return the font back to the default. Click on OK to change the font.

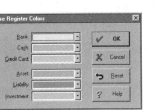

The Choose Register Colors window enables you to customize the colors used in the registers.

You can change the colors that Quicken uses for each type of account by clicking on the Colors button to open the Choose Register Colors window. Choose the color you want

Register Display Options

Display Option	Action When Option is Selected
Show Account Selector	Displays the Account Selector buttons in the line at the bottom of the Register window.
Show Description Bar	Displays the description bar with the names of the register fields at the top of the register.
Date in First Column	Displays the Date column first and the Num column second. By clearing this checkbox, you can reverse the order of these two columns.
Memo before Category	Displays the Memo column first and then the Category column. By clearing this checkbox, you can reverse the order of these two columns.
Color Shading	Displays the Register window with color shading in each transaction. A different color is used for each account. To change the colors used, click on the Colors button.
Transaction Toolbar	Displays the Record, Edit, and Split buttons next to the current transaction in the register. Clear this checkbox to turn the buttons off.

for each account type from the drop-down list alongside the account types. You may click on Reset to return the colors back to the default. Click on OK to change the colors.

The Miscellaneous Options

You can switch to the Miscellaneous register options by clicking on the Miscellaneous tab. See the sidebar "The Miscellaneous Options" for a summary of these options. An option is selected when a checkbox is displayed alongside its name.

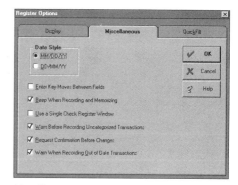

Miscellaneous options may be set in the Register Options window.

The Miscellaneous Options

Miscellaneous Option	Action When Option Is Selected
Date Style	You may choose one of two date styles by clicking on one of the radio buttons. The two date styles are MM/DD/YY and DD/MM/YY.
Enter Key Moves Between Fields	Uses the Enter key as well as the Tab key to move between fields in any account register and in the Write Checks window. (Note: The Enter key moves between fields in Quicken for DOS.)
Beep When Recording and Memorizing	Beeps after recording, deleting, or memorizing a transaction, or after memorizing a report.
Use a Single Check Register window	Allows only one Register window at a time. If you switch to another account, Quicken changes the open Register window to that account. If this option is not enabled, you can open multiple accounts, each in their own window.
Warn Before Recording Uncategorized Transaction	Prompts you to enter a category for the transaction that you are recording if you haven't already entered one. This helps you remember to always enter a transaction category.
Request Confirmation Before Changes	Requires you to confirm any changes made to a transaction or list before going to a new transaction or a new window.
Warn When Recording Out of Date Transactions	Warns you if you attempt to record a transaction with a date for a different year.

The QuickFill Options

QuickFill Option	Action When Option Is Selected
Automatic Memorization of New Transactions	Memorizes every new transaction you enter for a new payee (except investment transactions) and adds the transaction to the Memorized Transaction List. Quicken automatically turns off this option when the list of memorized transactions reaches half of Quicken's 2,000 memorized transactions limit.
Automatic Completion of Fields	Completes each field in a transaction as you type it. This feature works with Check Number (Num), Payee, Category, Class, Security Names, Investment Action, and transfer account names.
Automatic Recall of Transactions	Recalls a memorized transaction and fills in all the fields when you press Tab to leave the Payee field. This option is only available if you have also selected Automatic Completion of Fields.
Drop Down Lists Automatically	Displays the drop-down list for a field when you move the cursor to the field. If you find that the drop-down list gets in your way, you can disable this option and use Buttons on QuickFill Fields instead. That option lets you click on a button to drop down a list when you want.
Buttons on QuickFill Fields	Displays the drop-down list for QuickFill fields. Click the button to drop down the list. If you have this option turned off, you can still display the list by clicking with the right mouse button.
Auto Memorize to the Calendar List	Memorizes every new transaction to the Calendar list of memorized transactions.
Add Financial Address Book Items to QuickFill List	Found in Quicken Deluxe only, this option can add names and addresses from your Financial Address Book to items on the Memorized Transactions List.

The QuickFill Options

You can switch to the QuickFill register options by clicking on the QuickFill tab. See the sidebar "The QuickFill Options" for a summary of these options. An option is selected when a checkbox is displayed alongside its name.

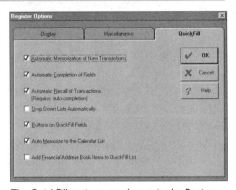

The QuickFill options may be set in the Register Options window.

QuickReports from the Register

From a register, you can click on the Report button to run a Quick-Report of the transactions in the register. The report initially lists all

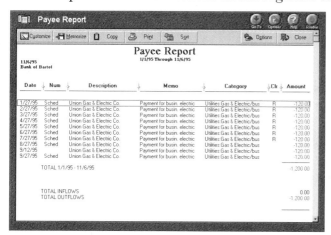

transactions in date order. However, as we shall see in Chapter 13, you can change the date range for the report, and sort by Payee or another field. As with other reports, you can double-click on any item in the report to return to the Register window and select that transaction.

The Register QuickReport shows all the transactions in the register.

Summary

To work with Quicken, you must set up accounts. In this chapter, we set up a checking account and explored the many options for its use. We looked at the various parts of the Register window, entered data using QuickFill, attached categories for the transactions, and memorized some of those transactions. We also customized the register using the register options, and created a QuickReport of the register contents.

Setting Up

5

COMING SOON FROM INTUIT

Anyone with a checkbook register and a calculator can keep track
of how much money they deposit and spend. But with Quicken,
you can not only keep track of your total expenses and income, you
can also easily find out exactly where your money is coming from
and going. It's as if you threw all your receipts into a big shoebox
and, in the middle of the night, a little elf came over to organize
them into categories. That little elf is Quicken's category feature.

Do you dine out a lot? By categorizing your dining expenses, you can
find out just how much you really spend at restaurants. How much
do you pay for gas and electricity? Quicken can tell you in seconds.
Auto repairs? What about the phone? Which of these expenses are
tax-deductible?

Keeping track of expenses can have some unexpected side benefits. As an experiment, my brother decided once to write down everything he spent—even pocket change. After awhile, he realized he was spending $5 a week on candy. He was shocked, not by the amount of money, but by the realization that he was eating so much junk food. He stopped buying candy on impulse and now he not only saves about $250 a year but he also avoids thousands of useless calories.

Using categories helps you figure out exactly where you spend your money and enables you to create category-specific reports and graphs. Reports help you summarize your income and expenses, while graphs can display trends in your spending that you might not have realized. It's amazing, but when you see that line graph or pie chart, you really do get a sense of things that you might not otherwise have noticed. Reports and graphs are covered more fully in Chapter 11, and budgets are covered in Chapter 17.

If you use Quicken to maintain a budget—a good idea, which I keep thinking I should start doing—you can set up budget amounts by category. Then, you can compare your actual expenses to your budgeted expenses within each category.

I don't prepare my own taxes, but I do take advantage of Quicken's category feature to create a report of all my tax-related income and expenses. I then take that report over to my accountant who, by the way, happens to be my brother Sandy—the same guy who used to eat too much candy.

What Is a Category?

A "category" is a way to classify the financial transactions you keep track of in Quicken. For example, you can classify a restaurant credit card bill as "Dining," an electronic funds transfer to your grocery store as "Groceries," your paycheck as "Salary," or a check to the local cable company as "Entertainment." You can also split a single transaction, such as a check you write to the drugstore, into several categories, such as "Medicine," "Household Goods," and "Gardening." If you deposit several checks at once, you also can split those into categories such as "Salary," "Book Royalties," or "Poker Winnings."

Working with Categories

When you install Quicken, you can include a set of business categories as well as home categories. If you include these preset categories, you will have a good list to begin with. However, you may want to add categories if the ones included with Quicken don't cover all your needs. By the same token, a lot of Quicken's categories will be irrelevant to you. That's what happens when a company writes a program for millions of users. The good news is that you can delete or edit any existing categories. Or, you can just ignore unused categories. They won't get in your way.

Setting Up Categories

There are three ways to set up new categories:

1. From the Category & Transfer List

2. From within a transaction in a register

3. From the Write Checks window

When you set up a new category from the Category & Transfer List, Quicken provides a lot of help in defining the new category or subcategory. Subcategories are discussed later in this chapter (see "What Is a Subcategory?") but, for now, suffice it to say that they're a way to get Quicken to track your expenses or income in greater detail than at the category level.

You can also set up a new category from the Register or the Write Checks window. This is very handy if you find yourself writing a check (or recording a credit card transaction) for an item that doesn't fit into an existing category. Instead of having to pull down another menu item, you can just enter it right then and there. Also, as we'll discover later, it can be quicker to set up a subcategory from the Register or Write Checks window than from the Category & Transfer List. Go figure.

Setting Up a Category from the Category & Transfer List

To create a new category from the Category & Transfer List, use the following steps:

1. Select <u>C</u>ategory & Transfer from the <u>L</u>ists menu. This will open the Category & Transfer List window, which will display a list of all the categories you have defined, as well as Quicken's prepackaged categories. The "Income" categories appear first in the list, followed by the "Expense" categories and a list of all your accounts.

Account names are included in the Category & Transfer List because you can transfer money between accounts by using an account name as your category. That way, when you write a check to, say, American Express, the information is tracked not only in your check register but in the credit card register you set up for your American Express

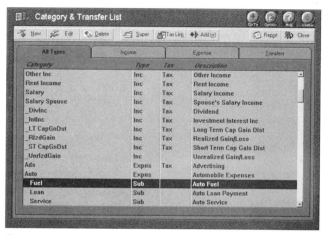

The Category & Transfer List window displays all your categories and accounts, as well as tools for working with them.

card. Don't worry: The information only shows up once in a report, so you won't be "double-billed" for one expense even if it is in two registers.

2. Click <u>N</u>ew. The Set Up Category window will appear.

3. Type the name of your category into the <u>N</u>ame line. You may use up to 15 characters for the category name.

Use the Set Up Category window to create new categories and subcategories.

4. Enter a description for the category or subcategory on the <u>D</u>escription line. You may use up to 25 characters for the category description.

5. Set the Type of Category. A category type may be Income, Expense, or a Subcategory of another category. (Subcategories are discussed later in this chapter.) Select one of the types by clicking on the little round circle (called a "radio button") next to Income, Expense, or Subcategory of.

6. If the category or subcategory is tax-related, click the Tax-related checkbox. Transactions with this category show up on Quicken's tax-related reports.

Note: If the category is tax-related, you may pick the tax form on which this category should be documented via the drop-down Form list. If the tax form you need is not available from the Form list or if you're not sure which form to use, leave the form selection blank. See Chapter 18 for information on working with computerized tax packages.

7. Select OK to add the category or subcategory to the list of available categories.

Setting Up a New Category or Subcategory from the Register or Write Checks Window

To create a new category or subcategory from a transaction in a Register or Write Checks window, simply click in the Category section of the transaction.

Begin typing in the category or subcategory. As you type, Quicken may try to fill in a matching category. Continue typing in the new category. If you wish to add a subcategory, end the category name with a colon (:), then type the subcategory name. You may continue adding subcategories of subcategories by adding colons at the end of each subcategory name and then typing the next subcategory name. Of course, you might want to avoid creating too many levels of subcategories. Life is complicated enough already.

Click in the Category section of the transaction to begin entering a new category.

Note: Quicken's ability to fill in information that matches what you type is called

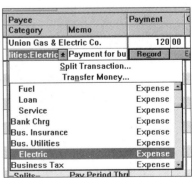

You may type a new category and its subcategories right into a register transaction.

"QuickFill." You can turn QuickFill on and off. QuickFill is discussed in Chapter 4.

When you record the transaction by clicking on the Record button at the bottom of the Register window, Quicken checks the category you entered. If it's a new category, Quicken displays the Set Up Category window. You may add additional information (such as "tax-deductible") in the Set Up Category window and then click OK to create the new category or subcategory. For example, if you created a new category by typing "Utility:Entertainment:TV" (and this entire category structure was new), Quicken would display the Set Up Category window three times: to set up the new category "Utility," to set up the new subcategory "Entertainment" of the category "Utility," and finally, to set up the new subcategory "TV" of "Utility:Entertainment."

Editing and Deleting Categories

Once you have set up categories and subcategories, you can modify them later. You can change the information about a category or sub-category, including the name, description, and tax status. Don't worry: If you change the name of a category, you won't delete the data. It will automatically be saved under the new category name.

You can delete a category or subcategory. You can also promote a subcategory (turning it into a category) or change a category into a sub-category. Finally, you can merge two categories together, turning them into a single category.

Changing Categories

To change the information about a category or subcategory:

1. Select Category & Transfer from the Lists menu to open the Category & Transfer List window.

2. Select the category or subcategory you want to edit.

3. Click on the Edit button. The Edit Category window opens. This window looks exactly like the Set Up Category window except for the title line, which reads "Edit Category" instead of "Set Up Category."

4. Make the changes you want in the Edit Category window. You can make the following changes:

- Change the Description or Name of the category. To change the description or name of a category or subcategory, edit the text for the Description or Name. All transactions attached to that changed category or subcategory will reflect the new name.
- Change the Tax-related status or Form. To change the tax-related status or tax form, click in the Tax-related checkbox or select another form from the Form drop-down list.
- Change the category type. To change the type of category from Income to Expense or from Expense to Income, click the radio button next to Income or Expense.
- Demote a category by making it a subcategory. To demote a category by making it a subcategory of either another category or an existing subcategory, click on the Subcategory of radio button and select the category or subcategory you want from the drop-down list.
- Promote a subcategory by turning it into a category. To promote a subcategory, select either the Income or Expense radio button. The subcategory will turn into a category.
- Move a subcategory from one category to another. To move a subcategory, select the name of the new category or subcategory from the Subcategory of list.

5. Click OK to close the Edit Category window and complete the changes.

Deleting Categories

If you no longer need a category or subcategory, you can delete it. When you delete a category, any transactions attached to that category aren't deleted, but they no longer have a category. When you delete a subcategory, you have the option of attaching the transactions to the parent category or subcategory.

Note: Quicken won't allow you to delete a category that has subcategories. You must promote the subcategories to categories or move them to another subcategory before you can delete the category. Strangely, you do this by "deleting" the subcategory though it doesn't really do that.

To delete a category or subcategory:

1. Select Category & Transfer from the Lists menu to open the Category & Transfer List window.

2. Select the category or subcategory you want to delete.

3. Click on the Delete button in the button bar at the top of the Category & Transfer List.

4. If you are deleting a category (with no subcategories), Quicken will prompt you to confirm that you want to delete the category. If you are deleting a subcategory, Quicken will display a dialog box with three choices on how to handle the transactions attached to the subcategory. If you select Yes, the subcategory's transactions are merged with the parent category or subcategory. If you select No, all transactions attached to the subcategory will no longer have a category. Finally, you may Cancel the deletion.

Quicken will confirm that you want to delete a category.

Quicken will ask you to decide what to do with transactions attached to a subcategory.

Merging Categories

If you start out with several similar categories, you may find that you want to merge them into a single category. Merging two categories is a two-step process. First, you make one of the categories a subcategory of the other. Second, you delete that new subcategory, at which point Quicken will attach all the subcategory's transactions to the category to which it had belonged.

Reporting on Transactions with a Specific Category

You can produce an instant report (referred to as a "QuickReport") that lists all the transactions in the current file that are attached to a single category or subcategory. A QuickReport can help you figure out how much you are spending on a certain category or subcategory. For example, you can quickly see how much you are spending on car repairs or dining out.

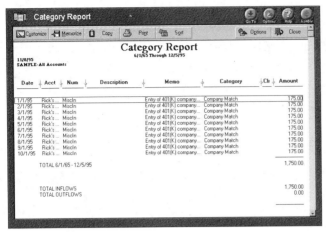

A QuickReport displays all the transactions in the open file attached to the selected category.

To create a QuickReport:

1. Select <u>C</u>ategory & Transfer from the <u>L</u>ists menu to open the Category & Transfer List window.

2. Select the category or subcategory that you want for the QuickReport.

3. Select Rep<u>o</u>rt in the button bar at the top of the Category & Transfer List window.

4. Quicken will display the report.
  Note: *By default, Quicken will not display any subcategories below the one you clicked.*

What is a Subcategory?

As the following steps indicate, using subcategories and supercategories can be more hassle than it's worth in some situations. But it can also be useful in helping you fine-tune how Quicken tracks expenses and income. So read on, at least for a little while, and decide for yourself.

When you set up categories, you have the option of setting them all up on a single level, or in a hierarchy where a subcategory belongs to a "parent" category. Take my restaurant charges, for example.

Not all meals are created equal. When I go out to dinner with my family, it's a personal expense. We had better enjoy the meal because I can't write it off. If I take out a business associate or eat a meal while on a business trip, it's another matter. Uncle Sam needs to know about that meal if I want to deduct part of its cost from my taxes. So, "dining" isn't just "dining."

That's where subcategories come in. When I get a restaurant bill it's always categorized as "Dining" (what else do you do at a restaurant?) but it usually has a subcategory. It can be "Dining:Personal," "Dining:Business," or "Dining:Travel."

By using subcategories, you can break down your expenses and income in finer detail.

Subcategories can also be useful when allocating tax-deductible expenses to the appropriate tax form. For example, you might have a category of "Computer Expenses" (if you ran a business that uses computers), with subcategories of "Hardware and Software," "Supplies," and "Equipment Repairs." While "Supplies" and "Equipment Repairs" are deductible on one form (most likely a Schedule C), the "Hardware and Software" expenses might have to be depreciated on another schedule. By using subcategories, you can keep all your computer-related expenses together, but still differentiate them. Subcategories appear on reports and in budgets. In graphs, the subcategories are summarized up to the parent category level.

Setting Up a Subcategory

You set up a subcategory in, more or less, the same way you set up a category, except for a couple of extra steps.

Before you can set up a subcategory in the Category & Transfer List section, you first have to have a category for which this is a subcategory. So, if you already have a category called Dining, you can easily set up a subcategory in the following manner:

I. Select Category & Transfer from the Lists menu to open the Category & Transfer List window.

2. Click New. The Set Up Category window will appear.

3. Type the name of your subcategory into the Name line. You may use up to 15 characters for the subcategory name.

4. Enter a Description for the subcategory on the Description line. You may use up to 25 characters for the subcategory description.

5. Click the radio button where it says Subcategory of.

6. Use the drop-down menu (by clicking on the arrow) to bring down a list of all your categories and select the category for which this is a subcategory. (Hint: You can type in the first letter of the category to skip right to the general area.)

7. If the subcategory is tax-related, click the Tax-related checkbox. Checking this box causes transactions that have this subcategory to show up on Quicken's Tax-related report.

8. If the subcategory is tax-related, you may pick the tax form on which this category should be documented by selecting the form from the Form drop-down list. The list of tax forms is not exhaustive, so you many not find the form you need.

9. Click OK to add the subcategory to the category.

What is a Supercategory?

Quicken enables you to group categories and subcategories together into "supercategories." You can use supercategories in your budget (see Chapter 17) and in budget reports to simplify the view of your budget by grouping items into larger categories. For example, you could combine all your travel-related items into a single supercategory, which would let you get a bird's-eye view of travel and still get all the detail you want.

Hint: Before you proceed, think about whether you really need to set up supercategories. First of all, you only use them for budgeting, so if you don't plan to use Quicken for that purpose, then there's definitely no reason. Even if you do create a budget, it might be just as easy (or even easier) to set up a budget with multiple regular categories.

Setting up a Supercategory

1. Select <u>C</u>ategory & Transfer from the <u>L</u>ists menu to open the Category & Transfer List window.

2. Click on the <u>S</u>uper button in the button bar at the top of the Category & Transfer List window. Quicken opens the Manage Supercategories window. On the right side of the window is a list of available supercategories.

3. Click on the category you want to join to a supercategory.

4. Click on the supercategory you want to join the category to.

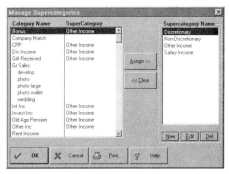

You can connect categories to supercategories and create new supercategories from the Manage Supercategories window.

5. Click the <u>A</u>ssign button. The connected supercategory appears in the Supercategory column alongside its category.

6. To remove a category's supercategory, select the category in the Category Name column, then click on the <u>C</u>lear button.

7. Click on OK to close the Manage Supercategories window and save your changes.

Editing a Supercategory's Name

1. Select the supercategory in the Supercategory Name column of the Manage Supercategories window.

2. Click on the <u>E</u>dit button to open the Edit Supercategory dialog box.

3. Edit the <u>S</u>upercategory Name, then click OK.

Creating a New Supercategory

1. Click on the <u>N</u>ew button in the Manage Supercategories window.

2. Quicken will open the Create New Supercategory window.

3. Enter a <u>S</u>upercategory Name, then click OK to add the new super-category.

Working with Classes

Classes are yet another tool that you may or may not use. I don't use them, though my accountant thinks I should. Oh well.

Classes enable you to further classify transactions beyond categories and subcategories. Classes are not used in place of categories; rather, they supplement categories by adding another dimension to graphs, reports, and budgets.

Hint: Classes, like supercategories and subcategories, are a relatively advanced feature. It's not that they're so hard to use-it's just that lots of people can live without them.

Classes can be used to specify:

- Who a transaction is for

    You can use classes to help bill expenses to particular clients, or to track income for salespeople (for example, commissions).
- Where a transaction applies

    You can use classes to specify sales by region, or to allocate expenses by property address. You can also track expenses by job, project, or department.
- What a transaction is for

    You can use classes to split expenses between business and personal, or by security names in an asset account.

Note: Quicken does not provide a preset list of classes.

Setting Up Classes

You can set up classes from the Class List or as you enter a transaction. Setting up a class in the Class List enables you to set up classes ahead of time, while setting up classes from the register enables you to create classes as you need them. You can also create "subclasses" to further define your transactions.

Setting Up Classes in the Class List

To create a class using the Class List, use the following steps:

1. Select Class from the Lists menu. Quicken will open the Class List window.

Quicken's Class List enables you to create and edit classes.

2. Click on the New button. The Set Up Class window will appear.

3. Fill in the Name and Description, then click OK to create the new class. The new class will appear in the Class List window.

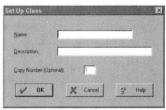

Use the Set Up Class window to create new classes.

Setting Up Classes in the Register

To set up classes directly in the register, simply enter the transaction as you would normally (refer to Chapter 4 for more information on using registers). Click in the Category field and enter a category. If you wish to add a subcategory, type a colon (:) after the category name and enter the name of the subcategory. Next, type in a forward slash (/) to separate the category information from the class information. Continue by entering the name of the class for this transaction. If you wish to add a subclass, type a colon (:) after the class name, then type in the subclass name. Continue adding any further subclasses you wish, separating the subclasses using colons.

Separate categories from classes with a slash (/), and classes from subclasses with a colon (:).

When you record the transaction by clicking on the Record button at the bottom of the Register window, Quicken checks the classes you entered. For each new class, Quicken displays the Set Up Class window. You may add a description for the new class if you wish. Unlike categories and subcategories, Quicken does not distinguish between classes and subclasses when you are setting them up. Instead, Quicken "knows" that a class is being used as a subclass because of its position in the register's Category field: after a class, and separated from the class by a colon.

Editing and Deleting Classes

You can easily edit and delete classes from the Class List window. To edit a class, select it and click the Edit button. The Edit Class window will appear. It looks exactly like the Set Up Class window except for the title bar. In the Edit Class window, you can change the name and description of the class. Any transaction that uses this class will automatically change to reflect the new name.

To delete a class, select it and click the Delete button. Click OK to confirm that you want to delete the class.

Reporting on Transactions with a Specific Class

You can create a QuickReport for a specific class, just as you can with a category. To produce a QuickReport from the Class List window, select the class you want a report for and click the Report button. The QuickReport will list all transactions that use the selected class—including transactions that use the class as a subclass.

Summary

Quicken provides many ways to classify and categorize your transactions so you can keep track of your expenditures. The program comes with a set of categories, and you can easily add your own to these. If you want to be even more precise with the way you break down your items, you can also nest categories within categories. In addition, categories can be specified as tax-related. Classes are useful for further classifying your transactions, and classes can also be nested within classes.

Writing and Printing Checks

"THE CHECK'S IN THE E-MAIL"? NICE TRY, SIR.

6

The most important activity in home banking is writing checks. Bill paying will always be a necessary evil, since no one wants their lights turned off, their mortgage foreclosed, or . . . well, I'm sure you get the idea without me adding to the list of depressing possibilities.

While this is never going to be anyone's favorite activity, Quicken has succeeded in taking the "writing" out of writing checks. In fact, with its new electronic banking options Quicken also takes the "checks" out of writing checks. Payments can be made totally in the electronic domain, with no paper exchanging hands.

Because we've all grown up struggling with a standard checkbook, however, Quicken uses the check register and "writing checks" metaphor for whatever type of payment you're making. This makes it easy to start using the program as a record-keeping adjunct to your traditional way of writing checks; to graduate to printing checks with your computer; and finally, to switch to online banking–all without learning anything new.

Quicken gives you three basic options for creating checks:

1. You can simply record the checks in the register, and write the checks by hand. This may be easier in certain circumstances: for example, when you are using page-oriented checks (see "Printing Checks," later in this chapter) and have only a single check to print. However, using handwritten checks does require entering the data on the check twice: once on the handwritten check, and once in Quicken.

2. You can let Quicken print the checks for you on special blank computer checks that you can buy from Intuit or (to save money) from a check printing company.

3. You can do as I do and send payments electronically. For several years, I've been using CheckFree to generate my checks. (There's a small service fee, but it's not much more expensive than writing and mailing checks.) CheckFree is still available, but there's now a complementary service from Intuit Services Corporation, plus all-out electronic banking from many different financial institutions (see Chapter 15 for more details on all of these options).

In this chapter, we concentrate on the second possibility: writing checks using the Write Checks window and then printing them on special check stock ordered from Intuit or several other firms.

Using the Write Checks Window

To write checks that will be printed by Quicken, you must open the Write Checks window by either clicking on the Check button in the icon bar or selecting Write Checks from the Activities menu. If you plan to write the checks by hand or transmit the data using one of the electronic banking options, you may use either the Write Checks window or the register. I use the Write Checks window because I find it easier to enter data in a familiar check form.

When you use the Write Checks window, you can enter all the necessary information onto a form that looks just like a check. When you're done filling out the check, click on the Record button and Quicken will add the check to the register. Quicken will indicate that the check is to be printed later by using "Print" as the check number. (If it's an electronic transaction, it will be transmitted the next time you connect to your bank via modem.) You don't enter the check number because the numbers are preprinted on the checks, and you must set the number for Quicken when you print the checks.

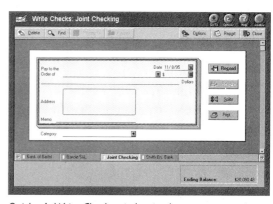

Quicken's Write Checks window is where you must write checks that you want to print with Quicken. You can, as an option, also use it to register checks you plan to write by hand or transmit electronically.

Note: *If you have a bank type of account open and selected when you open the Write Checks window, the check will automatically be drawn against that open account. However, if the open account is not a bank type of account (e.g., if it's a credit card, investment, or other type of account), or if no account is open, Quicken draws the check against the first bank account in the account list. The account that the check will be drawn against is displayed in the title bar of the Write Checks window.*

The Title Bar

At the very top of the Write Checks window is the title bar which also identifies which of your bank accounts the check will be drawn against. If the title bar shows the wrong account, you may select the correct account from the buttons that appear on the Account List line below the facsimile of the check. You may also close the Write Checks window, open the correct account, and reopen the Write Checks window.

The Button Bar

Just below the title bar (and Quicken's main icon bar, if you have it turned on) is the button bar. This button bar includes buttons to delete the current check, find user-defined information in the list of unprinted checks, set the Write Checks window options, run a QuickReport on checks, and close the Write Checks window. The toolbar button functions will be explored later in this chapter.

The Data Area

In the center of the Write Checks window is the data area. This area, which looks just like a paper check, is where you enter payment information. To the right of this "check" are four buttons: the Record button (which records, or saves, the transaction); the Restore button (like an "undo" command, it restores the transaction to its previous contents); the Splits button, which opens the Splits window to split the categories assigned to a check; and the Print button, which lets you print all the checks you have created without having to return to the register first.

The Account List Line

The Account List line stretches across the width of the Write Checks window below the data area. You can select accounts and rearrange accounts on the Account List line in the Write Checks window just as you can on the Account List line in the register (discussed in Chapter 4). However, the Account List line includes only bank-type accounts, since only these accounts can be used to write checks.

The Balance Amounts

Below the Account List line, you will see the dollar total of the "checks to print" and the ending balance for the register. If any transactions are postdated, Quicken also displays a separate "current balance," which is that day's account balance without the postdated transactions.

Writing Checks

To write a check, you must fill in the fields in the Write Checks window. You may write postdated checks, and you may review the checks you have written in the Write Checks window prior to printing them. As with the register, how each field in the Write Checks window responds to your data input may depend on the settings in the Write Checks window options.

To enter a check in the Write Checks window, you must enter the date, payee, category, and numeric amount. Quicken automatically translates the numeric amount to words for you. You cannot enter words directly on the spelled-out check amount line. If desired, you may also enter an address and memo.

Entering the Date

To enter the date, move the mouse pointer to the Date field and click to select it. You may type in the date, or use the pop-up calendar to enter one. If you chose to display buttons in QuickFill fields (see "Setting the Write Checks Options" window later in this chapter), you can click on the calendar button in the Date field to display the calendar pop-up. Or you can click on the Date field with the right mouse button to pop up the calendar.

To select a date from the currently displayed month, click on the date you want. You can move to the previous month by clicking on the Backward ([«]) button or move to the next month by clicking on the Forward ([»]) button.

You may use special characters to enter a date in the Date field (see the sidebar on page 52 in Chapter 4).

Entering the Payee

You may either type a name in the Payee field, or select the payee from a list of memorized transactions. Depending on the way you have set your register options, the Payee list will either pop up automatically when you select the Payee field, or you may display the list by clicking on the arrow button (if it is visible) or clicking with the right mouse button on the Payee field. Choose the payee you want from the list by clicking on your selection.

Unless you've changed the default register setup (by selecting Options from the Edit menu) to turn off automatic completion of fields, Quicken will fill in the first payee in a memorized transaction that matches your typed entry. As you continue to type, Quicken continues to try and match your entry to a payee in a memorized transaction. If your payee is not in the memorized transaction list, you can just ignore Quicken's entries and continue typing the full name of the payee. However, if the payee *is* on the memorized transaction list, you can just press the Tab key when Quicken correctly matches the payee's name. Quicken will fill in the rest of the fields (including Category, Amount, and Memo) from the memorized transaction. Of course, you can edit any of these fields before recording the transaction. None of this will happen, however, if you have turned off Automatic Recall of Transactions (by choosing Options from the Edit menu).

Entering the Category

You may type in the transaction's category or select it from a list of transactions. The list will appear automatically unless you've turned off this option. If you have, you can display it by clicking on the arrow button (if it is visible) or clicking with your right mouse button on the Category field. Choose the category you want by selecting it from the list. You can create a new category (and subcategory, if desired) by typing it into the Category field. If Quicken doesn't recognize the category name, it will prompt you for the additional information it needs to create the new category. If the transaction must be split into multiple categories, you may do so using the Splits button (as discussed in Chapter 5).

Note: As with the Payee field, if automatic completion of fields is enabled in the register options, Quicken will try to match your Category field entry to an existing category as you type. If the category you need appears in the Category field, you can press the Tab key to accept the category and move to the next field.

You can also enter another account name to indicate that money is being transferred to that account.

You can also enter a class and subclass in the Category field by separating the category information from the class information with a slash (/). If Quicken doesn't recognize the class, it will prompt you to enter the class information.

Entering the Payment Amount

You may enter the check payment amount by clicking on the field alongside the "$" and typing in the amount. You can also click on the Calculator button (if it is visible) or click with your right mouse button in the Payment or Deposit field to display the Calculator dialog box.

Entering a Memo

The Memo field enables you to enter additional information (up to 32 characters) about a transaction. This can be a lifesaver if you later need to recall what the check was *really* for. Do not put confidential information on the Memo field line, since it may show through the address window if you are using window envelopes. The Memo field will not show up on any checks that you transmit electronically.

Entering the Address

You may enter an address in the rectangular area in the middle of the check. This address is handy if you plan to print the check and mail it using a windowed envelope (available from Intuit and most office supply stores). To enter the name of the payee as the first line of the address, press the Quote key (') to automatically copy the payee name to the first address line.

Reviewing Checks You've Written

Once you've written and recorded your checks, you can review them in the Register window before printing or transmitting them. You can also scroll through them using the scroll bar in the Write Checks window. In the Register window, unprinted checks have the word "Print" instead of a check number; untransmitted checks have the word "Send."

If you review the unprinted checks by scrolling through them in the Write Checks window, you can adjust the address if necessary. The address information is not available from the Register window. Once you have printed the checks, you can no longer review them from the Write Checks window.

Note: *Once you have recorded your checks, you can delete them or void them using the appropriate selections from the* Edit *menu—just as you can with any other transactions in the register.*

Printing Checks

When you print checks with Quicken, you must use special checks that you order from Intuit or other sources. Checks are available for page-oriented printers (laser, ink jet, LCD) as well as for line-oriented printers (tractor-feed dot-matrix or daisy-wheel).

You can print checks as soon as you write them, or you can wait and print them later. Although it is possible to print one or two checks at a time (from a full page of three checks), it is often simpler with many page-oriented printers to "store up" a set of three checks to print. Printing a full page avoids having to deal with the vagaries of envelope feeders–although this has become easier with some late-model printers.

Moneysaving Hint: *Intuit would love you to buy checks from them, but lots of companies print checks compatible with Quicken. (See the end of this chapter.)*

Printing on an Ink Jet or Laser (Page-Oriented) Printer

To print checks on a page-oriented printer, such as an ink jet or laser printer, use the following steps:

1. Insert a full page of checks into the paper tray of your printer. If you are printing a partial first page of checks, see "Printing a Partial Page of Checks," later in this chapter. If you've never manually fed a sheet of paper through your printer, check your printer manual as this can sometimes be a bit tricky. Or, just experiment with a blank piece of paper so you don't waste any expensive preprinted checks.

2. Make sure that your printer is turned on and online.

3. Open the account from which you want to print checks via the Account List, the Account List line at the bottom of the register, or by double-clicking on a minimized account icon.

4. Choose Print Checks from the File menu. Quicken will open the Select Checks to Print window.
    Note: You can also open the Select Checks to Print window by clicking on the Checks to Print button in the Quicken Reminders window. The Quicken Reminders window opens automatically when you start Quicken, or you may open it by selecting Reminders from the Activities menu.

5. In the First Check Number box, type in the number printed on the first check in your printer.

6. Select the checks you want to print from the Print box. Click on one of the three choices:
- Choose All Checks to print all unprinted checks, including postdated checks.

Select the checks you want to print from the Select Checks to Print window.

- Choose Chec<u>k</u>s Dated Through to print all checks up to the selected date. You can type in a new date (the default date is the current date), or click on the Calendar button and choose the date from the pop-up Calendar dialog box.
- Choose S<u>e</u>lected Checks and click on the <u>C</u>hoose button to pick exactly which checks to print. The <u>C</u>hoose button opens yet another Select Checks to Print window. Quicken lists all unprinted checks in chronological order. By default, all non-postdated checks are selected for printing. You can change a check's print status by clicking on the check in the window or by pressing the spacebar. You may also select all checks by clicking on the <u>M</u>ark All button. You may clear the selection of all checks by clicking on the <u>C</u>lear All button.

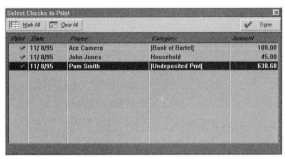

Choose the checks you want to print from the Select Checks to Print window.

7. Click on the <u>D</u>one button when you are through selecting the checks to print. Quicken returns to the main Select Checks to Print window.

This area of the second Select Checks to Print window lets you select the check type and number of checks on the page.

8. Select the correct check style from the Check St<u>y</u>le drop-down menu.

9. Choose the number of checks that are on the first page of checks by clicking on the Th<u>r</u>ee, T<u>w</u>o, or <u>O</u>ne button. For wallet and standard checks, there are normally three checks on a page, unless you have used one or more checks from the page. If your first page has only one or two of the original three checks on it, see "Printing a Partial Page of Checks," on page 98. Voucher checks only have a single check on each page—you don't need to select one of these numerical buttons for voucher-style checks.

10. Click on the Print your logo checkbox if you wish to include a logo (graphic) on standard or voucher checks (this option is not available for wallet-style checks). You must first have selected a .BMP file containing your logo from the Check Printer Setup option of the File menu. If you have a color logo and a color printer, the logo will even print in color.

Note: You may select Additional copies to print multiple (up to nine) copies of voucher checks only.

11. Click OK. Quicken prints your checks and presents a dialog box to verify that your checks printed correctly. Click OK, or type the number of the first check that didn't print correctly and click OK. Quicken makes these checks available for printing again. Correct the problem that caused the misprint and repeat the printing process.

Note: If only one check in the middle of a series of checks didn't print correctly, don't enter a number in this window. Instead, click OK, then

Quicken asks if all the checks printed correctly.

select the transaction in the register for the misprinted check, and type "Print" over the check number.

Printing a Partial Page of Checks

If you use standard or wallet checks in your page-oriented printer, you may sometimes find that a partial page of one or two blank checks remains after you have finished printing. To print a partial page of standard or wallet checks, use the following steps:

1. Make sure your printer is turned on and online.

Set up your printer to print checks using the Check Printer Setup window.

2. Choose Printer Setup from the File menu, and select the Check Printer Setup. Quicken displays the Check Printer Setup window.

3. Feed a single check into your printer the same way you feed an envelope. Check your printer manual if you aren't sure how to load an envelope into your printer. In the Partial

Page Printing Style section of the window, select the button that matches how your printer would handle a single check using its envelope feeder. There are three ways that you can feed a single check through the envelope printer:

- positioned on the left side of the envelope feeder, with the right or left edge of the check feeding into the printer
- centered in the envelope feeder, with the right or left edge of the check feeding into the printer
- centered in the envelope feeder, with the top or bottom edge of the check feeding into the printer

Note: If you are using standard or wallet checks and you need to print a partial page of checks, but your printer doesn't include an envelope option, you can use Intuit's Forms Leaders. Forms Leaders are pieces of 8.5-by-11-inch paper with a sticky edge, to which you can attach a single check so that it will go through your printer just like a regular sheet of checks. Although the Forms Leaders cost nearly $1 each, they can be reused multiple times.

4. Choose Print Checks from the File menu. Quicken will open the Select Checks to Print window. Be sure that the displayed first check number is the same as the first check on your partial page of checks. Select the checks you want to print from the Print box. You may print All Checks, Checks dated through (pick the date), or Selected Checks. If you choose Selected Checks, click on the Choose button to select the checks.

5. In the Checks on First Page section, choose the number of checks on the first page of checks.

6. Load the one or two checks into your envelope feeder or cassette as pictured in the Partial Page Printing Style icon you selected.

Note: Some printers, such as the HP LaserJet III, require you to load letterhead paper face down. For these printers, you must also load your check stock face down.

7. Click on OK to print the checks. If you selected a centered type of envelope feeder, Quicken asks whether or not you have removed the tear-off strip at the side of the page. Click on <u>Y</u>es or <u>N</u>o. This information affects the positioning of the checks.

8. Quicken asks if your checks printed OK. If they did, click on OK. If they did not print correctly, follow the instructions in Step 11 in the previous section to correct the problem.

Printing Checks on Continuous-feed Printers

You can use a continuous-feed (tractor-feed, or dot-matrix) printer to print your checks. However, unless you keep the printer loaded with checks all the time, you will need to reset the alignment of the checks in the printer every time you print checks. To print checks on a continuous-feed printer, use the following steps:

1. Make sure your printer is on and online.

2. If the printer is not loaded with checks, load the printer. Print a sample check to ensure that the checks are properly aligned. If they are not, follow the instructions in the Quicken manual for aligning the checks in the printer.

Note: If only one check in the middle of a series of checks didn't print correctly, don't enter a number in this window. Instead, click OK, then select the transaction in the register for the misprinted check, and type over the check number with the word "Print".

The rest of this procedure is the same as "Printing a Partial Page of Checks" on page 98, starting with step 3.

Setting the Checks Options Window

You can set the Checks Options window in Quicken to customize the way the window looks. To change the window options, click on the Options button in the Write Checks window button bar. Quicken will open the Check Options window. This window displays three sets of options—C<u>h</u>ecks, M<u>i</u>scellaneous, and Q<u>u</u>ickFill—split into three panels. To switch panels, simply click on the tab for the panel you want.

Check Options

The Check options are selected when a checkbox is displayed alongside the option.

Printed Date Style   *Default:* MM/DD/YEAR
Prints the date on the check in one of four common formats: MM/DD/YEAR, MM/DD/YY, DD/MM/YEAR, or DD/MM/YY.

The Check Options window enables you to customize how the register looks and works.

Allow Entry of Extra Message on Check
Default: No
Adds an extra message box on the check that isn't visible when you mail the check in an Intuit (or other standard) window envelope.

Print Categories on Voucher Checks   *Default:* Yes
Prints categories from a split transaction on the perforated attachment to voucher checks.

Warn if a Check Number is Re-used   *Default:* Yes
Warns you if you enter a check number that has already been used.

Change Date of Checks to Date When Printed   *Default:* No
The date on a check is normally the date you write it. If you set this option, Quicken changes the date on the check to the date on which you print the check.

Artwork on Check Entry Screen   *Default:* No
Displays the artwork you select from the drop-down menu in the Write Checks window. The artwork is not printed. Experiment with this to see if you like it—I don't because it makes the Write Checks window harder to read.

Miscellaneous options may also be set in the Check Window Options window.

Miscellaneous Options

You can switch to the Miscellaneous options by clicking on the Miscellaneous tab. The options are selected when a checkbox is displayed alongside the option.

Date Style *Default:* MM/DD/YY
Choose one of two display date styles by clicking on the radio buttons: M̲M/DD/YY or D̲D/MM/YY.

Enter Key Moves Between Fields *Default:* No
Uses the Enter key as well as the Tab key to move between fields in the Write Checks window.

B̲eep When Recording and Memorizing *Default:* Yes
Beeps after recording, deleting, or memorizing a check.

W̲arn Before Recording Uncategorized Transaction *Default:* Yes
Prompts you to enter a category for the check you are recording if you haven't already entered one.

R̲equest Confirmation Before Changes *Default:* Yes
Requires you to confirm any changes made to a check.

QuickFill Options

You can switch to the QuickFill options by clicking on the Quic̲kFill tab. The options are selected when a checkbox is displayed alongside the option.

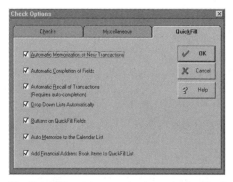

The QuickFill options may also be set in the Check Window Options window.

A̲utomatic Memorization of New Transactions *Default:* Yes
Memorizes every new check you enter for a new payee. Quicken automatically turns off this option when the list of memorized transactions reaches 1,000.

Automatic C̲ompletion of Fields
Default: Yes
Works with Payee, Category, Class, and transfer account names.

Automatic R̲ecall of Transactions *Default:* Yes
Recalls a memorized transactions and fills in all the fields (except for check number) when you press Tab to leave the Payee field. Available only if you have also selected Automatic Completion of Fields.

Drop Down Lists Automatically   *Default:* Yes
Displays the drop-down list when you move the cursor to the field. If the drop-down list gets in your way, you can use Buttons on QuickFill Fields instead.

Buttons on QuickFill Fields   *Default:* Yes
Displays the buttons for fields with QuickFill. If this option is off, you can still display the list by clicking with the right mouse button.

Auto Memorize to the Calendar List   *Default:* Yes
Memorizes every new transaction to the Calendar list of memorized transactions.

Add Financial Address Book Items to QuickFill List   *Default:* Yes
Found in Quicken Deluxe only, this option adds items from your Financial Address Book to the QuickFill list.

Ordering Checks

To print checks from Quicken, you must have special check stock that meets the requirements of financial institutions. This check stock must include your name, address, account number, bank name, check numbers, and all the information required by financial institutions. You can order checks from Intuit or from other sources that may provide the checks for less money.

Ordering from Intuit

You can order checks and other supplies from Intuit by mail, fax, or modem. You use the "Intuit Marketplace" to create an order, and then mail, fax, or transmit the order to Intuit.

An order form for checks is included in a booklet labeled "Quicken Checks" that comes in the box with your software. Send mail orders to:

Intuit Supplies
P.O. Box 34328
Seattle, WA 98124-9964
For fax orders, fax the order form to 206-925-9301 (U.S.A.) or 416-752-1140 (Canada).

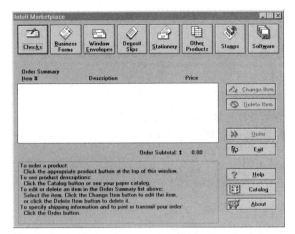

Use the Intuit Marketplace to order supplies from Intuit.

To create an order using the Intuit Marketplace, follow these steps:

1. Select Intuit <u>M</u>arketplace from the Online menu. Quicken will open the Intuit Marketplace window.

2. Click on one of the buttons across the top of Intuit Marketplace window to bring up the dialog box for ordering the item you want. For example, to order checks, click on the Chec<u>k</u>s button.

3. Continue clicking on buttons and filling out the requested information for each item until you have ordered everything you need. Quicken notes the price of each item and totals the order in the window.

    Note: For most items, minimal extra information is needed (for example, an address). However, ordering checks requires providing a substantial amount of information. If you are ordering checks for the first time, you must send a voided check from your checkbook to Intuit at the address listed above.

4. Click on the <u>O</u>rder button to start the placement of your order. Quicken presents the Delivery Address information window. Fill in your name, company, address, and phone number. Click on OK. Quicken opens the Payment and Delivery window.

5. Fill in the fields in the Payment and Delivery window. You can pay with a check or money order, but you must make sure to mail the payment right away to avoid holding up the order. You can also fill in credit card information to expedite the shipment. After you fill in your local sales tax rate, Quicken will compute the sales tax and shipping charges, and give you a total. Click on OK.

6. Quicken will open the Preview Order window. If you need to modify the order, click on the Back button to return to the Intuit Marketplace window.

7. To mail or fax the order, click on the Print button. To order by modem, click on the Transmit button. If you have never transmitted anything to Intuit before, you may need to Set Up Modem.

8. Click on Done when you are through ordering supplies.

Ordering from Other Sources

You may order supplies from sources other than Intuit, typically at a discount. Sometimes, the discount can be substantial! For example, Intuit charges $35.95 for a box of 500 wallet-size windowed envelopes, but you can pick up a box of envelopes with the same specifications at most office warehouse stores for about $18. Another example is the check stock: Intuit charges $47.95 for 250 standard-size checks, which can be ordered from other sources for as little as $30.

Other sources for checks include:
Designer Checks
P.O. Box 13387
Birmingham, AL 35202
800-239-4087
Sample price: $29.95 for 250 standard checks, page-oriented

Summary

Writing checks using Quicken saves you from having to enter information about a check twice. When you write checks in the Write Checks window, Quicken automatically records the information in the proper register. You can print checks on either a page-oriented or tractor-feed printer, and set the Write Checks window options to control how the window works. You can also order supplies from Intuit or other sources.

Balancing and Reconciling Your Checkbook

7

LIGHT AT THE END
OF THE FUNNEL

You may think you know how much money you have in your checking account, but your "official" balance is whatever the bank thinks it is. Though they may be built of glass, steel, or marble and often seem to have a heart of stone, banks really are staffed by people, who sometimes do make mistakes. That's why it's important to check those bank statements that come in the mail every month.

The first thing I do when my statement arrives is to look at the lower right corner of the checks–my bank returns canceled checks to me, although yours may not, depending on the type of account you have–to make sure that the number that's imprinted there matches the amount I wrote on the check. That number is magnetic ink that's read by the bank's scanners. It's put there by a human being who reads it from the amount of the check. That's the most likely error you'll find. If the amount was typed correctly, chances are very high that it was correctly entered into the computer.

But don't stop there. There are other things that can go wrong in a statement. You might get charged for checks or withdrawals that you didn't make, you may get service charges that don't seem fair, or there could even be a computer glitch that causes the bank to come up with the wrong answer.

Now you can get even. Banks have been using computers for many decades, and now you're using one, too. Take advantage of Quicken's Reconcile feature to make sure that your computer and their computer are in sync.

If your financial institution offers electronic banking, your computer and their computer can work things out on their own. Set things up right, and you'll be able to dial into their system and do an online reconciliation to make sure your records and theirs are in sync. For more information on this, see Chapter 15.

Perhaps you're not quite ready to take the electronic banking plunge, or perhaps your preferred financial institution doesn't yet offer the service. In that case, you'll still have to manually balance your check register against the bank's printout. However, the great news is that, thanks to Quicken, it's a pretty easy process.

Reconciling Your Account

The reconciling process begins when you receive a statement from your bank that lists all the transactions for your checking account for that month. The basic steps mirror the reconciliation process for your paper checkbook:

- Add any finance charges or interest earned that you didn't record previously.
- Compare your checkbook against the bank statement, and check off all cleared items.
- Calculate your closing balance, making adjustments for uncleared transactions.
- Compare your closing balance against the bank's closing balance.
- Resolve any discrepancies.

For the First Time

Typically, reconciling your account using Quicken is quite straight-forward. The first time you reconcile a Quicken-based checking account against the bank's records, there are a few extra steps that you must take to ensure that your checkbook balances accurately.

The best way to start using Quicken to track a checking account is to use the ending balance on the last available bank statement as the opening balance for that account in Quicken. To prepare and reconcile your Quicken checking account against the bank's records for the first time, follow these steps:

1. Enter all uncleared transactions in your account into Quicken. These are all the transactions in your checkbook that haven't yet appeared as cleared on a bank statement. After the first-time reconciliation, you will be recording transactions in Quicken as you make them.

2. Update the Opening Balance transaction in Quicken with the opening balance on your bank statement. This could also be the ending balance of your previous statement.

3. When you actually reconcile your account against the bank's records, record any transactions that show up on the bank statement that you haven't yet entered into Quicken. A common reason that this occurs on a first-time reconciliation is that the unrecorded transaction occurred during the previous month but hadn't cleared the bank yet. Another is automatic teller machines and other "on the fly" transactions that you may have neglected to record. If you don't do this, there will be an opening balance adjustment that you will have to make. This process is similar for a "regular" (non-first-time) reconciliation, but the likelihood of having to add unrecorded transactions is higher on a first-time reconciliation.

These steps are not all that different from paper-based methods. However, the advantage to using Quicken is that Quicken performs all the calculations for you, then recalculates the results as you make adjustments during the reconciliation.

Starting the Reconciliation

To begin your reconciliation, use the following steps:

1. Select the account you want to reconcile.

2. Choose <u>R</u>econcile from the <u>A</u>ctivities menu, or click on the Reconcile icon, which looks like an old-fashioned balance scale. This menu item is only available from the <u>A</u>ctivities menu if the open account is a bank-type account. Quicken will open the Reconcile Bank Statement window.

3. Compare the <u>O</u>pening Balance in Quicken to the opening balance shown on your bank statement. Your bank statement might call this number the "beginning" or "previous" balance.

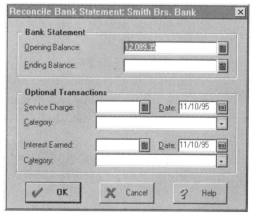

The amount in Quicken's <u>O</u>pening Balance should be the same as the previous balance on your bank statement. If these two numbers are *not* the same, correct the Quicken amount by entering the balance from the bank statement. Quicken will accept this new number, but will create an opening balance difference that you will need to resolve

The Reconcile Bank Statement window is where you enter the beginning information for a reconciliation.

later (see "If you have an Opening Balance Difference" on page 114).

Note: If this is the first time you have reconciled your Quicken account, the Quicken Opening Balance amount comes from the ending balance of your previous bank statement. Otherwise, the Quicken Opening Balance amount equals the total of all reconciled transactions in the check register.

The most common reasons for the Quicken Opening Balance amount and the bank statement opening balance to differ are that this is the first time you have reconciled your account, or that you haven't reconciled your account for some time. If you haven't reconciled in some time, it is important that you reconcile your account one month at a time (starting from the earliest unreconciled statement), using the bank statements for each month. This will prevent many of the most common errors that occur in reconciling a Quicken checking account.

4. Find the ending balance on your bank statement and enter it in the Ending Balance field in the Reconcile Bank Statement window. Your bank statement may call this amount the "current" or "new" balance.

5. If your bank statement lists any service charges that you haven't already entered in your Quicken register, enter the total amount in the Service Charge box, and then enter the date in the Date box. You can either type the date or click on the Calendar button and pick a date from the pop-up calendar.

6. Enter a Category in the Category box. Quicken remembers the category you choose for the service charge, and inserts it in the Category field the next time you reconcile. If you don't have one entered, start typing "Bank" and Quicken will fill in "Bank Charge."

7. If your bank statement shows interest earned during this period that you haven't entered in your Quicken register, enter the amount in the Interest Earned box. Also enter a date in the Date box. You can either type the date or click on the Calendar button and pick a date from the pop-up calendar.
   Note: *Be careful about entering interest. Some banks display the interest earned year-to-date, or even "Interest Paid This Period" when no interest has been credited to your account during the month in question.*

8. Enter a category in the Category box. Quicken remembers the category you choose for the interest earned, and inserts it in the Category field the next time you reconcile.

9. Click OK to complete filling out the initial Reconcile Bank Statement window. The next Reconcile Bank Statement will appear. This window is discussed in the next section.

Marking Cleared Transactions

Next, compare the bank statement to your Quicken register, and mark all the transactions that appear on your bank statement. For convenience, Deposits are shown in a list on the right side of the Reconcile Bank Statement window, while Payments and Checks are shown in a list on the left.

To mark your cleared transactions, use the following steps:

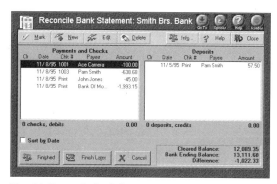

Use this Reconcile Bank Statement window to mark cleared transactions.

1. Match each transaction on your bank statement with the corresponding transaction in the Reconcile Bank Statement window, and mark the transaction as cleared. To clear a transaction (or unclear a cleared transaction), you can click on the transaction or select it with arrow keys, and either press the spacebar or click the Mark button. You can also drag the mouse pointer over a range of transactions.

A cleared transaction is displayed with a small yellow check mark to the left of the transaction. As you mark transactions, the Cleared Balance amount is updated in the lower right corner of the Reconcile Bank Statement window. The Difference between the Cleared Balance and the Bank Ending Balance is also updated.

Note: *If your records agree with the bank's, the Difference amount will be zero when you are done.*

2. If a transaction on your bank statement doesn't appear in the list of uncleared transactions, enter it now in the check register. To do so:

    a) Click New to move to the blank transaction at the end of the register.

    b) Enter the information for the transaction in the register, then hit the Enter key to record the transaction.

    c) Click Close to return to the Reconcile Bank Statement window.

    d) Mark the transaction as cleared in the window.

3. If a transaction contains an incorrect amount or other error, correct it in the check register. To do so:

    a) Click on the transaction in the Reconcile Bank Statement window and click the Edit button, or double-click on the transaction. Quicken will display the transaction in the register.

    b) Correct the error in the register, then hit the Enter key.

    c) Click Close to return to the Reconcile Bank Statement window.

    d) Mark the transaction as cleared.

Completing Reconciliation

When you've finished checking off cleared transactions, look at the Difference amount in the lower right corner of the Reconcile Bank Statement window. This difference can have one of three possible results, as discussed below. How you proceed to finish the reconciliation depends on the final Difference amount.

If the Difference amount is zero, and there is no Opening Balance

Congratulations. You've successfully reconciled your account. Click on the Finished button to complete the reconciliation. Quicken will ask

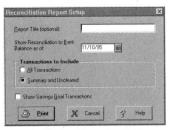

The Reconciliation Report Setup window enables you to run a report that shows the reconciled balance.

you if you want to create a reconciliation report. If you want a reconciliation report, click Yes; otherwise, click No. If you click Yes, Quicken will open the Reconciliation Report Setup window.

You can configure the Reconciliation Report to show the Bank Balance as of a date other than the current date by changing the date in the Bank Balance as of field. You can also decide how much information to include in the report by selecting All Transactions or Summary and Uncleared. You can add an optional title by typing the title in the Report Title field. Click on Print to print the report.

If the Difference is not zero

Oops. Either you or the bank made a mistake. No offense, but it's probably you. At this point, there are two ways you can proceed: Find the problem and correct it, or have Quicken enter an adjustment to bring the account back into balance with the bank's records.

If you decide you wish to correct your records, here are some things you can check:

- Did you miss recording an transaction in the check register? This is rare, because you usually find such transactions as you mark cleared items.
- Did you miss marking an item as cleared?
- Did you mistakenly mark an item as cleared?
- Did you enter any transaction in the register twice?
- Did you enter a deposit as a payment, or a payment as a deposit?

The problem may also be in the dollar amount recorded for a transaction. Compare the dollar amounts for each transaction between the bank statement and your Quicken account. If a dollar amount doesn't match, either you or the bank made a mistake. Look at the returned check to verify the amount.

If you made the mistake, correct the mistake by editing the transaction in the register. Quicken automatically recalculates the Cleared Balance and the Difference amounts.

If the bank made the mistake, you can either adjust the transaction amount in the register, or have Quicken adjust the balance as discussed below. Then, call the bank and have the transaction adjusted. This adjustment will appear on the next bank statement assuming, of course, that the bank agrees. You account will be off by the same amount at the end of the next reconciliation. Have Quicken make another adjustment when you finish reconciling the next statement.

Another option, which I use if the discrepancy is relatively small, is to just accept the fact that life isn't always perfect and let Quicken make a balance adjustment for you. This act won't impress any CPAs or bookkeepers, but hey, life is too short to spend your evenings searching to see how you misplaced a dollar or two.

If you decide to go this route:

1. Click on Finished. Quicken will tell you the amount of the discrepancy.

2. Click Adjust to record an adjustment transaction in the check register. This transaction is equal to the difference between your cleared items and the bank statement.

Note: You can delete the adjustment transaction later if you find the error that resulted in the difference.

If you have an Opening Balance Difference

The Opening Balance Difference is the difference between the total of all reconciled items in the register and the opening balance shown on your bank statement. An Opening Balance Difference is usually attributable to one of the following causes:

- You are balancing your Quicken account for the first time. You should be able to resolve any Opening Balance Difference by following the instructions for "Reconciling Your Account for the First Time," earlier in this chapter.
- You were using Quicken and reconciling your account, and then started recording earlier transactions in Quicken. To properly enter earlier transactions in Quicken, you should work from earlier bank statements, and record every transaction, reconciling each statement as you go.
- You started reconciling with the current month's bank statement, but you didn't reconcile each of the previous month's statements. You must reconcile one month at a time, starting with the earliest month.
- You changed or deleted a previously reconciled transaction. Quicken warns you when to change or delete a previously reconciled transaction, because it can result in an Opening Balance Difference. You should only go ahead and change or delete the reconciled transaction if you plan to enter an adjustment. Or, you can have Quicken record an adjustment transaction when the reconciliation is complete.
- A crazy person broke into your computer room and deliberately wreaked havoc with your Quicken files. Just kidding.

Although Quicken notes the Opening Balance Difference in the Reconcile Bank Statement window, the program does not offer to make an automatic adjustment to correct for this discrepancy. Instead, it simply updates Quicken so the next month will match the bank statement.

Catching Up

Sigh. If you have used Quicken for a number of months, but have not reconciled against your bank statements, you might want to catch up by reconciling your Quicken register against the bank statements. To make your Quicken account current, you need to reconcile each month individually, starting with the earliest month. Another option is to forget about old account activity and just go back a month or two.

BARRY BRACES FOR A CALL
FROM HIS BANKER.

Summary

Reconciling your Quicken checking account against the bank statement is important if you want to ensure that your records are accurate every month. Reconciling involves comparing your opening balance against the bank's and clearing all the transactions that appear in the bank statement (and adding or editing missing or erroneous transactions). Keep your records current by reconciling against the bank statement every month.

Setting Up
Other Types of Accounts

8

INSTEAD OF SAVING FOR YOUR COLLEGE EDUCATION, YOUR FATHER AND I ARE ENDOWING YOU WITH A COPY OF QUICKEN.

HECK, YOU MAY NOT EVEN NEED COLLEGE.

If *you're like most users, you'll probably use your checking account the vast majority of the time. But, as I'm reminded every time my credit card bills arrive, checking accounts aren't the only way to spend or keep track of money. Fortunately, Quicken handles lots of account types, including Credit Card, Savings, Cash, Money Market, Investment, Asset, and Liability accounts. In this chapter, we will discuss how to create each of these account types and how they differ from a checking account.*

Creating a New Account

Creating a new account is done from the Create New Account window. The easiest way to open the Create New Account window is to click on the Accts button on the toolbar and select <u>N</u>ew. Other options include:

- From the Account List window, click New.
- From the Activities menu, click Create New Account.

Once the Create New Account window is open, click on the button for the type of account you want to create.

Create new accounts in Quicken with the Create New Account window.

Creating a Savings Account

Savings accounts are used to keep track of bank savings accounts (they're sometimes called "passbook accounts," but these days, some banks are too cheap to issue passbooks). Within Quicken, they work identically to Checking accounts: You may even enter a check number in the Num column, and reconciling the account to the bank statement works exactly the same.

To create a Savings account:

1. Click on the <u>S</u>avings button in the Create New Account window. Quicken will open the Savings Account Setup window. Click the Next button to continue.

2. You will be prompted to enter a name, and optionally, a description for this account. Otherwise, Quicken will come up with a pretty nondescript name, such as "Savings." To make it more useful, you can type a new name, such as "Dollars R Us," into the

The Savings Account Setup window features five tabbed dialog boxes.

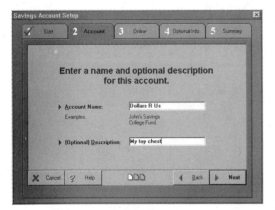

Use this window to name your Savings account.

Account Name field. If you wish, enter additional information in the Description field, then click the Next button.

Note: *Remember, the keyboard shortcut for the Next button is the Enter key. Use this in case you're feeling mouse-ridden.*

3. Quicken will ask if you have the last statement for this Savings account. If you click No, it will create an account with a balance of $0 and skip you to Step 5. Don't worry—you can easily pump up the account balance later. If you do have a statement, or a bank receipt from having opened a new account, click Yes. Then click the Next button.

4. Quicken will ask you to input the relevant balance and date information. Do so using the Statement Date and Ending Balance fields, then click the Next button.

Note: *If you made a mistake during any part of this process, you can return to previous screens using the Back button at the lower right of the Savings Account Setup window.*

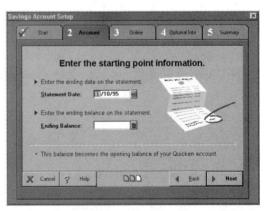

Quicken makes it easy to enter an existing balance and date.

5. Quicken will now ask you if you've signed up to use an online service with your account. For the purposes of the rest of this chapter, we'll assume you haven't—though the sign-up process only adds a couple of extra steps (for more details, see Chapter 15). If you do not plan to use an online service at the moment, click No and then click Next.

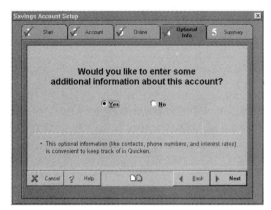

Use this dialog box to indicate if you want to add further account information . . .

6. Next, the program will ask if you want to add any additional information about your account. You may answer No and click the Next button, or answer Yes, in which case you'll be presented with a screen where you can enter the information.

. . . and this one to enter the information itself.

7. If you choose to enter additional information, enter it into the Financial Institution, Account Number, Contact, Phone Number, Comments, and Interest Rate fields. Click the Next button to continue.

8. A Summary screen will let you review all the information you've entered. You may return to previous fields to modify information by pressing the Back button.

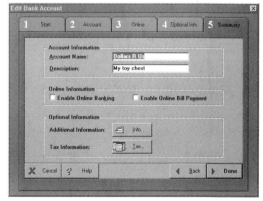

You may review or change entered information using this Summary screen.

Creating a Credit Card Account

Credit Card accounts are used to keep track of the transactions you bill against a credit card. You will need one Credit Card account for each credit card you use. To create a Credit Card account:

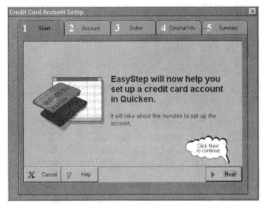

The first Credit Card Account Setup window.

1. Click on the Credit Card button in the Create New Account window. Quicken will open the first Credit Card Account Setup window. Click on the Next button to continue.

2. Enter a name for the account. Usually this is the name of the bank or credit card company. Then enter an optional Description if you wish. Click Next to proceed to the next screen.

3. Quicken will now ask for a "starting point" for this account. If you have your last credit card statement, select Yes. If not, select No and skip to Step 5; you'll be able to easily make changes later.

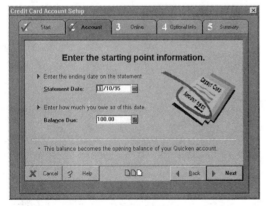

Enter your last statement date and balance due on this screen.

4. Enter the Statement Date and the Balance Due, then click Next.

5. Quicken will now ask if the credit card is one whose transaction information you can download electronically. The answer is Yes if you have a Quicken credit card or another that's been set to use electronic banking. For now, we'll assume the answer is No (but see Chapter 15 for more information). Click Next to continue.

6. The next screen will offer you the (optional) chance to enter your credit limit. If you do so, Quicken will then automatically display your remaining credit. This can be of some use, although for most of us the

problem with credit cards is not bumping up against the credit limit, but rather getting lulled into owing more than we ought to. If you're one of those people who get seduced by a lofty credit limit, maybe you ought to leave this line blank. Either way, click the Next button to continue.

7. You will now get the chance to enter additional information about the account. Even more than with an ordinary Checking account, this is worth filling in. It lets you record a card's expiration date, interest rate, and the all-important number to call in case the card gets stolen.

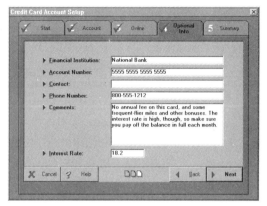

The new Credit Card account.

Thoughts about Credit Card Record-Keeping

Credit Card accounts work similarly to Checking accounts. However, before going ahead, think about the level of detail you really need. You can, of course, write down every credit card transaction, either as you spend the money or when you get your statement. There's nothing wrong with that, but it can be time-consuming. First decide whether you really need a computerized record of each transaction. Remember, you already have the printed credit card statement.

Of course, if you use electronic banking, this is all moot because Quicken will automatically enter all your transactions from the data that comes in from your modem or from the floppy disk you get each month in the mail.

Creating a Cash Account

Cash accounts, as the name implies, are used to keep track of Cash transactions. You create a Cash account the same way you create a Checking or Savings account, so there's no need to repeat all the steps.

Typically, money is placed in a Cash account by transferring it from another

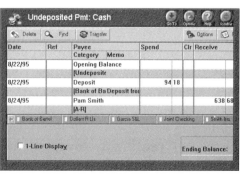

The register from a Quicken Cash account.

account. Such transfers might include an ATM withdrawal from your Checking or Savings account, or a cash advance against a credit card.

Another way money could be "deposited" in your Cash account is via a "deposit" of some or all of a check you received. If the entire check is cashed, you can show the check as a deposit to the Cash account. However, if only part of the check goes to cash, it is best to handle the transaction as follows:

- Show the total check amount—less the amount you took as cash—as a deposit to the account in which you are depositing the balance of the check.
- Open the Splits window to document the category.
- Enter the total check amount on the first line of the Splits window. The second line of the Splits window will show a negative amount that is equal to the amount you took in cash.

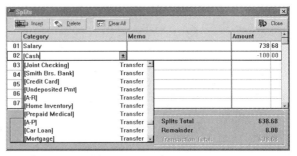

The transfer to your Cash account is displayed as a negative number.

- Use the name of the Cash account as the category on the second line of the Splits window. Quicken will create the balancing transaction in the Cash account.

Creating a Money Market Account

Money Market accounts, which are discussed in Chapter 23, are generally used for savings. The difference is that they're not federally insured and you usually get a higher interest rate.

You set up a Money Market account in Quicken the same way you set up a Savings account. These accounts work identically to Checking and Savings accounts: You can enter a check number in the Num column if you wish, and reconciling the account to the bank statement works exactly the same.

Creating an Investment Account

Before you spend a lot of time setting up your Investment accounts, think about your goals and the type of information you really need.

And think about all the information your brokerage sends you. If you're like me, you're inundated with paper from those guys.

I think it has something to do with federal reporting laws, but it never ceases to amaze me how many reports and statements I get each month from Fidelity and the other investment companies I use for IRAs and mutual funds. My point is, the investment companies already do your record-keeping for you with either monthly or quarterly reports.

Of course, you can use Quicken to get a snapshot of how your investments are doing. That's a good idea from time to time, but, if you're investing for the long haul (as you should be), then it really doesn't matter much if Consolidated Software is down ¼ of a point or Aggregate Cow Manure is up by an eighth.

I don't bother tracking my investments to the penny, but I do like to have a general idea of my net worth. So I use Quicken to enter my securities. I've been using Quicken Quotes (which came with Quicken Deluxe, Version 5) to download the values from CompuServe. Quicken Quotes no longer is included with Quicken Deluxe, but there are a variety of new online links. More on this topic later.

Setting up an Investment account in Quicken is surprisingly simple. You use the same EasyStep interface that led you through creating Checking, Savings, and other account types previously.

1. Click on the Investment button in the Create New Account window. Quicken will open the Investment Account Setup window. Click on the Next button.

2. Enter the Account name, and optionally, an account Description. Then click on the Next button to continue.

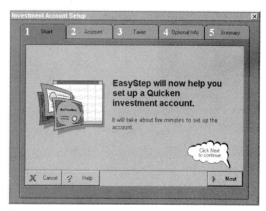

The Investment Account Setup window.

3. Most mutual fund companies will let you aggregate several funds into a single account, which may be true in your situation. An Investment account that tracks a single mutual fund allows you to reconcile your account by share balance. If your account contains a single mutual fund, select <u>Y</u>es. Click on the Next button to continue.

4. Quicken will now ask if the Investment account provides features such as check writing, ATM cards, or automatic fund transfer. If so, click <u>Y</u>es. In either case, select Next to continue.

5. You will now enter the Taxes tabbed dialog box. If this is a tax-deferred account (such as an IRA, 401(k), SEP, or KEOGH), click <u>Y</u>es, then select Next to continue.

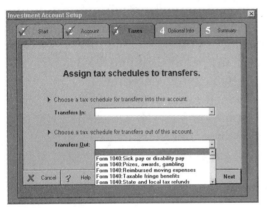

Drop-down menus let you automatically link your investment account to any required tax forms.

6. If you need to report transfers into or out of this account on any tax forms, select <u>Y</u>es. Then use the drop-down menus to the right of the Transfers <u>I</u>n and Transfers <u>O</u>ut boxes to select the appropriate forms.

7. As with the previous types of accounts, Quicken will ask if you wish to enter additional information, such as a contact number, interest rate information, or comments. If you do, select <u>Y</u>es and fill in the form. Either way, click Next to continue.

8. The Summary screen will allow you to double-check the information you've entered and change it if necessary. If you do need to make changes, move back through the set of tabbed dialog boxes by clicking on the <u>B</u>ack and Next buttons. When you are satisfied with all the answers, click Next and then Done.

9. If you are tracking a single mutual fund (that is, if you answered Yes in Step 3), Quicken will open the Set

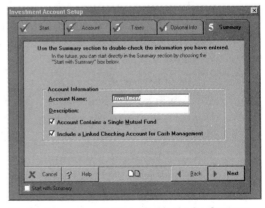

The Summary screen lets you double-check information about your Investment account.

Up Mutual Fund Security window. In this window you may specify:

The Set Up Mutual Fund Security window.

- **Name:** This is the name of your mutual fund, stock or other investment.
- **Symbol:** This is the symbol for the stock, as designated on the stock exchange on which the stock appears. This is especially important if you track your securities online, because Quicken looks up the value of each security by its symbol.
- **Type:** Select a security type. By default, Quicken provides Bond, CD, Mutual Fund, and Stock security types. However, you can add security types to the list, as discussed in Chapter 14.
- **Goal:** You have the option of selecting an investment goal. By default, Quicken provides College Fund, Growth, High-Risk, Income, International, and Low-Risk goals. However, you can add goals to the list, as discussed in Chapter 14.
- If this is a tax-free security, make sure a check mark appears in the Tax-Free Security checkbox . Tax-free securities are not displayed in Capital Gains reports.
- **Est Annual Income:** You have the option of entering the amount you expect to earn from this stock (the expected annual dividend per share). This figure is displayed in some Portfolio Views.

10. Click OK. Quicken will create the Investment account.

11. The first time you open the Investment account from the Account List window, Quicken will open the Create Opening Share Balance window.

Quicken will use the information in the Create Opening Share Balance window to create an opening balance in the Investment account register, and set the market value on the opening date. You may fill in the quantities in this window only if you *don't* need historic cost basis and performance reports. If you *do* need accurate cost basis, capital gains, and historic performance reports, do *not* fill in this window. Instead, click Cancel, then enter all transactions for the mutual fund from the date you first bought it.

If you choose to fill in the Create Opening Share Balance quantities, do the following:

- Enter the date on which you want to create the opening balance in the Create Opening Balance as of field. You may either type in the date or click on the Calendar button and choose the date from the pop-up calendar.
- Enter the number of shares purchased in the Number of shares field.
- Enter the price per share in the Price per share field. Quicken uses the number of shares and the price per share to calculate the opening balance (market value).
- Click OK to close the Create Opening Share Balance window and place the opening balance in the investment account register.

Use the Create Opening Share Balance window only if you don't need historic cost basis or performance reports.

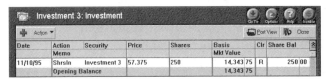

A single Mutual Fund register with an opening balance.

As mentioned earlier, Investment accounts are significantly different from other account types. They are discussed further in Chapter 14.

Creating an Asset Account

Your "net worth" consists of more than cash, bonds, and stock. Non-liquid assets include a house, art or stamp collection, or even your car. Transactions that take place in an Asset account tend to increase or decrease the estimated value of the asset—or convert part or all of the asset to cash through selling the asset.

To create an Asset account:

1. Click on the Asset button in the Create New Account window. Quicken will open the EasyStep interface you've become accustomed to by now. Just click on the Next button to begin.

2. To change the account name, type the new name into the Account Name field. Enter an optional description in the Description field. Then click on the Next button.

3. If you know how much the asset is worth, click on the Yes button. (Otherwise, click No and skip to Step 5. You can always add the valuation later.) Click on the Next button to continue.

4. Enter the date you want to start with in the As of Date field. Then enter the value of the asset in the Value field. Click on the Next button.

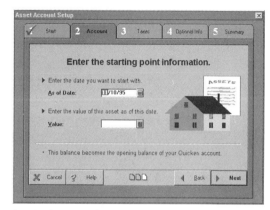

5. Now, Quicken will ask if you are using this account to track a tax-deferred investment (such as an IRA). If you're not, click No and skip to Step 7. Otherwise, select Yes and click on the Next button to continue.

Initial information for an Asset account.

6. Do you need to record transfers into or out of this account on any tax forms? If so, select Yes and press the Next button. (If not, click No and skip to Step 7.) Simply use the drop-down menus in the screen that will appear to select the forms for Transfers In and Transfers Out. When you're done, click Next.

7. As with the previous types of accounts, Quicken will ask if you wish to enter additional information, such as a contact number, interest rate information, or comments. If you do, select Yes and fill in the form. Either way, click Next to continue.

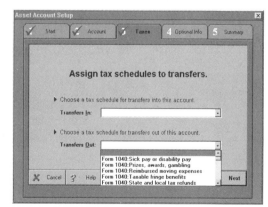

Use the drop-down menus in the Asset Account Setup to record transfers on any tax forms.

8. Once again, a Summary screen will allow you to double-check the information you've entered and change it if necessary. If you do need to make changes, move between the fields by clicking on the Back and Next buttons. When you are satisfied with all the answers, click Next and then Done.

Asset accounts have a register very similar to a Checking account. Below is a summary of the differences:

- The second column in the register is called "Ref" (for "Reference"). Unlike the Num column in a check register, the Ref column has no predefined list of values.

- The Decrease and Increase columns function identically to the Payment and Deposit columns in a check register. The Decrease column is used for transactions that decrease the value of the asset (such as the sale of part of a collection). The Increase column is used for transactions that increase the value of the asset (such as additions to a house).

- The Activities menu doesn't have a Reconcile function. This is because an Asset account is not tracked by anyone other than you, so (oh joy!) there is no statement to reconcile against.

- To update your account balance, choose Update Cash Balance from the Update Balances item in the Activities menu. Use this item to periodically update the value of your asset. This could be handy if, for example, your house were reappraised periodically.

The Asset account register.

When you select Update Cash Balance, Quicken opens the Update Account Balance window. Type in the new amount in the Update Balance to field. Specify the date for the adjustment in the Adjustment Date field. You may either type in the date or click on the Calendar button and enter the date from the pop-up calendar. Optionally, choose a category for the adjustment in the Category for Adjustment field.

The Update Account Balance window.

Creating a Liability Account

We're sorry, but we had to get to this part of the book eventually. Sometimes life gives us more than assets. Many of us also have debts.

Not surprisingly, a liability looks just like all the other accounts, except in reverse. In this case, your "balance" is how much you owe rather than what you have. The one difference is that once you've filled the main screen, you get the option of setting up an amortization schedule which lets you track how a loan is being paid off, over time. If you're paying off a loan in regular installments, this will allow you to get a quick view of where you stand at any point during the life of the loan.

To set up a Liability account:

1. Click on the Liability button in the Create New Account window. Quicken will open the EasyStep interface once again. Click on the Next button to continue.

2. To change the account name, type the new name into the Account Name field. Enter an optional description in the Description field. Then click on the Next button.

3. If you know how much you currently owe, click on the Yes button. (Otherwise, click No and skip to Step 5. You can always add the valuation later.) Click on the Next button to continue.

4. Enter the date you want to start with in the As of Date field. Then enter the amount you owe in the Balance field. Click Next.

5. Now, Quicken will ask if you wish to enter additional information, such as a contact number, interest rate information, or comments. If you do, select Yes and fill in the form. Either way, click Next.

6. Once again, a Summary screen will allow you to double-check the information you've entered and change it if necessary. If you do need to make changes, move back through the fields by clicking on the Back and Next buttons. Although EasyStep did not prompt you for any tax-related information, you can link transfers into and out of this Liability account by clicking on the Tax button on the Summary screen. Then select any relevant tax forms from the drop-down menus that appear. When you are satisfied with all the answers, click Next and then Done.

7. Quicken now asks if you want to set up an amortized loan for this account. Select No if you don't want to do this now (you can always do

Specify the loan factors in the Loan Setup window.

it later). If you select Yes, Quicken will open the Loan Setup window.

8. Enter the origination date of the loan in the Opening Date field. You may either type in the date or click on the Calendar button and enter the date from the pop-up calendar. Enter the original loan balance in the Original Balance field. Then click on the Next button.

Note: *In order for Quicken to calculate the split between interest and principal correctly, you must use the opening date and opening balance of the loan, not the date of the last statement you have for this account.*

9. Quicken will now ask if the loan includes a balloon payment—one that's much bigger than the regular payments—at the end. Click Yes or No as appropriate, then click Next to continue.

10. Enter the length of the loan (in years) in the Original Length field. In order to include months in the length of the loan (for example, a loan length of 5 years, 6 months) you must enter the months as a fraction of the year (for example, 6 months = .5 years). Click Next to continue.

Note: *Enter the length of time for which payments are made, not the length of time over which the loan is amortized. The loan can be due in less time than the "length" of the loan if a balloon payment is due after a certain period. For example, you might have a 30-year mortgage on your house, but the loan is due after 10 years. At the end of 10 years, you would owe a "balloon" payment for the remaining balance on the loan. If you chose to refinance at that time, you would need to refinance the amount of the balloon payment. For a "30-in-10" loan such as this, enter "10 years" here.*

11. Enter the amortized length of the loan in the Amortized Length field. For example, if you have a 30-year loan or a "30-due-in-7" loan, enter "30" here. You can also ask Quicken to calculate the amortized length for you if necessary. Click Next to continue.

12. Enter the payment period for the loan. If it is not monthly, use the drop-down menu to select another interval, or click on the <u>O</u>ther period button and enter the payments per year. Click Next.

13. Now enter the compounding period—how often the amount of interest owed is recalculated—for the loan. This may be daily, monthly or semi-annually, though the "monthly" default choice is usually correct in the United States. If you need to change the value, do so using the drop-down menu. Click Next to continue.

14. Enter the current balance and date, taken from your last loan statement. Enter the date in the Current Balance <u>D</u>ate field. You may type in the date or click on the Calendar button and enter the date from the pop-up calendar. Enter the balance in the Current Balance <u>A</u>mount field. If you are setting up a new account, you should leave this field blank. Click Next to continue.

15. Enter the due date of the next scheduled loan payment. You may type in the date or click on the Calendar button and enter it from the pop-up calendar. Click Next.

A pop-up calendar helps you visualize your next loan payment.

16. Quicken will ask you if you know the amount of your next loan payment. If you do not, Quicken will calculate it for you. However, it is better to answer <u>Y</u>es at this point if possible, because methods for calculating loan payments can vary. Click Next to continue.

17. Now you should enter the loan payment amount, but only the principal plus interest. The amount should not include other fees, such as mortgage insurance or payments to escrow accounts (such as property taxes or homeowner's insurance). You will enter these other fees in the Edit Payment window. Click Next.

18. Enter the interest rate for the loan. If it is an adjustable-rate loan, enter the rate that will be applied to the next payment. Click Next.

19. Quicken will now display two consecutive Summary screens. Review the information you've entered, and if necessary, return to previous screens using the Back button. Click Next.

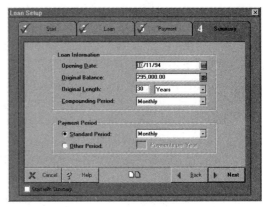

The Summary screen displays the loan information you've entered.

20. Quicken will now display the Set Up Loan Payment screen. At the top left of this screen, you will see the interest rate and P+I (principal plus interest) amounts that you

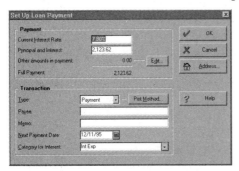

The Set Up Loan Payment screen.

previously entered. If there are other fees that need to be added into your payment—such as mortgage insurance or payments to escrow accounts—click on the Edit button. You can specify these fees using the Splits window that will appear.

At the bottom left of the Set Up Loan Payment screen is the area devoted to the transaction. This is where you specify how you are making, or are going to make, loan payments. Using the Type drop-down menu, specify Payment if you plan to write checks yourself, or Print Check if you plan to have Quicken write your check. (If Quicken is going to write checks, you can click on the Address button to open a Printed Check Information window.)

Now click on the Pmt Method button. Quicken will open the Select Payment Method window. You can set the payment as a Scheduled Transaction, Memorized Transaction, or Repeating Online Payment. (If you are not currently set up for online banking, the latter choice is grayed out.) If you choose Scheduled

Use the Select Payment Method window to either schedule or memorize your payment information.

Transaction, you can use the Register Entry drop-down menu to specify whether the check will be printed automatically or whether you will be prompted before the check is entered. You can also use the Account to Pay from field to specify the account from which you want to pay the liability. The Days in Advance field lets you set the number of days Quicken will prompt you *before* the scheduled payment.

When you are done updating the Select Payment Method window, click OK. You will be returned to the main Set Up Loan Payment window. Click OK again when you're satisfied with all the entries.

Note: *More information on scheduling payments is in Chapter 9.*

21. At this point Quicken will normally return you to the Account List window. If you would like to reconfirm details of your loan—it's probably the largest expense you'll ever enter in Quicken, after all— open the View Loans window. You do this by selecting Loans from Quicken's main Activities window. The View Loans window will show the payment history and the projected payments for the loan.

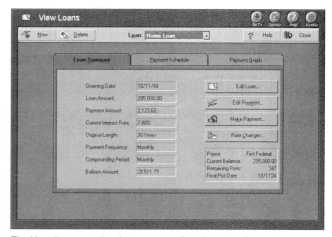

The View Loans window lets you reconfirm those touchy loan details.

Summary

Quicken has many types of accounts, including Checking, Savings, Credit Card, Cash, Money Market, Investment, Asset, and Liability. Setting up and using most of these accounts is similar to the steps for a Checking account, covered in Chapter 4. However, Investment and Liability accounts do work differently. Investment accounts are covered further in Chapter 14, and Liability accounts in Chapter 10.

Scheduling Transactions and Using the Financial Calendar

9

THANKS TO QUICKEN'S NEW "BEYOND-THE-GRAVE BANKING," RALPH **DID** TAKE IT WITH HIM.

If you're like me, you tend to forget things—especially when it comes to paying bills. Besides, a lot of the transactions you record in Quicken occur on a regular basis, and there's no reason to repeat every procedure each time.

If you use electronic banking to pay your bills, then you might not need to use the Quicken Financial Calendar since you can schedule fixed (recurring payments) or pay an individual bill up to a year in advance. Quicken doesn't actually touch your money until the due date arrives. But if you handwrite or print your checks, you might find the Calendar useful to make sure you don't forget anything.

If you get your paycheck or other income on approximately the same day each month, it might also be worthwhile to use the Calendar to record your deposits.

Quicken has the ability to schedule transactions individually or in a group. With scheduled transactions, you don't need to remember to pay your bills or deposit your paychecks—Quicken reminds you on dates that you specify.

This chapter reviews how to set up scheduled transactions using both the Scheduled Transaction List and the Financial Calendar. We will also discuss how you can use the Financial Calendar to review past and future transactions, and modify them directly from the Calendar—without opening the appropriate register.

What is a Scheduled Transaction?

A scheduled transaction is a transaction that you set up ahead of time. There are two types of scheduled transactions: one-time and recurring. A one-time scheduled transaction appears in your register only once, serving as a convenient reminder to pay a particular bill. A recurring scheduled transaction appears in your register on a regular basis, based on the schedule that you set up.

For example, your monthly mortgage payment is a likely candidate for a recurring scheduled transaction. A bill arriving on the 5th of the month that isn't due until the 21st is a good candidate for a one-time transaction.

When a scheduled transaction comes due, Quicken can either enter it in the register automatically or remind you of the bill—leaving the decision about whether or not to enter the transaction in the register up to you. Because the reminder also gives you a convenient way to edit the transaction before entering it in the register, you can easily be reminded about bills that vary from month to month, such as your phone and utilities bills.

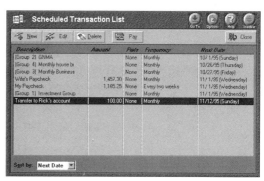

Setting Up a Scheduled Transaction

To set up a scheduled transaction using the Scheduled Transaction List, follow these steps:

1. Select Scheduled Transaction from the Lists menu. Quicken will open the Scheduled Transaction List.

The Scheduled Transaction List is one way to create and edit scheduled transactions.

2. Click on the <u>N</u>ew button. Quicken will open the Create Scheduled Transaction window.

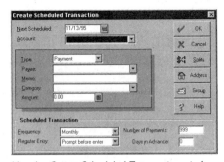

Use the Create Scheduled Transaction window for new scheduled transactions.

3. Fill in the date for the next time the transaction is due in the <u>N</u>ext Scheduled field. You may either type in the date or click on the field button and enter the date from the pop-up calendar. For recurring transactions, Quicken will update this date every time the transaction is entered into the register.

4. Click on the down arrow to the right of the <u>A</u>ccount field icon to select the account. Quicken will automatically debit or credit that account.

5. Select the type of transaction from the <u>T</u>ype drop-down menu. The transaction types are:
- Payment: Use Payment for a check you intend to handwrite.
- Deposit: Use Deposit for an amount you are depositing in this account.
- Print Check: Use Print Check for a check you will print from Quicken. A Print Check transaction is entered in the register with Print as the check number.
- Online Pmt: Use Online Pmt for an electronic payment that will be sent by CheckFree or other online banking systems.

Note: *See Chapter 15 for other ways to schedule online payments.*

6. Type the name of the payee in the Pa<u>y</u>ee field or select it by clicking on the down arrow icon. If you have QuickFill turned on, Quicken will try to match the name of the payee from the memorized transactions list as soon as you start to type.

7. Enter any memo you want in the <u>M</u>emo field.

8. Enter the category for the transaction in the <u>C</u>ategory field. If you have QuickFill turned on, Quicken will try to match the category you type to the list of valid categories. If you need to split the transaction into multiple categories, click on the Splits button at the right to open the Splits window. Enter the categories and amounts in the Splits window as described in Chapter 5.

9. Enter the amount of the transaction in the Amount field. You may either type in the amount or click on the field button and enter the amount in the pop-up calculator.

Note: If you entered split categories and amounts in the Splits window, the Amount field will not be available, since in a split transaction, the amount is set by the total of the amounts in the Splits window.

10. To select a payment frequency, click on the down arrow to the right of the Frequency field of the Scheduled Transaction section (at the bottom of the Create Scheduled Transaction window). The available frequencies are:

- Only Once: The transaction will be recorded only once—on the date indicated in the Next Scheduled field.
- Weekly: The transaction will be recorded every week, on the day of the week that corresponds to the day on which the Next Scheduled date falls. For example, if the next scheduled payment is December 22, 1996, and that date is a Sunday, then the transaction will be recorded automatically every Sunday.
- Every Two Weeks: The transaction will be recorded every two weeks, on the day of the week that corresponds to the day on which the Next Scheduled date falls.
- Twice a Month: The transaction will be recorded twice every month. The first occurrence in any give month will correspond to the date indicated by the Next Scheduled field. The second occurrence will be half a month (between 14 and 16 days, depending on the month) later.
- Every four weeks: The transaction will be recorded every four weeks, on the day of the week that corresponds to the day on which the Next Scheduled date falls.
- Monthly: The transaction will be recorded every month on the date indicated in the Next Scheduled field.
- Every two months: The transaction will be recorded every other month on the date indicated in the Next Scheduled field.

- Quarterly: The transaction will be recorded once every quarter (every three months). The actual date on which the transaction will be recorded will be the month and date that corresponds to the *position* (within the quarter) of the date specified in the Next Scheduled field. For example, if the next scheduled date is December 22, 1996 (the last month of the fourth quarter), then the transaction will be recorded on the 22nd of the last month of every quarter.
- Twice a Year: The transaction will be recorded every six months on the date specified in the Next Scheduled field.
- Yearly: The transaction will be recorded once every year, on the date specified by the Next Scheduled field.

11. Specify how you want Quicken to enter the scheduled transaction in your register by making a selection from the Register Entry field. The selections are:

- Automatically enter: Quicken will enter each transaction in the register as it comes due.
- Prompt before enter: Quicken will prompt you (when you start the program or use Quicken Reminders) to verify the information and verify that you want the transaction entered in the register. For more information on this feature, see "Using Quicken Reminders," later in this chapter.

12. Select the number of times you want Quicken to record this scheduled transaction by entering the number in the Number of Payments field. To have Quicken continue to record this payment indefinitely, leave the default entry of "999."

13. In the Days in Advance field, enter the number of days in advance you want Quicken to prompt you or enter the transaction in the register. Quicken can enter the transaction in the register ahead of time, although the date on the transaction will still be the date specified in the Next Specified field. When you enter a number in the Days in Advance field, you are creating a postdated transaction.

14. If the transaction is a printed check, you can click on the Address button to enter an address to be printed on the check.

15. Click OK to enter the new scheduled transaction.

Tip: To temporarily disable a scheduled transaction that you will use later, edit the scheduled transaction and enter 0 for the number of payments. Quicken will not record any more transactions in your register until you enter a new number in the Number of Payments field. However, the transaction will remain in your Scheduled Transaction List.

Working with the Scheduled Transaction List

The Scheduled Transaction List permits you to work with all your scheduled transactions using the buttons in the button bar located across the top of the window. In addition to the New button discussed in the previous section, you can perform the following actions:

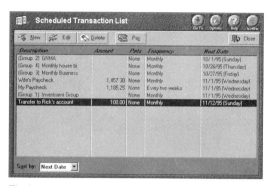

The buttons at the top of the Scheduled Transaction List let you edit, delete, and pay scheduled transactions.

- Edit an existing transaction by clicking on the Edit button. Quicken will open the Edit Scheduled Transaction window. This window contains the same fields as the Create Scheduled Transaction window discussed above. You can change any of the fields.

- Delete a scheduled transaction by clicking on the Delete button. Confirm that you want to delete the transaction by clicking OK in the confirmation dialog box.

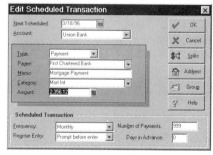

Use the Edit Scheduled Transaction window to change any field for a scheduled transaction.

- You may pay a scheduled transaction at any time (including prior to its due date) by clicking on the Pay button. Quicken will display the Record Transaction Group window. You may edit any of the data in the window. Editing the data affects only this occurrence of the scheduled transaction. Click on either Record or Skip. If you click on Record, Quicken will enter this payment in the account register and change the transaction's next scheduled due date. If you

Use the Record Transaction Group window to edit and either pay or skip over a scheduled transaction.

click on S<u>k</u>ip, Quicken will skip the transaction (does not record it) for this occurrence—and update the next scheduled due date.

Setting Up a Transaction Group

Some people have groups of bills that they pay regularly at the same time every month. For example, you might make both your house and

car payments on the 15th of each month, or perhaps you pay your phone, gas, electric, and cable TV payments on the 1st of every month. You could set up each of these payments as a scheduled transaction. However, you also can group transactions into a recurring "transaction group" that contains all the bills that you pay regularly at the same time. A transaction group reduces the clutter in your

Transaction groups are displayed in the Scheduled Transaction List.

Scheduled Transaction List, since each transaction group (you can have up to 12) appears just once in the list.

When a transaction group is due to be recorded, Quicken will enter each transaction of the group into your register. You may then open the register and make modifications to each transaction separately.

Note: *Unlike individual memorized transactions, you cannot edit the transactions that make up the transaction group prior to recording them. You also cannot choose to record only some of the transactions in the group—you must either record the entire group or skip the entire group. Of course, you can record the group, then remove individual transactions from the register.*

Before you can include a transaction in a group, Quicken has to memorize the transaction.

To set up a transaction group, use the following steps:

1. Choose Sc<u>h</u>eduled Transaction from the <u>L</u>ists menu. Quicken will open the Scheduled Transaction List window.

2. Click on the <u>N</u>ew button. Quicken will open the Create Scheduled Transaction window.

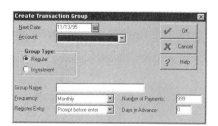

Use the Create Transaction Group window to create a new transaction group.

3. Click on the Grou<u>p</u> button. Quicken will open the Create Transaction Group window.

4. Select the date on which all transactions in the group should next be paid in the <u>N</u>ext Date field. You may either type in a date or click on the field button and choose the date from the pop-up calendar.

5. Select the account from the <u>A</u>ccount field. All transactions in a group affect the same account.

 Note: *When you use the memorized transaction list to choose a transaction you want to include in a group, all memorized transactions are listed, regardless of whether they affect the account to which the group is attached.*

6. Choose the type of group from the radio buttons in the Group Type box: Regular or In<u>v</u>estment. All groups are "Regular" unless the transactions in the group are investments.

7. Type in a name for the group in the Group Na<u>m</u>e field.

8. Enter the transaction scheduling information in the <u>F</u>requency, Register Entr<u>y</u>, Num<u>b</u>er of Payments, and Days <u>i</u>n Advance fields, as discussed in "Setting Up a Scheduled Transaction in the Scheduled Transaction List," above.

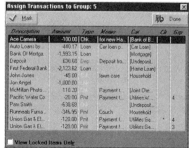

The last step in building a transaction group is assigning memorized transactions to the group.

9. Click OK. Quicken will open the Assign Transactions to Group window. This window contains a list of all the memorized transactions.

10. Mark the transactions to be included in the group. To mark a transaction, either double-click on it, or select it and click on the <u>M</u>ark button. Each marked transaction will show the number of the group it is attached to in the Grp column. A transaction can be attached to just one transaction group.

11. Click on Done. Quicken will create the transaction group and display it in the Scheduled Transaction List window. The Description column indicates that a scheduled transaction is a group by including the word "Group" and the group number in square brackets. The Amount and Pmts columns are empty, because a group usually involves multiple transactions.

> **Note:** *If you delete a memorized transaction that is included in a transaction group, Quicken will automatically remove it from the transaction group. However, deleting a transaction group does not remove the memorized transactions from the transaction list.*

Working with a Transaction Group

Editing and paying transaction groups in the Scheduled Transaction List works slightly different from regular scheduled transactions. To edit

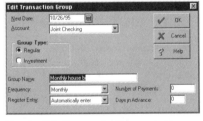
Use the Edit Transaction Group window to change any field for a transaction group.

a transaction group, use the following steps:

1. From the Scheduled Transaction List window, select the group you want to edit and click on the Edit button. Quicken will open the Edit Transaction Group window, which will include all the same information as the Create Transaction Group window.

2. Edit any of the fields in the Edit Transaction Group window. When you are through, click OK.

> **Note:** *If you change the Next Date or Frequency information, all future occurrences of the transaction group are affected. For example, if you change the date from the 22nd to the 25th (and the frequency is monthly), the group will come due on the 25th of every month for all future occurrences.*

3. Quicken will open the Assign Transactions to Group window. You may add more transactions to the group by marking them (double-click them, or select them and click Mark). You may also remove transactions from the group by unmarking. To unmark a transaction, double-click on it, or select it and click Mark. The group number will be removed from the Grp column.

4. When you have made all your changes, click Done.

To pay a transaction group, use the following steps:

1. From the Scheduled Transaction List, select the group you want to pay and click on the Pay button. Quicken will open the Record Transaction Group window.

The Record Transaction Group window is the first step in paying a group transaction.

2. If you wish, you may change the Due Date and Account. This changes the due date and account *for this payment occurrence only.* Future due dates are still calculated from the date and frequency that you used when you set up the group or changed by editing the group later.

3. Make your choice from the three buttons at the bottom of the Record Transaction Group window:

- If you click Record, Quicken will record all the transactions that form the group in the specified account for the specified date. If you need to make any changes to individual transactions (such as change the amount), you must open the register window and make the changes in the register.
- If you choose Skip, Quicken will skip paying all the transactions. It will update the due date to be the next due date.
- If you choose Edit, Quicken will open the Assign Transactions to Group window. You can add (mark) transactions to the group, and remove (unmark) transactions from the group. However, unlike the date and account changes in the Record Scheduled Transaction window, the changes you make in the Assign Transactions to Group window *do* affect all future occurrences of the group.

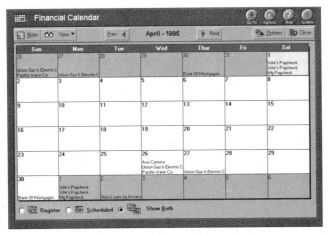

Quicken's Financial Calendar provides a visual record of your account activity.

Working with the Financial Calendar

Quicken contains a Financial Calendar that provides a visual record of both past and scheduled transactions. You can configure the Financial Calendar to display the memorized transaction list as well as a graph of your account balances for the current month. You can also attach a note to a date, and have Quicken display that note. You can schedule transactions in the Financial Calendar, and you can create new transactions. You can even edit or delete existing transactions without opening the register to which they belong.

To open the Financial Calendar, click on the Calendar button in the icon bar or select Financial Calendar in the Activities menu. Across the top of the Financial Calendar is the button bar, containing the buttons for configuring the calendar. The buttons are:

- Note: Enables you to add a note to a date (see "Adding Notes to Your Financial Calendar," later in this chapter).
- View: Enables you to display the memorized transaction list and/or the account balances graph (see "Scheduling a Transaction" and "Viewing the Account Balances Graph," later in this chapter).
- Prev: Click on this button to move to the previous month.
- Next: Click on this button to move to the next month.
- Options: Opens the Financial Calendar Options page (see "Modifying the Financial Calendar Options," later in this chapter).
- Close: Closes the Financial Calendar window.

You may select the type of transactions you want to see in the Financial Calendar by using the radio buttons across the bottom of the window:

- Select Register to see only past transactions (transactions that have already been entered in your account registers).
- Select Scheduled to see only future scheduled transactions. These transactions are the same ones that appear in the Scheduled Transactions List.
- Select Show Both to see both Register and Scheduled transactions.

Scheduling a Transaction

To schedule a transaction in the Financial Calendar, you must have the memorized transaction list available in the window. To open the memorized transaction list, click on the View button in the Financial Calendar button bar and select Show Memorized Txns. Quicken will shrink the calendar and display the memorized transaction list to the right side.

Note: *You can open the memorized transaction list to make changes to memorized transactions by clicking on the Manage List button.*

Once the memorized transaction list is open, you can schedule a transaction in the Financial Calendar by clicking the appropriate date and dragging in the payment. Here's how to do it:

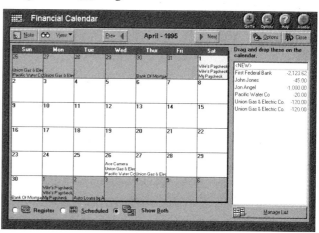

1. Using the Prev and Next buttons, select the month in which you wish to schedule a transaction.

2. Move the mouse pointer
over the list of transactions on the right. The pointer will turn into a hand to show that you are ready to pick a transaction.

Quicken can display the memorized transaction list on the right side of the Financial Calendar.

3. Click on the transaction you want, hold down the left mouse button, and drag the transaction onto the calendar. If you want to schedule a transaction that is not present in the memorized transaction list, click on the <NEW> entry at the top of the list instead of picking an existing transaction.

4. Position the pointer over the date on which you want to schedule the transaction. If the date is in the future, the mouse pointer will change to a calendar to indicate that the transaction will be a scheduled transaction. If the date is in the past, the mouse pointer will change to a register to indicate that the transaction won't be scheduled, but instead will be added to the register as an existing transaction.

    Note: Dragging an existing transaction or a <NEW> transaction onto a past date in the Financial Calendar is a technique for recording existing transactions in the Financial Calendar.

5. Release the mouse button. Quicken will open the New Transaction window. If you chose an existing transaction, information from that transaction will be displayed. If you chose <NEW> from the transaction list, the fields in the New Transaction window will be empty, waiting for you to enter the information.

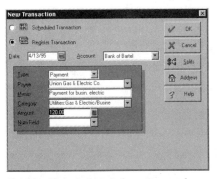

The New Transaction window appears when you use drag and drop to schedule or record payments or deposits from the Financial Calendar.

6. Select the type of transaction using the radio buttons in the upper left corner of the New Transaction window. As mentioned earlier, Quicken will select the Scheduled Transaction button if you dropped the transaction on a future date, or it will select the Register Transaction button if you dropped the transaction on a past date. However, you can change that selection here.

    Note: If you take a future-dated transaction and convert it to a register transaction by selecting Register Transaction, Quicken will enter the transaction in the register with the future date— this transaction will be a postdated transaction. Quicken will not use the Scheduled Transaction information at the bottom of the Drag and Drop Transaction window. If you convert a past transaction to a scheduled transaction by selecting Scheduled Transaction, Quicken will enter the past transaction in the register, and also schedule future occurrences.

7. Fill out the rest of the information in the New Transaction window as detailed in "Setting Up a Scheduled Transaction in the Scheduled Transaction List," earlier in this chapter.

8. Click OK to enter the scheduled or register transaction.

Viewing the Account Balances Graph

Quicken can show you a graph of your account balances from the Financial Calendar window. To view the graph, click the View button and select Show Account Graph. Past dates are shown in yellow, future dates are shown in blue, and the currently selected date (if any) is shown in green.

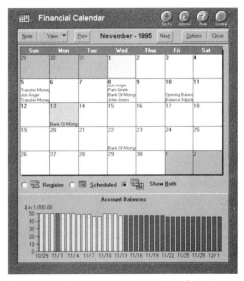

    Note: *If your account balance doesn't change a lot from day to day in terms of a percentage of the whole—lucky you!—it may be hard to discern much from the graph using its default size. To increase the amount of screen area the graph uses, you can click on the line separating the calendar area from the graph area and drag it upwards.*

The Account Balances graph is available from the Financial Calendar.

Checking or Changing a Transaction

You may check or change any transaction visible in the Financial Calendar. To check or change a transaction, use the following steps:

1. Double-click on any day in the calendar, or click with the right mouse button on a day. Quicken will open the Transactions on window. The Transactions on window displays a brief listing of every transaction that occurred or will occur on the selected day. If no transactions occurred or will occur on that day, the window will be empty. If the transactions are scheduled, the word <SCHED> will appear next to the transaction details in the window.

Quicken displays transactions for a selected day in the Transactions on window.

2. Choose the action you want to take by selecting it from the buttons at the bottom of the Transactions on window. The actions you can take are:

- To create a new transaction, click on New. Quicken will open the New Transaction window described above. Fill out the window and click OK to create the new transaction.

    Note: If there are no transactions for the selected day, only the New button will be available.

- To edit a transaction, click on Edit. You will get different results depending on whether the transaction is a register transaction, a scheduled transaction, or part of a transaction group.

    - If the transaction is a past (register) transaction, Quicken will open the Edit Register Transaction window. You may edit the fields in the window and click on OK to complete the edit.

    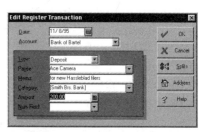

    Use the Edit Register Transaction window to edit register transactions.

    - If the transaction is a scheduled transaction, Quicken will open the Edit Scheduled Transaction window. You can make any changes, as detailed earlier in this chapter, and click on OK. Changes you make in the Edit Scheduled Transaction window affect all future occurrences of this scheduled transaction.

    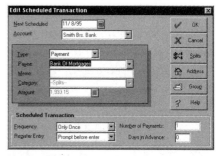

    Use the Edit Scheduled Transaction window to edit scheduled transactions.

    - If the transaction is a group, Quicken will open the Edit Transaction Group window. You may then edit the details of the transaction group, as discussed earlier in this chapter, and click on OK. Quicken will open the Assign Transactions to Group window where you can add (mark) or remove (unmark) transactions from the group. Any changes you make to the transaction group affect all future occurrences of this scheduled transaction.

    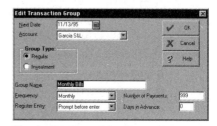

    Use the Edit Transaction Group window to edit transaction groups.

- To delete a transaction, click on <u>D</u>elete, then click on OK to confirm the deletion. For scheduled transactions (including transaction groups), this deletes only the single occurrence and does not affect future occurrences.
- If the transaction is a register transaction, you can click on the <u>Reg</u>ister button to open the account register to which the transaction belongs. This button is not available for scheduled transactions.
- If the transaction is a scheduled transaction (including a transaction group), you can pay the transaction now by clicking on the <u>Pa</u>y Now button. For a transaction group, Quicken will open the Record Transaction Group window. You can modify the fields in the window and then either <u>R</u>ecord or <u>S</u>kip the transaction group. For a non-group scheduled transaction, Quicken will open the Record Scheduled Transaction window. You can modify the fields in this window and then either <u>R</u>ecord or <u>S</u>kip the scheduled transaction.

Adding Notes to Your Financial Calendar

You can add reminder notes to a date in the Financial Calendar. These notes can be used to remind you of important tasks. You can color-code the notes to indicate their topic (for example, olive for business and red for personal). However, each date can contain only a single note. A date with a note attached displays a small rectangle in the upper right corner. To add a note to a date in the Financial Calendar, follow these steps:

1. Select a day by clicking on it.

2. Click on the <u>N</u>ote button. Quicken will open the Note window.

The Financial Calendar's Note window enables you to attach a note to a date.

3. Type the contents of the note into the Note window.

4. Select a color from the <u>C</u>olor drop-down menu.

5. Click <u>S</u>ave to save the note and close the Note window.

To view the note, click on the small square in the date. To delete the note, first click on the small square to open the note, then click on <u>D</u>elete.

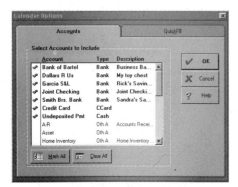

The Calendar Options window enables you to customize how the Financial Calendar looks and works.

Modifying the Financial Calendar Options

You can set the Financial Calendar options in Quicken to customize how the calendar works. To change the Financial Calendar options, click on the Options button in the Financial Calendar button bar. Quicken will open the Calendar Options window. This window displays two sets of options: Accounts and QuickFill, split into two panels. To switch panels, simply click on the tab for the panel you want.

The Account Options

You can switch to the Account options of the Financial Calendar by clicking on the Accounts tab.

To show the contents of an account register in the Financial Calendar, mark the account by clicking on it (or pressing the spacebar) to place a yellow check mark at the left end of the account line in the Calendar Options window. To exclude a marked account, click on it (or press the spacebar) to unmark it and remove the yellow check mark. You may also click on Mark All to display every account in the Financial Calendar, or click on Clear All to unmark all the accounts.

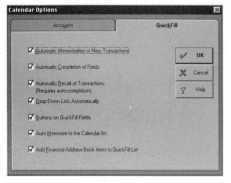

The QuickFill options may also be set in the Calendar Options window.

The QuickFill Options

You can switch to the QuickFill options of the Financial Calendar by clicking on the QuickFill tab.

A QuickFill option is selected when a checkbox is displayed alongside the option.

Note: *As with the register fields discussed in Chapter 4, the fields in the scheduled transaction windows behave differently depending on the settings in the QuickFill options. For example, if you have enabled Drop Down Lists Automatically, any field with a drop-down list will display that list automatically when you tab to the field or click on it with the mouse.*

The QuickFill Options

QuickFill Option	Action When Option Is Selected
Automatic Memorization of New Transactions	Memorizes every new transaction you enter for a new payee (except investment transactions) and adds the transaction to the memorized transaction list. Quicken automatically turns off this option when the list of memorized transactions reaches half of Quicken's limit of 2,000 memorized transactions.
Automatic Completion of Fields	Completes each field in a transaction as you type it. This feature works with Check Number (Num), Payee, Category, Class, Security Names, Investment Action, and transfer account names.
Automatic Recall of Transactions (Requires auto-completion)	Recalls a memorized transaction and fills in all the fields when you press Tab to leave the Payee field. This option is only available if you have also selected Automatic Completion of Fields.
Drop Down Lists Automatically	Displays the drop-down list for a field when you move the cursor to the field. If you find that the drop-down list gets in your way, you can disable this option and use Buttons on QuickFill Fields instead.
Button on QuickFill Fields	Displays the drop-down buttons for fields with QuickFill. Click the button to drop down the list. If you have this option turned off, you can still display the list by clicking with the right mouse button.
Auto Memorize to the Calendar List	Memorizes every new transaction to the Calendar list of memorized transactions.
Add Financial Address Book items to QuickFill List	Appearing in Quicken Deluxe only, this option lets you select whether or not your Financial Address Book items appear in QuickFill lists.

Using Quicken Billminder

If you're the forgetful type, you can program your computer to remind you when it's time to pay a bill. Quicken has three ways to do this: It can remind you as soon as you boot your computer; it can remind you as soon as you run Windows; or it can remind you when you start Quicken.

- If you enable Billminder to run when you first boot your computer, Billminder will present a message on your screen informing you that you have overdue transactions. This message will appear in character mode before Windows 95 or Windows 3.1 starts up.

To get such a message, modify your AUTOEXEC.BAT file using the Edit program that comes with DOS (or the Notepad program that comes with Windows) to add the following command:

C:\QUICKENW\BILLMNDW.EXE C:\QUICKENW /p

This assumes that Quicken is installed on drive C in the QUICKENW directory (or folder, in Windows 95 terminology). If you installed Quicken somewhere else, substitute that drive and directory for C:\QUICKENW (in both places where it appears in the above command).

- If you enable the Billminder program to run when you first start Windows, it will load as an icon (minimized application). By clicking on this icon, you can find out whether you have overdue transactions without having to load Quicken. To enable Billminder, do the following:

  If you have Windows 3.1, use Notepad or a similar text editor to modify your WIN.INI file. Add the following command:

  LOAD = C:\QUICKENW\BILLMNDW.EXE

  If there are already other entries on the LOAD = line, you may add this one at the end. (The wording given assumes that Quicken is installed on drive C in the QUICKENW directory. If you installed Quicken somewhere else, substitute that drive and directory for C:\QUICKENW in this command.)

  If you have Windows 95, click with the right mouse button on the Task Bar at the bottom of the screen. Then select Properties from the pop-up menu that will appear. Next, from the Task Bar Properties window, click on the Start Menu Programs tab; then click on the Add button. In the Create Shortcut window that appears, type the following:

  C:\QUICKENW\BILLMNDW.EXE

  Again, this assumes that you installed Quicken for Windows in the default folder. If not, substitute the Quicken program's name manually or use the Browse button to locate it on your hard drive. Then click on the Next button.

  You will now see the Select Program Folder window. Use your mouse to scroll down the list until you see the StartUp folder.

Click on that folder, then on the Next button. A Select a Title for the Program window will ask you to name the shortcut: You can type in "Quicken Billminder" or anything else you like. Click on Finish to leave this window, then on OK to close the Task Bar Properties window.

The Select Program Folder menu helps you place the Billminder program in Windows 95's startup menu.

- If you enable the Billminder program to run when you first start Quicken, it will let you know about overdue transactions, and you won't have to check manually.

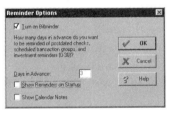

Quicken's Reminder Options window.

Arrange this by pulling down the Edit menu in Quicken, then selecting Options.

Click on the Reminders button in the Options window that will appear, and you will see the Reminder Options window. Click on the Turn on Billminder button, and Quicken will display a special Scheduled Transactions Due window when you first load the program. It will not only remind you of transactions due, but will also let you work with them immediately by clicking on the Record or Edit buttons.

Quicken's Scheduled Transactions Due window.

Note: *If you're really forgetful, you can use both the above forms of Billminder— the separate program that runs when Windows first loads and the Scheduled Transactions Due window. In fact, you could also load the initial character-mode Billminder to appear when you boot up your computer, but then you'd probably be too exasperated to do anything by the time you had the Quicken register open!*

Using Quicken Reminders

Quicken Reminders are still another way to remind you about Quicken transactions that need your attention. Quicken Reminders can be set to run automatically when you start Quicken. Reminders are also available by selecting Reminders from the Activities menu. Either way, Quicken will open the Quicken Reminders window.

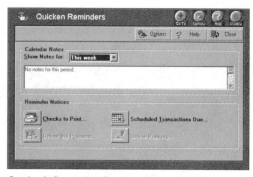

Quicken's Reminders function alerts you about transactions needing your attention.

In the Quicken Reminders window, you will see the following:

- The Calendar Notes section. (This does not appear by default; you need to enable it via the Reminder Options window (see "Setting Quicken Reminder Options," below). To set which notes you want to see, select a time period from the Show Notes for drop-down list. You can select to show notes for a variety of time periods, including Last Week, This Week, Next Week, Last Month, This Month, and Next Month. You can also select to see notes from the next 7 or 14 days. If you use Calendar notes for miscellaneous "to-dos," these last two options are the most useful.
- Checks to Print shows you the checks you need to print. For more information, see "Printing Checks from Quicken Reminders," below.
- Scheduled Transactions Due presents a list of scheduled transactions that are now due. For more information, see "Handling Scheduled Transactions from Quicken Reminders," below.

Printing Checks from Quicken Reminders

To print checks from the Quicken Reminders window, use the following steps:

Choose the account you want to print checks from.

1. Click on the Checks to Print button. If you have checks to print in more than one account, Quicken will present the first Checks to Print window to find out which account you want to print checks from.

Note: *If there are no checks to print, the Checks to Print button will not be available.*

2. After you have selected an account, Quicken will open the Select Checks to Print window. Verify that the First Check Number is correct.

3. From the Print section, select the checks to print. You may print All Checks, Checks Dated Through (pick the date), or Selected Checks. If you pick Selected Checks, click on the Choose button to pick the checks you want to print.

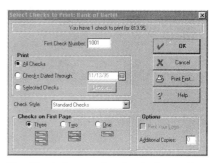

4. Click Print to print the checks.

    Note: You may also print checks by selecting Print Checks from the File menu.

Use this window to select the checks to print.

Handling Scheduled Transactions from Quicken Reminders

When you click on the Scheduled Transactions Due button in the Quicken Reminders window, Quicken will let you record or edit any scheduled transactions for which you have set the Register entry to "Prompt before enter." Scheduled transactions with a Register entry of "Automatically enter" do not show up in the Scheduled Transactions Due list, because Quicken handles those transactions without any help from you.

    To work with your scheduled transactions from the Quicken Reminders window, use the following steps:

1. Click on the Scheduled Transactions Due button. Quicken will open the Scheduled Transactions Due window.

    Note: If there are no scheduled transactions due, the Scheduled Transactions Due button will not be available.

2. To record a transaction, select the transaction and click on Record. Quicken will record the transaction in the register and remove it from the Scheduled Transactions Due list.

The Scheduled Transactions Due window.

    Note: Quicken will not prompt you to confirm that you want to Record the transaction, even if you have the scheduled transaction set to "Prompt before enter."

3. When you have finished working with the scheduled transactions, click on the Done button. Any scheduled transactions you have not worked with will remain on the Scheduled Transactions Due list.

You can delete a scheduled transaction from the list by selecting the transaction and clicking on Delete. This deletes only the current occurrence of the transaction—it does not affect future occurrences.

You may also edit a transaction in the Scheduled Transactions Due window by selecting the transaction and clicking on Edit. If you make changes, however, you *must* click on the Record button before you leave the Scheduled Transactions Due window—otherwise your changes will be ignored without warning.

Setting Quicken Reminder Options

You can turn Billminder on and off and set how Reminders work by selecting the Options button in the Quicken Reminders window. Quicken will display the Quicken Options window.

You can have Quicken warn you ahead of time about upcoming checks to print and scheduled transactions. Set the number of days ahead that you want to be warned in the text box.

To have the Reminders window open when you run Quicken, make sure you have placed a check mark in the Show Reminders on Startup checkbox. If you want the Reminders window to show Calendar notes, place a check mark in the Show Calendar Notes.

Summary

One of the most powerful features of Quicken is its ability to schedule both individual transactions and groups of transactions ahead of time. You can set up scheduled transactions from the Scheduled Transaction List and from the Financial Calendar. The Financial Calendar also provides a graphical view of your Quicken activity. You can add new transactions and reschedule transactions without ever opening a register. Quicken also includes several methods of reminding you that transactions need your attention.

Loans and Mortgages

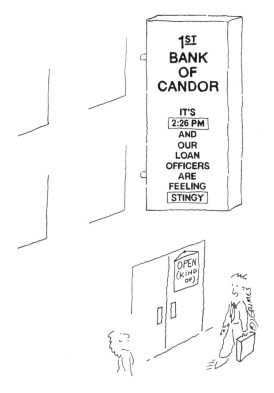

10

William Shakespeare once wrote "neither a borrower nor a lender be, for loan oft loses self and friend." Well, Shakespeare never had to spend six figures for a house or five figures for a car. Today, almost everyone is a borrower.

If Will Shakespeare were writing today, he'd probably give you the same advice that my co-author, Louis Fortis, gives in Chapter 25. If you are going to borrow, make sure that it's for something you really need and at interest rates that are competitive. Just as important, keep track of that loan because if you don't control it, it will find a way to control you. Fortunately, Quicken gives you plenty of tools to help you keep track of loans.

I kind of agree with Will's advice about being a lender but, if you're inclined to lend money and don't worry about your loan "losing self and friend," you can also use Quicken to keep track of money you lend to other people. Of course, many people do lend money to banks, in the form of savings accounts (discussed in Chapter 8).

This chapter covers using Quicken to set up and keep track of loans such as home mortgages and car loans. Credit cards—the other way most of us get into debt, are covered in Chapter 12.

Setting Up a Loan

Quicken tracks your loan by setting up an account. If you're the one borrowing money (which is usually the case), Quicken will set up a liability account. If you are lending money, Quicken will set up an asset account.

The example I'm using is for a car loan, but the same steps apply for mortgages and other types of consumer loans (except credit cards).

To set up a loan:

1. Go to the Activities menu and select Loans.

2. Quicken will show you a summary screen for an existing loan if you have one. If this is your first loan, the loan data on the screen will be blank.

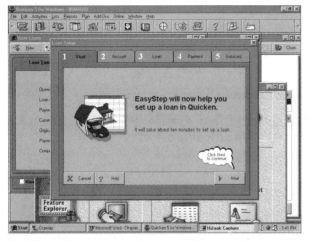

3. Click New to start the Easy-Step process that, in seven steps, will walk you through creating a loan account. Or, if you dislike the walk-though process and like filling out forms, just click on the Summary tab and enter the information yourself, avoiding EasyStep.

EasyStep guides you through the process of setting up loans.

4. Click Next and tell Quicken if you wish to Borrow Money or Lend Money. For this exercise, we'll borrow.

5. Quicken will now be ready to set up your loan account. If it's a new loan, click New Account and give the loan a name. I'm calling mine "Car Loan 1." (I put in a "1" because I might want to take out a second loan for my wife's car.)

6. Quicken will now want to know if you've made any payments. For this example, I am assuming that we're tracking an existing loan, so I'll check Yes.

Getting Information About an Existing Loan

If you're going to use Quicken to track an existing loan, you'll need the following information about the loan: the date it originated, the original balance, the interest rate, the original length of the loan, how often it is compounded, whether there's a balloon payment at the end, and the date of your next payment. You will also be asked to provide the current balance (how much you now owe), but if you don't know the amount, Quicken will calculate it for you. If you're like me, the loan papers you signed when you bought your car or house are probably several inches thick and buried deep in some filing cabinet. You could dig them out, but it might be easier to call the lender. Most companies that lend money have 800 numbers that you can call to get information about your loan. They'll ask you for identifying information (such as your Social Security number or your mother's maiden name), and then they'll tell you whatever you need to know.

7. Quicken will now want to know both the original balance and the date that you took out the loan. This information is on your loan papers. If you want to try to enter the information from memory, keep in mind that the original loan balance is not necessarily the full price you paid (because you probably made a down payment).

8. Quicken will next want to know if you have a balloon payment. That's not the price you pay for party favors; rather it's a lump-sum payment that some lenders apply after regular payments stop. You probably won't have a balloon payment with a car loan, so check No.

9. Enter the length of the loan. The default is in years, but you can enter the length in months, weeks, or number of payments. You can check years even if you plan to pay off the loan in monthly installments. Car loans are typically paid off over four or five years, so I've entered "5."

10. Enter the standard payment period for the loan—usually monthly.

11. Enter the compounding period of the loan. This is how often interest is calculated. The more frequently interest is calculated, the higher the cost of the loan. Interest is usually calculated monthly, but not always, so check with your lender.

12. Quicken will now ask for the current balance of your loan. You can get this information from your lender. Sometimes you don't even have to speak to anyone—just call the lender's 800 number, punch your loan number and other data into your Touch-Tone phone, and a machine will tell you the balance.

If you know the balance, check Yes, click Next, and enter the amount. Otherwise, click No and Quicken will calculate it based on the information you have already entered.

13. Enter the date of your next payment.

14. Quicken will now ask if you know the amount of your next payment. If you don't know, check No and Quicken will calculate it. Otherwise, check Yes and enter the amount.

15. Enter the interest rate. If it's 8.25%, just enter 8.25 (not .0825). The "%" sign is optional. If you have an adjustable loan, enter the rate as of your next payment.

16. Quicken will now present you with a series of summary screens. Review the information and make any necessary changes. You can make the changes directly on the summary screens (which is the easiest way) or you can click the Back button to go back to the setup screen you want to revisit. Don't worry—Quicken will remember everything you've typed, so you don't have to re-enter any information if you go back to a previous screen.

17. Click Done and Quicken, if necessary, will calculate your balance and loan payment and bring you to the Set Up Loan Payment window.

The Set Up Loan Payment window, as generated by Quicken's EasyStep.

Checking and Completing the Loan Payment Screen

You've done most of the work, but you're not quite finished. You now need to enter the payment type, payment method, payee, and a category for the interest.

1. Enter the payment type. Select Payment if you plan to pay the bill by writing a check. Select Print Check if you plan to use Quicken to print your checks. Select Online Pmt if you plan to transmit your payments through Check-Free or one of Quicken's other electronic bill payment services.

The Set Up Loan Payment process includes a place to enter the payment type.

2. Go to the Payment Method screen by clicking on the Pmt Method button. Select Scheduled Transaction if you wish to have Quicken enter the payment for you automatically. Select Memorized Transaction if you want Quicken to memorize the payment information so you can easily recall it manually when you're ready to make a payment. You should also select Memorized Transaction if you're using an electronic bill payment service and choose to have the service pay your bill automatically. Click OK.

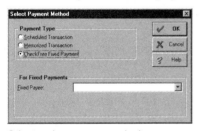

Selecting the payment method.

   Note: *Choosing Memorized Transaction means that you can manually recall the transaction without having to enter the data. It does not automatically pay the bill for you—choose Scheduled Transaction for that option.*

3. If you plan to have Quicken print a check for you, click on Address and enter the necessary information.

4. Enter the name of the payee in the Payee field exactly as you want it to appear on the check or electronic transfer.

5. Enter an optional memo in the Memo field. The memo will appear in your register.

6. In the Category for Interest field, enter the category that you want your interest applied to. This is very important if you plan to deduct your interest payments. You can type in the category or click on the down arrow and select one from the list.

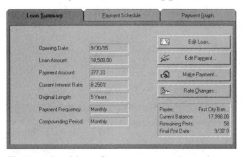

The completed Loan Summary screen shows the details of a loan.

7. Click OK. The Loan Summary screen will appear.

If there are any problems in the loan itself, click Edit Loan. If there are problems in the payment setup, click Edit Payment.

Payment Schedule

The Payment Schedule screen, which you can access by clicking the Payment Schedule tab to the right of the Loan Summary tab, tells you how your payments will be allocated over the life of the loan. At first, you'll see that most of your money goes toward interest. But as you scroll down the list, you'll notice that, as the loan ages, more and more of your payment goes to paying off the principal.

This screen can also be used to edit your loan or payment, make a payment, or change the interest rate (Rate Changes). You will need to change the interest rate every time a variable or adjustable (non-fixed-rate) loan has a rate change.

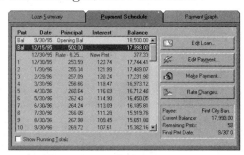

The Payment Schedule screen shows how a loan is allocated over time.

Special Considerations for Mortgages

Mortgage loan accounts have some special considerations. First, a lot of mortgage loans these days have a variable or adjustable interest rate. If you have one of these loans, set up the loan based on the current rate, but remember to change the interest rate setting as the rate changes.

Negative Amortization

Second, some mortgages have negative amortization, which means that the principal actually goes up rather than down. This is to keep the payments from rising as rates rise. I'm not thrilled about these types of loans, but if you have one of them, be sure to follow these steps:

1. When you set up the loan, enter the length of the loan as the original length of loan.

2. After you enter the interest rate in the Set Up Loan Payment window, modify the Principal and Interest amount so that it's the amount you are actually paying. If that amount is lower than the actual interest on the loan, the payment schedule will reflect the increase in principal over time.

Tracking Loan Accounts and Making Payments

When you set up a loan, Quicken will automatically create a loan account that is, essentially, just like any other account. The difference is that the balance decreases as you make payments.

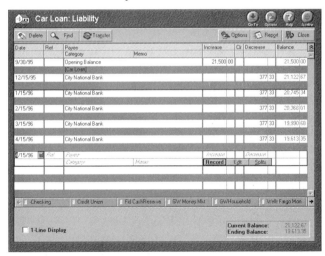

Making Payments

If you have set up automatic online payments, Quicken will pay the loan bill each month, deduct the payment amount from the paying account (probably your checking account), and credit the payment amount to the loan account. If you are pay-

The Loan Account register shows a decrease in the balance as you make payments.

ing manually, you can do so from your check register or by using the Write Checks window. Specify the loan account name as the category, and Quicken will credit the account when the payment is made.

When you use the Write Checks window to make a payment to the lender, Quicken will display a screen informing you of the split between principal and interest. If it looks correct to you, click OK.

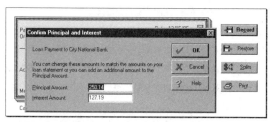

Quicken displays the breakdown between principal and interest when you make payments.

Deleting, Paying Off, or Refinancing a Loan

I know you think the day will never come, but at some point in the future, you might actually pay off some of those loans. When the loan is fully paid, you can delete it from the View Loans window. Quicken will ask if you wish to save the account associated with the loan for your records. Click Yes if you feel you need to keep a record of your loan and payments, or No if you're ready to let it go to data heaven.

If you refinance your loan, you'll need to set up a new loan account with a different name. Enter all the necessary data for the new loan. Then go into the account for the old loan and adjust the balance to zero (choose Update Balances from the Activities menu, select Update Cash Balance, and set the amount to zero).

Summary

While there's nothing pleasant about being in debt, the ability to borrow money, keep track of it, and pay it back in a timely manner can greatly enhance both your buying power and your economic power. Quicken won't make you creditworthy, but it will help you manage your loans and assets and keep track of your payments.

Setting Up Reports

11

Q*uicken's report feature gives you a great deal of control over the ways you can view and print your information. A report, in a sense, is like a filter. It lets you sort information any way you want and select only the information you want to see.*

For example, you can print out a list of all your tax-deductible expenses, or sort transactions by date. You can customize the layouts of reports, and select which account or categories to include. This chapter details how to create and customize reports to meet your needs.

You don't necessarily have to print out a report. Reports can be handy even if you just want to look at the information onscreen. Another important aspect of reports is that they can be "memorized." So, once you've created a report that you like, you can save that format for later use. Any changes in your data will affect the *content* of your report, but not the way it looks or the type of information it includes.

Beware of False Data

Before creating any reports, consider the old computer adage: "Garbage In, Garbage Out." I'm not suggesting that you would deliberately enter any garbage into Quicken, but if any information is inaccurate or incomplete, the report will reflect that. This is especially important to remember if you're creating investment or net worth reports that assume that all of your records are complete and up-to-date. It's not uncommon for Quicken users to be a bit behind or to just decide not to enter certain information. That's fine, but don't expect reports that depend on that information to be accurate.

Creating a Report

To create a report, use the following steps:

1. Click on the Reports button in the icon bar. Quicken will open the Create Report window.

2. Quicken splits its available reports into groups or "families." You can see them in the tabs at the top of the Create Report window: EasyAnswers, Home, Investment, Business, Other and Memorized. The first of these, EasyAnswers, is not actually a report type, but rather a simple, "plain-English" guide (new in Quicken Version 6) that helps you access the most commonly used reports. Before you use EasyAnswers, you need to understand the other report types. Therefore, we'll skip this feature for the moment (see "Using EasyAnswers" later in this chapter).

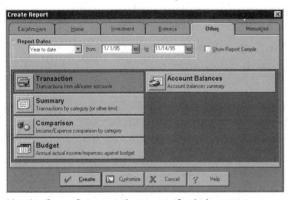

Use the Create Report window to specify which report you want to see.

To choose a report family, just click on one of the tabs. (For more information on the report families, see "Types of Reports in Quicken" later in this chapter.) Then click once on one of the buttons in the middle of the Create Report window.

If you put a check in the Show Report Sample field, the area to the right of each report name displays what the report will look like (the data displayed is not your data). If Show Report Sample is turned on, not all of the report types in the current family will fit in the Create Report window; you will need to use the scroll bar at the right to see them all.

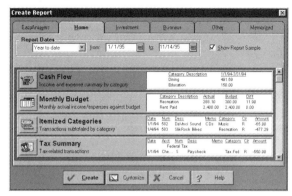

3. Select a date range for the transactions to be included in the report. The details of the date range will vary depending on the type of report. For transaction

When you are displaying sample reports in the Create Report window, use the scroll bar to show all report types in the current family.

reports, you may specify an opening and closing date for the range. For comparison reports, you must specify the two date ranges for which the report will compare the results. For "as of" reports (for example, net worth as of a certain date), you need only specify the "as of" date you want Quicken to use.

To set the date range:

- For reports that require an opening and closing date, type the dates into the from and to fields. You may also click on the field buttons for the date fields and select the date from the pop-up calendar.
- For reports that require two date ranges, type the first period dates into the from and to fields, and then type the second period dates into the same from and to fields. You may also click on the field buttons for the date fields and select the dates from the pop-up calendar.
- For "as of" reports, type the date into the Report Balance as of field.
- For most reports, you can also select a date range from a drop-down list of predefined ranges. If you make a selection from the predefined set of date ranges, the dates that appear in the date fields change to match your selection. For example, if you select "Last Year" from the drop-down list, the date fields will contain January 1 and December 31 of the previous year.

4. If you wish, you may customize the report layout by clicking on the Customize button. You can either customize the report now or

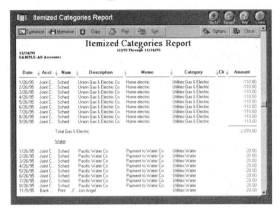

after you create it. For more information on customizing reports, see "Customizing Reports" later in this chapter.

5. Click on OK. Quicken will search the current file for transactions that meet the date range criteria (and any other criteria you may have set using the Customize button) and will display the report on the screen.

A sample report created using Quicken's Create Report window.

Working with the Report Window

Each report window displays a button bar across the window. The buttons on the button bar are:

- Customize: For more information on customizing a report, see "Customizing Reports" later in this chapter.
- Memorize: You can have Quicken remember a particular report, complete with date settings and any other customization. Once you memorize a report, you can choose it by clicking on the Memorized tab at the right of the Create Report window, then selecting it from the Memorized Reports list.

  When you click on the Memorize button, Quicken will open the Memorize Report window. You may enter the name of the report in the Title field. If a memorized report already has the same title, Quicken will ask you to confirm that you want to overwrite the existing memorized report. You can also choose the date range for the memorized report. There are three choices:

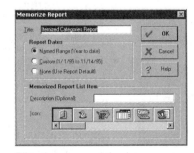

Fill in the name and the date range in the Memorize Report window.

  1) If you select Named Range (for example, Month to Date), the report will always run with a date range that corresponds to the named range at the time you run

Once you memorize a report, you can select it from the Memorized Reports list.

the report. This option is only available if you selected the date range using the drop-down list of named ranges when you created the report.

2) If you select <u>C</u>ustom, the report will run with the same date range as when you first memorized it, regardless of when you run it.

3) If you select <u>N</u>one, the report will run with the default date range for that report.

- Cop<u>y</u>: Copies the entire contents of the report to the clipboard. This is the easiest way to insert Quicken data into other Windows programs. (See also "Sending Data to Other Programs" later in this chapter.)

    Note: If you copy a report and paste it into a Windows word processing program, you may have to adjust the tabs within the word processor. Quicken will automatically insert a tab between each column.

- Pri<u>n</u>t: Prints the report.
- S<u>o</u>rt: (Transaction Reports only). Enables you to sort the transactions in the report. You can sort by the criteria summarized in the sidebar "Sort Criteria for Reports."
- E<u>x</u>port: (Tax Schedule report only). Enables you to export the tax schedule report for use in tax preparation software. See Chapter 18 for more information on using Quicken for preparing your taxes.
- Options: Lets you customize the default settings for any report you generate. For more information on setting the options for a report, see "Changing Report Options" later in this chapter.

Sort Criteria for Reports

Sort by	Means
None	Transactions actually are sorted by account type, then account name, then date.
Date/Acct	Sorts transactions first by date, then by account type, then by account name.
Acct/Chk#	Sorts transactions first by account type, then by account name, and then by check number.
Amount	Sorts transactions from smallest to largest amount.
Payee	Sort transactions alphabetically by payee name.
Category	Sorts transactions alphabetically by category.

Types of Reports in Quicken

As mentioned above, Quicken divides the reports it can generate into four types: Home, Investment, Business, and Other. Summarized below are the reports included in each family.

Home Reports

Home Reports are reports that the average home user of Quicken would be most likely to use. The available Home reports are summarized below.

Quicken's Home Reports

Report Name	Description
Cash Flow	Summarizes income and expenses by category.
Monthly Budget	Compares actual income and expenses against budgeted income and expenses, by month.
Itemized Categories	Lists transactions from all your accounts, grouped and subtotaled by category.
Tax Summary	Lists tax-related transactions from all your accounts except tax-deferred accounts (such as IRAs or 401(k) accounts), grouped and subtotaled by category.
Net Worth	Calculates your net worth on the basis of all accounts in the Quicken file. Net Worth is the difference between your assets and your liabilities. For an accurate picture, you must have created accounts for all assets (for example, your house, car, etc.) and all liabilities (mortgages, etc.).
Tax Schedule	Lists transactions with categories assigned to tax schedule line items, grouped and subtotaled by tax form name and line item. By default, tax-deferred accounts are excluded, although you can add them back into this report. For this report to work, you must click on the Options icon in Quicken's icon bar, select the General button, and then click on the Use Tax Schedules with Categories checkbox.
Missing Checks	Lists payments in the current account by check number. This report highlights any breaks in check number sequence and shows duplicate check numbers.
Comparison	Compares your income and spending for two different periods. You can display the difference between the two time periods in dollars, as a percentage, or both.

Investment Reports

Investment Reports show the performance of securities, stocks, bonds, and other investments. The available Investment reports are summarized below.

Quicken's Investment Reports

Report Name	Description
Portfolio Value	Shows the value of each of your securities on a specified date. It also shows unrealized gain in dollars and has options for subtotaling by account, security type, or investment goal.
Investment Performance	Shows the average annual total return of your securities in a specific period. This return includes account dividends, interest, and other payments you receive, plus increases and decreases in the market value of your securities. The average annual total return is the internal rate of return (IRR).
Capital Gains	Shows long-term and short-term capital gains for securities sold in a specific period. For an accurate report, specify when you bought the shares you sold and the actual cost basis of those shares. If you sold only part of your shares of a security in one account, Quicken assumes that the ones you sold are the shares you held the longest, unless you specify otherwise. *Note: To use this report for Schedule D, subtotal by short-term vs. long-term gain. It excludes nontaxable accounts (for example, IRAs).*
Investment Income	Shows dividend income (taxable and tax-exempt), capital gains distributions, realized gain or loss, unrealized gain or loss (as an option), and margin interest and other investment expenses for a specific period. *Note: To use this report to gather information for Schedule B, be sure you've entered all investment transactions for the year. Select only those accounts for which you must report income (for example, exclude IRAs). Subtotal by security. Create one report for all your reportable income, taxable and tax-exempt. Then create a second report, selecting only securities that generate reportable but tax-exempt income. Again, subtotal by security. Do not include unrealized gains.*
Investment Transactions	Shows how transactions in a specific period have affected the market value or the cost basis of your investments and the cash balance in your investment accounts. If you don't include unrealized gains, the report shows the change in cost basis of your investments between the beginning and the end of the period. If you choose to include unrealized gains, the report shows the change in the market value of your invest-ments between the beginning and end.

Business Reports

Business Reports cover the reports used by people who track their business records using Quicken. The available business reports are summarized below.

Quicken's Business Reports

Report Name	Description
P&L (Profit and Loss) Statement	Summarizes the revenue and expenses of a business by category—first by income, then by expense.
P&L Comparison	Compares profit and loss for the month-to-date to the year-to-date.
Cash Flow	Summarizes income and expenses by category.
A/P (Accounts Payable) by Vendor	Summarizes the dollar amount of all unprinted checks in your bank accounts by payee name. If you don't use Quicken to write checks, this report will still work if you enter all your payables as printable checks. When you pay the bill, go back to the register and record the actual check number in the Num field.
A/R (Accounts Receivable) by Customer	Summarizes uncleared transactions in all your Quicken asset accounts by payee.
Job/Project	Summarizes your income and expenses for each job, property, client, project, or other Quicken class. You must set up each job, project, etc., as a class.
Payroll	Summarizes income and expenses by category. This report has a column for each payee and is restricted to transactions with payroll categories, and transfers to payroll liability accounts. Quicken will only use category or transfer account names that begin with "Payroll."
Balance Sheet	Shows the assets and liabilities, and equity (or capital) of a business as of a specific date.
Missing Checks	Lists payments in the current account by check number. It highlights any breaks in check number sequence and shows duplicate check numbers.
Comparison	Compares your income and spending for two different periods. You can display the difference between the two periods in dollars, as a percentage, or both.

Other Reports

Quicken has five standard reports. All other reports that Quicken provides are based on these reports. These standard reports are summarized below.

Quicken's Other (Standard) Reports

Report Name	Description
Transaction	Lists transactions from one or more registers.
Summary	Summarizes transactions from your accounts by category or any other criteria.
Comparison	Compares your income and spending for two periods, breaks down your finances by category, and lets you define the periods displayed.
Budget	Compares your actual expenses with your budgeted expenses for each category. You must have set up a budget before running this report.
Account Balances	Lists and totals the balances for all accounts in the current file. For investment accounts, the balances include unrealized gains.

QuickReports

You can display a QuickReport from within various registers and lists by clicking on the Report icon for that register or list. The Report icon does not appear on the general button bar but rather within the special button bar associated with the specific window you're in. If you don't see a button bar within a register window click on the chevron in the upper right corner of the window.

The upper right hand corner of a register window, showing the Report button and the chevron that activated the button bar.

QuickReports are actually standard reports that are filtered to provide the appropriate information. Once you display a QuickReport, it can be customized, as described in "Customizing Reports," below.

You can display QuickReports for the following windows:
- Category and Transfer List
- Class List
- Register (lists all transactions for a certain payee)
- Memorized Transactions List (payee report)
- Portfolio View (lists all transactions for a certain security)

Customizing Reports

You can customize any report by changing its layout, the accounts covered, and the transactions included by categories, classes, and supercategories. Exactly which options are available depends on the type of report. For example, transaction reports (reports that include transactions) have different options from account balance or summary reports.

To customize a report:

1. Create a report as described on page 166 of this chapter.

2. Either click Customize in the Create Report window, or click OK to create the report, then click the Customize button on the Report button bar.

3. Quicken will open the Customize Report window. Although the Customize Report window is similar for most reports, there are some small differences for certain reports. Since all Quicken reports are variations of the "Other" category reports (Transaction, Summary, Budget, Account Balances, and Comparison), the differences in the Customize Report windows are generally discussed in terms of the "Other" category reports that they pertain to.

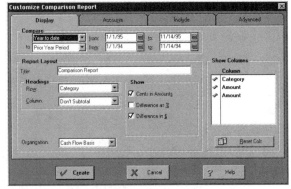

4. By clicking on one of the tabs—Display, Accounts, Include, or Advanced—at the top of the Customize Report window, choose the aspect of

You can modify how a report looks and works using the Customize Report window.

the report that you want to change. (The Report Dates fields appear on each one of the tabbed dialog boxes.) See the sections later in this chapter for complete details on the various settings.

5. Click Create. Quicken will apply your changes to the report.

When a report is displayed on the screen, you can change the title, date range, or included accounts. To change the report, move the mouse pointer over the report. When it turns into a magnifying glass with a "C" (for "customize") in it, double-click on the title, date range, or accounts label. Quicken will open the Customize Report window so that you can make modifications to these fields—and anything else that appears in the Customize Report window.

Changing the Report Dates

For all reports except Comparison reports, the Report Dates area appears at the top of the tabbed dialog box. To modify the date range, type dates into the from and to fields. You may also click on the field buttons for the date fields and select the date from the pop-up calendar.

In Comparison reports, this area of the screen is labeled Compare, and has two rows for entering date ranges instead of one. To modify the report dates for a Comparison report, type the first period's dates into the first from and to fields, and type the second period's dates into the second from and to fields. You may also click on the field buttons for the date fields and select the date from the pop-up calendar.

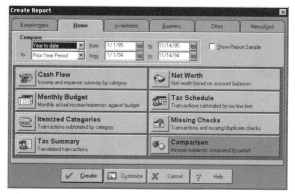

The screen for customizing a Comparison report has two date ranges instead of one.

You may also select a date range from the drop-down lists of predefined ranges. These values include current month, quarter, and year; to-date for month, quarter, and year; earliest-to-date; and all dates. If you make a selection from the predefined set of date ranges, the dates that appear in the date fields change to match your selection. For example, if you select "Last Year" from the drop-down list, the date fields will contain January 1 and December 31 of the previous year.

Changing the Report Layout

To change the report layout, click on Report Layout in the Display section of the Customize Report window. What you see on the right side of the window depends on the type of report you are modifying.

The options for the Report Layout section of the Customize Report window are summarized in the "Report Layout Options" table on the next page.

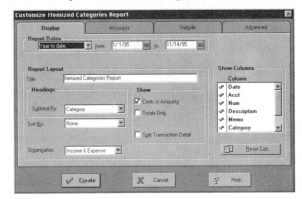

The Report Layout for an Itemized Categories report.

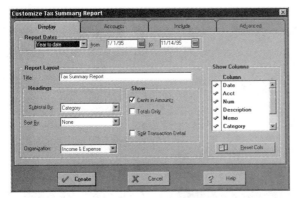

The Report Layout for a Summary report.

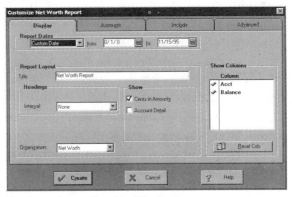

The Report Layout for a Net Worth report.

Report Layout Options

Option	Appears in Report	Description
Title	All	Displays and prints as the title on the report.
Row Headings	Summary	Creates a row for each category, class, payee, or account.
Column Headings	Summary, Budget, Account Balance	Creates a column for each week, two weeks, half month, month, quarter, half year, category, class, payee, account, or tax schedule. Can also suppress subtotaling.
Subtotal By	Transaction	Groups and totals transactions by week, two weeks, half month, month, quarter, half year, year, category, class, payee, account, or tax schedule. Can also suppress subtotaling.
Interval	Account Balance	Can create one total for account balances based on the ending date (by choosing None); or creates a column and totals account balances for each week, two weeks, half month, month, quarter, half year, or year.
Sort By	Transaction	Sorts the results by None (account type, account name, and date); Date/Acct (date, account type, account name); Acct/Chk# (account type, account name, check number); Amount (smallest to largest); Payee (alphabetically by name); Category (alphabetically by category).
Max Short-Term Gain Holding Period	Investment Capital Gains	Defines how many days you must have held a security before selling it for the resulting capital gain to qualify as a long-term gain.
Organization	See Description	*Income and Expense* (all reports except Account Balance): Totals income, expense, and transfer transactions in separate sections of your report.

Cash Flow Basis (all reports except Account Balance): Groups and totals inflows and outflows (including expenses and transfers out of an account).

Net Worth Format (Account Balance reports): Prints the net worth as the last item.

Balance Sheet Format (Account Balance reports): Prints net worth as a liability ("equity") with total liabilities and equity last.

Supercategory (Budget reports): Groups and totals budget amounts by supercategory instead of inflows and outflows. |
Show Cents in Amounts	All	Determines whether cents are shown in amounts. If not shown, Quicken rounds to the nearest dollar.
Amount as %	Summary	Shows amounts as a percentage of total.
Difference as %	Comparison	Shows the difference between the two column amounts as a percentage of the first column amount.
Difference in $	Comparison	Shows the dollar difference between the two column amounts.
Show Totals Only	Transaction	Displays only the total dollar amount of transactions that meet the criteria you set.
Show Split Transaction Detail	Transaction	Displays the details from the Splits window.
Account Detail	Balance Sheet, Net Worth, Account Balance	Displays subtotals by class (or security) for all selected accounts.
Show Cash Flow Detail	Investment Performance	Shows all transactions that contribute to the Average Annual Total Return.

Selecting Accounts to Include

To set the accounts for which transactions will be included in the report, click the Accounts tab to bring this section of the Customize Report window to the foreground. Quicken will display a Selected

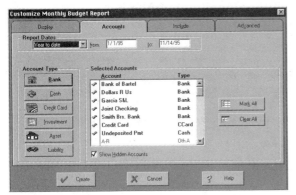

Accounts section in the right side of the window. Depending on the type of report, certain accounts may be preselected in the Selected Accounts section. For example, a cash flow report automatically pre-selects all your Bank, Cash, and Credit Card accounts.

Pick the accounts to include in the report from the Selected Accounts section of the Accounts window.

You may mark or unmark an account by clicking on it with the mouse, or selecting it with the arrow keys and pressing the spacebar. A marked account is displayed in bold type, with a yellow check mark to the left of the account name. You may also click on the Mark All button. To unmark all accounts click on the Clear All button. Finally, you can mark all accounts of a certain type by clicking on the Account Type button for each account type: Bank, Cash, Credit Card, Investment, Asset, and Liability.

Selecting Transactions to Include

To filter the transactions that Quicken will include in the report, click on the Advanced tab to bring this section of the Customize Report win-

dow to the foreground. Quicken will display a Transactions section in the left side of the Customize Report window. The choices available in the Transactions section are summarized in the "Options for Selecting Transactions" table on the next page.

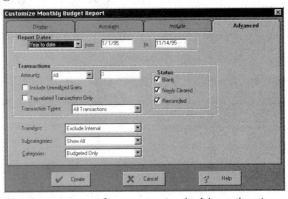

Filter the transactions for a report using the Advanced section.

Options for Selecting Transactions

Option	Description
Amounts	Includes all transaction amounts less than, equal to, or greater than an amount you enter.
Include Unrealized Gains	Includes unrealized gains. This determines whether Quicken will generate additional transactions (in transaction reports) or income/inflow lines (in summary reports) to represent the impact of price increases and decreases for securities. This item only appears if you have set up investment accounts.
Tax-related Transactions Only	Includes only transactions that have been categorized with tax-related categories.
Transaction Types	Allows inclusions of payments only, deposits only, unprinted checks only, or all transactions. For nonbank accounts, payments are decreases to cash and other asset accounts, and increases to credit card and other liability accounts.
Status	Refers to a transaction's entry in the Clr (cleared) field. By inserting or deleting check marks, you can include blank (unreconciled), newly cleared, or reconciled items.

Three lines at the bottom of the Advanced window provide further control over which transactions will be shown. The Transfers line allows you to include All transfers, Exclude All transfers, or Exclude Internal transfers (a transfer between accounts included in the report). The Subcategories line allows you to Show All subcategories and subclasses grouped under their main categories, Hide All subcategory and subclass information, or Show Reversed subcategory. This last option displays subcategories with the main categories grouped under them. Finally, the Categories line, available on Budget reports only, allows you to include All categories from the list (whether or not you've used them in a transaction); Non-Zero Actual/Budgeted (categories already used in transactions, and all categories with budgeted amounts assigned); or Budgeted Only (only categories that have budgeted amounts assigned).

Selecting Column Information

To change the number of columns that appear in a report, click on the Display tab of the Customize Report window. A list of the column headings in your report will appear in a white box at the right side of the screen. The number of headings depends on the type of report you are modifying.

To remove a heading, click on it to remove the yellow check mark from beside it, scrolling down the list with the scroll bar if necessary. If you ever need to return to the default of "all headings selected," click on the Reset Cols button.

Another way to remove a column—obviously, removing a column heading also removes the values that would have appeared in that column—is to create a report. Then click the marker to the right of any column's heading and drag the marker to the left past the leftmost column marker to delete it.

Note: *To widen any column, click the column marker to the right of the*

Click on the markers at the top to resize or remove a column in a report.

column heading and drag the marker to the right. To make the column narrower, drag the marker to the left. (The widths of all other columns in the report will remain unmodified.)

Selecting Categories, Classes, and Supercategories to Include

To set the categories, classes, and supercategories for which transactions will be included in your report, click on the Include tab in the

Pick the categories and classes to include from the Select to Include section of the Include window.

Customize Report window to bring this section to the foreground. Quicken will display the Select to Include section in the left side of the window.

To choose which list you want to work from, click on one of the radio buttons to the right of the list. You can select to view the list for Categories, Classes, or Supercategories. (Supercategories are only available for Budget reports.)

Quicken will display the appropriate list of items.

You may mark or unmark an item by clicking on it with the mouse, or selecting it with the arrow keys and pressing the spacebar. A marked item is displayed in bold type, with a yellow check mark to the left of the account name. You may also click on the Mark All button. Unmark all items by clicking on the Clear All button.

Using Matches to Filter Transactions

You can select transactions for inclusion in a report that match specified criteria in certain fields, such as Payee, Category, and Memo. To filter transactions for inclusion in a report based on the contents of these fields, enter criteria in the Matching section on the right side of the Customize Report window .

Note: For Investment reports, you can filter the report based on the Security Contains or Memo Contains fields. For the Security Contains field, you can type in the criteria or select from a drop-down list.

To make a selection in the Payee Contains, Category Contains, or Class Contains fields, you can type in your criteria and let QuickFill complete your entries if desired. The Payee list is programmed with payees from all memorized transactions. The Category and Class lists are programmed with all the categories and classes you have set up using either the Category and Transfer List or the Class List. For the Memo Contains field, you must type in the complete search criteria—QuickFill does not operate on this field.

In addition to typing a specific payee, category, class, memo, or security name, you can type in a partial string and use special characters called "wildcards." (While the Quicken manual calls them "match characters," they are called "wildcards" in virtually all other computer books and manuals).

A wildcard matches any one or more unspecified characters. For

Wildcards for a Quicken Match in a Report

Symbol	Matches
=	An exact match (includes only transactions that match exactly what you type).
.. (two periods)	A match that contains unspecified characters wherever you type two periods.
?	A match with one unspecified character (for example, C?T could match Cat, Cut, Cot, etc.).
~ (tilde)	Excludes all transactions that match the text you typed.

Note: *Wildcards can be combined. For example, the combination of ~.. would search for fields that are blank, while ..tax.. would search for any fields that contain the word "tax" anywhere in the text.*

example, "T..X" would match Tax, Trix, and any other words beginning with "T" and ending with "X." Quicken's wildcards are summarized on the previous page.

Changing Report Options

You can change certain portions of a report after you have created it by clicking on the Options button.

Quicken's preset reports display only the names of accounts or categories. By clicking on the buttons at the top of the Report Options window, you can have Quicken display the descriptions instead, or both names and descriptions.

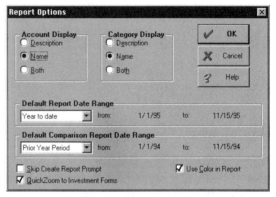

After you have created a report, you can invoke this Report Options button for further changes.

Setting Your Own Default Date Range

In the Default Report Date Range section of the Report Options window, you can select the date range each time you create a report. You can also create your own default date range, which Quicken will then display each time you create a report. To set up your own default report date range:

1. Click on the drop-down button in the Default Report Date Range field.

2. Select Custom Date (at the bottom of the scrolling list).

3. Select the starting date in the range by clicking on the from drop-down list. There are more options in this list than in Quicken's preset date ranges. Extra options include beginning of the month, quarter, or year; beginning of last month, quarter, or year; the first of every month; and a month or year ago.

4. Select the ending date in the range by clicking on the to drop-down list. Again, there are more options than in Quicken's preset date range. Extra options include End of month, quarter, or year; end of last month, quarter, or year; and the end of every month.

5. Select the custom start and end date from the Default Comparison Report Date Range field in exactly the same manner as illustrated in Steps 2–4.

6. Click OK to record your changes.

Note: If you memorize a report after using your own default date range to create the report, Quicken doesn't memorize the named range. Instead, it memorizes the actual dates that correspond to the named range at the time you memorized the report. For example, if you memorize a default date range of Beginning of the Year to End of the Year, the report will be memorized with the From date of January 1 and the End date of December 31 of the year in which the report was memorized.

Changing Other Report Options

Three other options appear at the bottom of the Report Options window. You can modify any of these simply by clicking on the box to create or remove a check mark. The options are:

- Skip Create Report Prompt: This option enables you to create reports from the Reports menu without first displaying the Create Report window. The default date range will be used. If necessary, you can change any setting by clicking on the Customize button on the Report button bar after the report is created.
- QuickZoom to Investment Forms: From an Investment Income or Investment Transactions report, QuickZoom to the entry forms instead of to the Investment register.
- Use Color in Report: With this selected, Quicken displays positive numbers in blue, and negative amounts in red.

Using EasyAnswers

Quicken's new EasyAnswers feature provides you with quick access to the above report types. It has been programmed to give you answers to "the most commonly asked questions" so that you don't have to configure reports manually.

To create an EasyAnswers report, use the following steps:

1. Click on the Reports button in the icon bar, click on the word "Reports" on the Home-Base screen, or select EasyAnswers from Quicken's main Reports menu. Quicken will open the Create Report window with the EasyAnswers tab at the top.

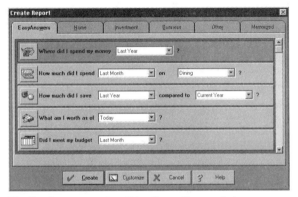

The EasyAnswers section of the Create Report window.

2. Quicken offers eight possible EasyAnswers (you need to use the scroll bar at right to view the three that do not appear onscreen), each with blanks you can fill in with a variety of values:

- **Where did I spend my money?**
  This EasyAnswer report tells you what you spent your money on during the period of time you specify. It is similar to a Cash Flow Home report.
- **How much did I spend on ... ?**
  This EasyAnswer report tells you how much you spent on a category of expenses that you specify. It is similar to an Itemized Categories report.
- **How much did I save compared to ... ?**
  This EasyAnswer report compares how you spent your money during two periods of time you specify. It is similar to a Comparison Home report.

- **What am I worth as of ... ?**
  This EasyAnswer report tells you how much money is in all your accounts as of a date you specify. It is similar to a Net Worth Home report.
- **Did I meet my budget?**
  This EasyAnswer report compares your spending with your budget. It is similar to a Budget Home report. (You must have created and saved a budget for this EasyAnswer report to work.)
- **What taxable events occurred?**
  This EasyAnswer report tells you what transactions were tax-related during the period of time you specify. It is similar to a Tax Summary Home report.
- **How did my investment do**?
  This EasyAnswer report shows you the average annual total return of an investment during the period of time you specify. It is similar to a Performance Investment report. (This EasyAnswer question appears only if you have already created and saved an Investment account.)
- **What are my investments worth**?
  This EasyAnswer report tells you the value of all your investment accounts as of a date you specify. It is similar to a Portfolio Value Investment report, and appears only if you have already created an Investment account.

3. Pick the EasyAnswer you desire and use the down arrow to fill in the blank field or fields until your question is complete. Then click on Create.

4. Quicken will show you the resulting report. Since it is a standard Quicken report, you can use all the tools—accessible via the Customize and Options buttons at the top—for customizing it that we covered in previous sections of this chapter.

    Note: *If the criteria you selected in the EasyAnswer window resulted in a report with no entries, Quicken will ask if you would like to change report settings. If you answer "No," you will exit EasyAnswers. If you answer "Yes," you will be taken to Quicken's Customize Report dialog box to make changes.*

Sending Data to Other Programs

Once you have created a report, you have the option not only to send it to your printer, but also to send it to another software application. At

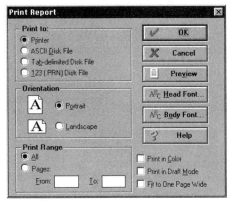

The Print Report dialog box lets you send output to a printer or to a disk file.

tax time, the most important of these will be your tax preparation software. Tax preparation is covered in Chapter 18. At other times of the year, however, you might wish to export information to your word processor (for informal reports or perhaps to enforce your manifestos to other family members) or to your spreadsheet for some "what-if" operations.

As I have mentioned above, you can export report data to the clipboard simply by creating a report, then clicking on the Copy button. The clipboard data is simple ASCII text, with tabs used to separate columns: It can be readily accepted by any word processor or spreadsheet.

For more control over the data you export, click on the Print button. The Print Report dialog box will appear. In the Print to area of this dialog box, change the default from Printer to either ASCII Disk File, Tab-delimited Disk File, or 123 (.PRN) Disk File.

The ASCII Disk file option creates a file that simulates the appearance of your report by using spaces to position the columns. For sending data to most other software programs, this option is best avoided. If you're sending data to a word processor, use the Tab-delim-

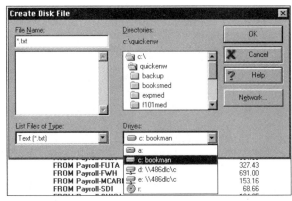

The Create Disk File window lets you specify where to send output from Quicken.

ited Disk File option instead. When using tab-delimited output, you may need to reset the tabs in your word processor to have the report look the way you expected, but you'll have much greater flexibility in formatting and choice of fonts, and you won't have to delete any stray characters. The 123 (.PRN) Disk File option produces comma-delimited output (each line uses commas within it to delineate where columns fall), which is compatible with most spreadsheets and database programs.

Click OK, and the Create Disk File window will appear. Enter a name and location for the disk file you are creating, then click OK again to complete the process.

Using Graphs

Giant corporations and governments have long known that there's no better way to make financial trends clear than to use a graph. Thanks to Quicken, you can now easily produce professional-quality graphs to celebrate (or mourn) what's happening in your own financial life.

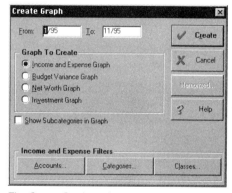

The Create Graph window.

By using the procedures in the previous section, you can send data from Quicken to a program such as Excel or PowerPoint for graphing. This is not really necessary, however, since Quicken's own graphing capabilities are so versatile. To create a graph, click on the Reports and Graphs icon in HomeBase, click on the Graphs icon in the button bar, or select Graphs from Quicken's main Reports menu. The Create Graph window will appear.

The Graph to Create section of the Create Graph window offers you four different graph types: Income and Expense Graph, Budget Variance Graph, Net Worth Graph, and Investment Graph.

Income and Expense Graphs

An Income and Expense graph helps you answer questions such as:

- Is my income changing over time?
- Is my income covering my expenses?
- Where does my money come from?
- Where does my money go?

The upper part of an Income and Expense graph compares your total monthly income against your total monthly expenses over time. Each bar represents either a month's income or a month's expenses. The bottom part (Expense Comparison) shows your total income, broken down by what you spent and what you didn't spend.

To create an Income and Expense graph, do the following:

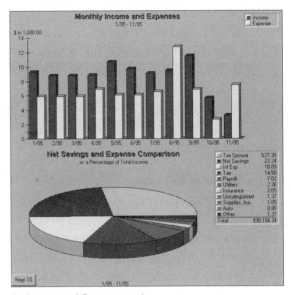

An Income and Expense graph.

1. From the Create Graph window, choose Income and Expense.

2. Enter the beginning and ending dates for the period of time you want the graph to cover.

3. To include subcategories in this graph, select Show Subcategories in Graph.

4. To limit your graph to certain accounts, click Accounts. Then choose which accounts to include. Similarly, to limit it to certain categories, click Categories, or to choose only certain classes, click Classes.

5. Click Create.

For more detail on any of the graphs, move the mouse pointer—which will display a magnifying glass icon—onto any of the bars or pie chart segments. Then double-click to view another graph devoted to that particular item. To return to the original overall graph, click the Close button.

Budget Variance Graphs

Budget variance graphs compare actual spending and income with budgeted spending and income. Quicken will calculate the difference in dollars between the two so you can see how you are actually doing compared to the budget.

Before you create this graph you must first set up a budget. If you haven't done this yet, see Chapter 17. If you already have a budget, do the following:

1. From the Create Graphs window, choose Budget Variance graph.

2. Enter the beginning and ending dates for the period of time you want the graph to cover.

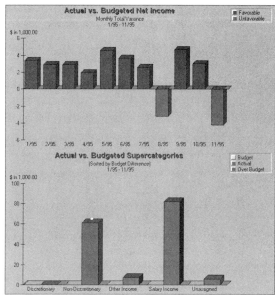

3. To include subcategories in this graph, select Show Subcategories in Graph. Or, to include supercategories, select Graph Supercategory Budgets.

4. To limit your graph to certain accounts, click Accounts. Then choose which accounts to include.

A Budget Variance graph.

Similarly, to limit it to certain categories, click Categories, or to choose only certain classes, click Classes.

5. Click Create.

For more detail on any of the graphs, move the mouse pointer—which will display a magnifying glass icon—onto any of the bars or pie chart segments. Then double-click to view another graph devoted to that particular item. To return to the original overall graph, click the Close button.

Net Worth Graphs

Net Worth graphs help you answer these questions:
- Do I own more than I owe?
- What are my largest debts?
- How is my net worth changing over time?

They show you your assets, liabilities, and net worth during the period of time you specify. Each month has two bars in the graph.

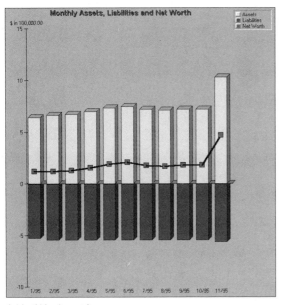

A Net Worth graph.

Each bar that extends above the horizontal axis represents the value of your assets on the last day of the month. Each bar that extends below the axis represents the value of your liabilities on the last day of the month. The line that connects the square points on the graph represents your net worth as it changes from month to month. Each point on the line is your net worth on the last day of a particular month.

To create a Net Worth graph, do the following:

I. From the Reports menu, choose Graphs, and then choose Net Worth.

2. Enter the beginning and ending dates for the period of time you want the graph to cover.

3. To limit your graph to certain accounts, click Accounts. Then choose which accounts to include. Similarly, to limit it to certain categories, click Categories, or to choose only certain classes, click Classes.

4. Click Create.

For more detail on any of the graphs, move the mouse pointer—which will display a magnifying glass icon—onto any of the bars or pie chart segments. Then double-click to view another graph devoted to that particular item. To return to the original overall graph, click the Close button.

Investment Graphs

Investment graphs help you answer these questions:

- Is my portfolio value increasing?
- How are my stocks and bonds doing?

The upper graph (monthly portfolio value) shows how the value of your investment portfolio has changed over time. The lower graph (average annual total return) shows how well each part of your portfolio has performed compared to the average return of your portfolio as a whole.

To create an Investment graph:

1. From the Create Graphs window, choose Investment Graph.

2. Enter the beginning and ending dates for the period of time you want the graph to cover.

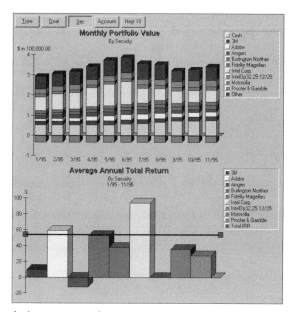

An Investment graph.

3. To limit your graph to certain accounts, click Accounts. Then choose which accounts to include. Similarly, to limit it to certain securities, click Securities.

4. Click Create.

When the graph appears, you can change how it breaks down the value of your investment portfolio by clicking one of the buttons explained in the table on the next page.

Investment Graph Button Bar Options

Type	Clicking this button changes the graph so that it shows the types of investments you have made, such as stocks, bonds, or CDs.
Goal	Clicking this button changes the graph so that it shows the investment goals you have established.
Sec (this is the default)	When you click this button, the graph shows individual securities.
A**c**count	Clicking this button changes the graph so that it shows individual Investment accounts.
Ne**x**t 10	If there are more than ten investments, goals, securities, or accounts to be shown, click on this button to see the next group of ten values.

Summary

Quicken has many different types of reports, split into "families." These families include Home, Business, Investment, and Other. You can run a report from the Reports menu or from the Report button on the icon bar. It is possible to customize the reports in many ways, such as specifying the date range, specifying columns, filtering which transactions to include, and sorting the transactions. The customizing options vary, depending on type of report.

Tracking Credit Cards

12

"**Congratulations! Your superlative record** of: a) having a pulse, and b) staying out of prison, means **you've earned** a First Bank of Candor **Gold Card**. Now you can **enjoy** even **more great stuff you want** but don't need, at usurious rates much higher than what **we pay** to borrow it from the **U.S.** Government..."

In Chapter 8, which covers setting up Quicken accounts, I mentioned that you can create a credit card account. Now, it's time to talk more about why you would want to do this.

Most people enjoy the freedom, convenience, and ability to handle emergencies (such as an auto repair or urgent travel) that a credit card gives them. However, many also allow that credit card to become a Grim Reaper within their wallet, decimating their savings.

You might or might not need to cut that card in half. However, there's no better way to find out than by using Quicken to get it under control.

To Track or Not to Track

The first question you have to ask yourself is whether you want to bother tracking your credit card purchases. If you only use your credit card for real emergencies or major purchases such as a new refrigerator, you may not need a record of each transaction. You might just want to keep track of the payment of the credit card bill itself and not bother with anything else.

If you use your credit card for a variety of smaller purchases, however, you may want to keep closer tabs on it. This is especially true if you use the credit card for many tax-deductible expenses, or business expenses that should be reimbursed by your employer. Just keep your credit card receipts and, when you're at the computer, enter them in the credit card register (I'll tell you how later in this chapter). That way, you'll always know how much you've spent.

You'll want to keep the closest tabs of all if you already know you have a problem with credit card overuse. By entering each purchase carefully, you'll not only know the raw amount of credit card debt you have, but you'll also know where the credit card purchases fit into your budget. Are you charging things on the credit card that are frivolous expenses, or are you trying to make ends meet by charging things you really needed anyway? Tracking your expenses will tell you the answer.

Are you charging things on the credit card that are frivolous expenses, or are you trying to make ends meet by charging things you really needed anyway? Tracking your expenses will tell you the answer.

If you use the Quicken credit card, American Express, or another credit card that is set up for online banking, then tracking becomes a moot issue. Quicken will do it for you. All transactions on these credit cards can automatically be entered into your Quicken register and even categorized. You can elect to receive your statements via modem or by floppy disk. Either way, it's easy and painless to keep track of all your expenses and payments.

For years my strategy has been to use my Quicken credit card for all tax-deductible expenses so I never have to worry about losing track of a business expense. I charge my personal expenses to different credit cards and don't bother to keep a record of each item.

Choosing and Setting Up a New Credit Card

I have already covered the basic process of setting up a credit card account in Quicken in Chapter 8, "Creating a Credit Card Account." The procedure detailed in that section applies to both:

- setting up an account for a credit card you've had for a long time
- setting up an account for a credit card you just received in the mail

Now I'd like to review the same ground, but with an emphasis on the second activity—setting up an account for a new credit card. I'd also like to suggest very strongly that you consider getting a credit card with an online link that will automatically download transactions into your Quicken register. The advantages of this are covered more fully in Chapter 15, "Online Banking." For now, let's just say that since all your credit card transactions are automatically entered into the bank's computer when you make purchases, there's really no point in your having to type them into a computer all over again when you don't have to.

Choosing a Card

The Quicken credit card, which used to be called IntelliCharge, is now part of online banking and works like any other online banking account. If you had IntelliCharge before, Quicken 5 took account of this when you installed the program and has automatically updated your account to online banking.

As you probably know, credit cards can vary greatly in interest rates, annual charges, and perks such as automatic insurance on your purchases, frequent flier miles, and much more. An entire book could be written on the subject of picking a credit card—except that it would be out of date the minute it was printed. While the Quicken card used to be your only choice if you wanted online statements, a number of card issuers now offer them.

Note: *One way to get the latest information on the credit card companies that offer online statements is via the Quicken Financial Network at http://www.intuit.com. For more information, see "The Quicken Financial Network" in Chapter 15.*

Setting Up a New Account

If you've taken my advice and now have a spanking-new credit card with an online link, the first thing you need to do is create a Quicken credit card account for it:

The first Credit Card Account Setup window walks you through the process.

1. Click on the Credit Card button in the Create New Account window. Quicken will open the first Credit Card Account Setup window. Click on the Next button to continue.

2. Enter a name for the account. Usually this is the name of the bank or credit card company. Then enter an optional Description if you wish. Click on Next to proceed to the next screen.

3. Quicken will now ask for a "starting point" for this account. Since this is a new account, select No. Click on Next to continue.

4. Quicken will now ask if the credit card is one whose transaction information you can download electronically. The answer is Yes if you have a Quicken credit card or another card that's been set to use electronic banking. Click on Next to continue.

5. Enter the financial institution you have signed up with using the drop-down menu. Click on Next to continue.

6. Enter your new credit card number. Depending on the institution you have chosen, a drop-down menu may also appear, asking you whether your Account Type is a Credit Card or a Line of Credit. Click on Next to continue.

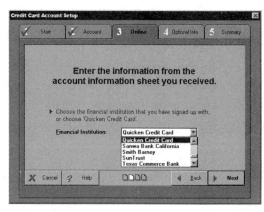

Enter your financial institution here.

Note: A revolving line of credit is based on your average daily balance with a financial institution. The bank calculates your credit limit each day. Because there is always a time lag, you can't track your credit limit at home. In other respects, the line of credit account is basically the same as a credit card statement, and you can reconcile it the same way.

7. If you have a Quicken credit card, the next screen will ask you if your statements are being sent to you via modem or diskette. The choice you make must match what you presently have on file at Travelers Bank (issuer of the Quicken card). To change from diskette-based statement delivery to modem delivery, see below under "Getting Quicken Credit Card Data." If you have another type of credit card, you can receive statements *only* via modem. Click on Next to continue.

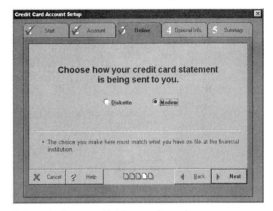

Select whether your Quicken credit card statements come via modem or diskette.

8. Quicken will now request your Social Security number, plus a routing number. The routing number should have been supplied by the bank issuing your credit card; if you can't find it, call them directly. If you have a Quicken credit card, enter your Social Security number plus a personal identification number (PIN).

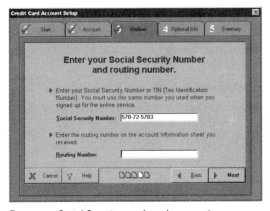

Enter your Social Security number plus a routing number or ...

... a personal identification number (PIN).

9. The next screen will offer you the (optional) chance to enter your credit limit. If you do so, Quicken will then automatically display your remaining credit. Click on the Next button to continue.

10. You will now get the chance to enter additional information about the account. This lets you record a card's expiration date, interest rate, and the all-important number to call in case the card gets stolen.

11. Three different summary screens will now let you review the information you've entered. After you step through them all by clicking on Next and then Done, you will be returned to the Account List window.

You have the option of entering additional information about an account.

Entering Transactions in the Credit Card Register

To enter transactions in the credit card register, save your transaction slips when you charge items and enter transactions as they occur through the month. This method gives you your current credit card balance at all times, and also lets you double-check your charges against those listed on your credit card statement.

Frankly, though, most of us are not going to be that meticulous, and will pick the other way of operating: waiting until we get our monthly statement and then entering in the transactions. This method is OK if you don't need to know your balance throughout the month. You can also enter only major transactions that you know will have a big impact on your available credit.

Once you've set up a credit card account, you have to select it in order to use it. That's because Quicken makes it possible to have several different credit card accounts and it needs to know which one you want to use.

1. Select the account by pressing the Accounts icon to bring up a list of all your accounts and double-clicking on the credit card account to bring up its register.

2. The rest is pretty straightforward. Enter the date of the transaction, the name of the business, and the amount of the charge.

3. (Optional) Select a category from the Category field and write a brief description of the charge in the Memo field. Even though this is optional, I suggest you enter this information if it's a tax-deductible expense.

4. Click the Record button or press Enter. You will hear a "beep" and Quicken will record the transaction.

Of course, if you have selected a credit card with an online link, you don't need to enter transactions at all. You can do so, of course, but most people will prefer to go online every few days and let Quicken update the credit card register automatically. As well as entering each purchase, Quicken will now categorize each for you, as explained below.

Automatic Categorization

If you use your credit card extensively, you'll appreciate the new automatic categorization feature available with online banking. When Intuit's online banking center gets credit card data from your financial institution, that data includes a merchant code for each transaction. The online banking center reads the merchant code and converts it to a Quicken category.

Quicken may or may not use that category, depending on the payee. Before adding the transactions to your register, it checks to see which merchants you have already created categories for. If you've already assigned a category to a merchant, Quicken sticks with your category. However, if you have not assigned a category to a merchant, Quicken supplies the category based on the merchant code.

Reconciling Your Account

The process of reconciling a credit card account is pretty much the same as with a checking account, only you're working with your credit card bill instead of a bank statement.

1. Be sure you've selected the credit card account.

2. Click on the Recon icon or select Reconcile from the Activities menu. If this is an
online account, the Reconcile Online
Account window will appear. If it is not, the
Credit Card Statement Information window
will appear instead.

The Credit Card Statement Information window.

You now must decide whether to reconcile to your Paper State-
ment or to your Online
Balance. You can't do
both because Quicken presents your statement's
opening balance based on the balance to which you
last reconciled. If you reconcile to your *online* balance during the month, then the Quicken opening
balance will always disagree with the opening balance on the *paper* statement. In addition, if you reconciled during the month, Quicken will have
removed all the reconciled transactions from the Reconcile window.
Therefore all these transactions will appear to be totally missing when
you try to reconcile to your paper statement.

The Reconcile Online Account window.

3. Choose a balance to reconcile to, either Paper Statement or Online
Balance. If you choose Paper Statement, you need to enter the ending
statement's date, plus the charges or cash advances, the payment, and
the statement's ending balance. If you choose Online Banking, simply
click OK to begin reconciling.

If you use online banking and have been reconciling throughout the
month, there may be little to do at this point. If you are reconciling to
your paper statement, however, Quicken will now display the Pay
Credit Card Bill window. Your job is to click on charges that are listed
in the credit card bill (just as you clicked on checks that cleared the
bank when reconciling your bank statement). You can place a check on
an item by clicking on it once. If you want to see the item in the register, just click twice.

Note: *To mark a range of transactions instead of just one, click on the
first transaction you'd like to mark. Move the mouse pointer down to the*

last transaction in the range and hold down the Shift key while you click on the transaction. Quicken will mark all the transactions between these two points.

If you find any transactions on the credit card bill that are missing from your statement, you can enter them at this time by clicking on the New button and entering the information. Miraculously, any transactions you

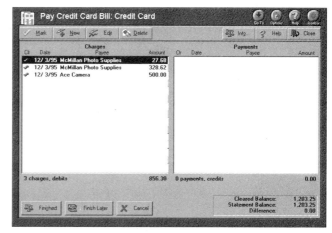

The Pay Credit Card Bill window.

enter at this point will automatically appear as uncleared transactions when you return to the Pay Credit Card Bill window. When you return to the Credit Card register at the end of the process, an "R" will appear in the CLR field for each entry you have reconciled.

At the end of the process, the Difference shown in the lower right corner of the window should be zero. You also have the option of ignoring any charges that you don't want to record. I don't particularly recommend this when it comes to balancing your checkbook, but it's not always necessary to have everything balance when it comes to credit card bills—just so long as you're sure that you're not being charged for anything that you didn't authorize.

If you do wish to ignore any charges or discrepancies, Quicken will automatically enter an adjustment that makes your balance equal that of the credit card company. Remember, this is your choice. The more "prudent" recommendation is that you stare at your bill and register until you can figure out the discrepancy, and, once you've found it, either make the correction in your register or convince the credit card company to fix the mistake on their end (good luck). But, life doesn't always have to be prudent. As long as you're convinced that there are no fraudulent charges on your account, you may be better off living with the differences between your records and those of the credit card companies.

Paying Your Bill

The folks who wrote Quicken must agree with the financial advice in Chapters 20 through 25 of this book, because they prompt you to pay your credit card bills in full each month. But, don't worry, you still have

The Make Credit Card Payment window.

the choice of supporting that plastic by not paying the bill in full. Your credit card company will be happy because it will love collecting the finance charges.

The Make Credit Card Payment window will appear as soon as you have finished reconciling your account. Select the bank account to pay from by using the drop-down menu. The payment will be recorded as a transfer to the credit card account from whichever bank account you select. Then choose a payment method: Printed Check, Handwritten Check, or Online (if available).

If you choose Handwritten, the appropriate account register will open so you can verify payment entry. If you choose Printed Check or Online, the Write Checks window (see Chapter 6) will open instead.

Getting Quicken Credit Card Data

For more information on how to transmit payments online or receive credit card statements, see Chapter 15. The online banking process—which requires registering for an Intuit membership and setting up a modem—is identical, whether or not you have a credit card account.

There are, however, special considerations for people who already have Quicken credit cards. If you had a Quicken ("Intel-liCharge") card before you upgraded to Quicken 5, your account is still set up for diskette delivery. To retrieve the data from the diskette, do the following:

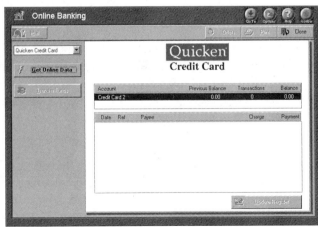

The Quicken credit card has been selected for getting online data in the Online Banking window.

1. From the Online menu, select Online Banking.

2. Select Quicken credit card as the financial institution name in the Online Banking window.

3. Click on Get Online Data. (This is the same way you retrieve a statement via modem if the account is set up for modem delivery.)

4. In the window that will appear, enter the letter for your floppy disk drive, and then click on OK.

This window lets you retrieve data from a floppy disk.

To change your delivery method from diskette to modem, you need to call Travelers Bank at 800-772-7889. Then change your setting in Quicken as follows:

1. From the Lists menu, choose Accounts.

2. In the Account List window, select the credit card account.

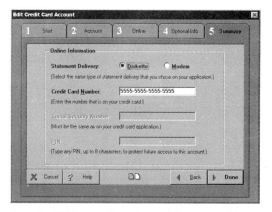

3. Click on Edit, then click on Next. You'll see that the Diskette radio button is chosen; click on the Modem radio button to make the change. Then click on Done, and you'll be returned to the register.

Changing Quicken credit card data delivery from diskette to modem.

Summary

Although Quicken might not single-handedly get your credit card spending under control, it provides the best shot at it you've ever had. The new options for online data delivery, which encompass American Express as well as a variety of other issuers, make entering transactions into your credit card register completely automatic. Remember that credit cards are just one part of Quicken's online banking options. You'll find information about the rest in Chapter 15.

Tracking Cash

13

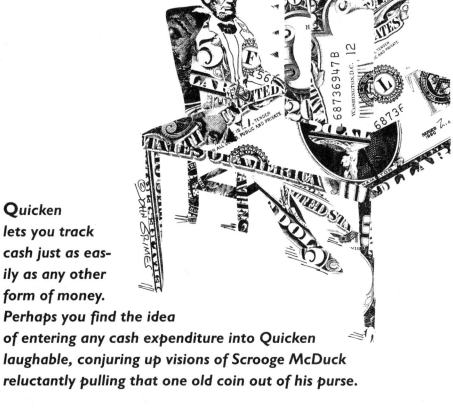

*Quicken
lets you track
cash just as eas-
ily as any other
form of money.
Perhaps you find the idea
of entering any cash expenditure into Quicken
laughable, conjuring up visions of Scrooge McDuck
reluctantly pulling that one old coin out of his purse.*

Whether or not you really need to set up a cash account in Quicken
depends on how much cash you spend. That seems like an obvious
point, but think about it: If you rarely carry cash in your wallet, only
breaking into the odd $5 or $10 for a magazine, a box of cough drops,
or a restaurant tip, you probably aren't spending enough to significantly affect your budget. The advent of supermarkets and service
stations that accept ATM cards for payment means that most of us can
live without carrying cash at all. On the other hand, if you routinely
withdraw $40, $60, or more as "mad money" each time you use an
ATM—and, looking back on it, you don't really know where that cash
goes—you've got a problem.

Who should track cash?

If you've set up an account in Quicken for your checking or savings account, as both this book and the Quicken manual suggest, you're already making entries in your register every time you withdraw cash from an ATM, supermarket, or teller. Therefore, you can find out how much cash you spend each month just by asking Quicken to produce a report (see Chapter 11).

The amount of cash you can spend without having to worry about it is obviously related to your income. It's a little like an oil stain on the floor of a garage: A puddle that would be nothing to worry about for the owner of a Peterbilt truck might be a major disaster for someone driving a Geo Metro.

I can't tell you how much cash you should or shouldn't spend. However, if the "puddle" looks bigger than you're comfortable with, it's time to evaluate your cash spending. You can begin to control your pocket money by setting up a Quicken cash account, as described in this chapter. Estimate how much cash you'll spend this week and transfer that amount from your checking account into the new cash account. At the end of the week, open your wallet and your cash account. Subtract what's left in your wallet from the amount you "received" at the beginning of the week, and enter the result in the Spend field. After several weeks of this, you'll have a better feel for how much cash you're spending.

If you find that you have very few cash expenses, maybe you *don't* need a cash account. Just enter the transactions you want to track in your checking account. Even if you do have a cash account, there's no requirement that you enter every single transaction for the cash that you spend. Do make sure, though, that you enter a transaction for the cash you *receive* (of course, this is done automatically if your cash "deposits" take the form of transfers from another account).

If you often pay for things in cash or get paid in cash, you may well need a meticulously maintained cash account. Small business can use Quicken cash accounts to track petty cash.

Don't overlook the possibility that you might want more than one cash account in your family. The online help for Quicken Deluxe contains an anecdote from a father who set up cash accounts for each of his kids to help them manage their allowances. By doing this, and letting them write "checks" drawn on the accounts using an old set of check forms, he helped teach them budgeting—and also avoided trying to convince a real bank to deal with such small deposits.

A computer set up with a Quicken cash account could also act as the banker for your family's next Monopoly game—no, come to think of it, there are still a few times that handling money is best done by hand.

Creating a Cash Account

To create a cash account, follow the same procedure that you would for creating any other Quicken account. Details on how to do this appear in Chapter 4, but here's a brief review:

1. Select Create New Account from the Activities menu.

   or

   Open HomeBase (select the Homebs icon in the icon bar, choose the HomeBase Quick Tab at the left of the screen, or choose HomeBase from the Activities menu), then click on the Account List icon. Then select New at the top of the Account List window.

The Create New Account window lets you create a cash account as easily as any other type of account.

   or

   Open the Account List window (select the Accts icon in the icon bar or choose the Accounts Quick Tab at the left of the screen), then click on the New button.

2. In the Create New Account window, click on the Cash button.

3. Click on the Next button, then enter an Account Name and optional Description. Click on the Next button again.

4. Quicken will now ask for a starting point for this account (for example, how much cash you have). Answer Yes or No. In fact, it's likely that the answer will be No if you're setting up this account to be fed by transfers from a checking account. (And how else are you going to get money into it? You can't very well shove that pile of greenbacks into

your computer's floppy disk drive.) Then click on Next to proceed until you are looking at the Optional Info tab.

5. Use the Optional Info screen to enter any special information about this cash account. In this case, you won't use the Financial Institution or Account Number fields, but you might want to include notes to yourself on how the account should be used. When you're done, click on Next to continue.

6. Use the Summary screen to review the information you've entered, then click on Done to create your new cash account.

If you created the account from the Account List window, the window will remain open and the new account will be listed. If you created the account from HomeBase or the Activities menu, the new cash account register will open on the screen for you to work with.

Note: You may not be able to see your new account in the Account List window. This will occur if you have created an account type that is not the same as the type currently being displayed in the Account List window. For example, if you create a new cash account, but the Account List window is displaying Credit accounts, you won't see the new account appear in the list. To see the new account, select the All Types tab.

The Cash Register

Quicken's cash register resembles the registers for all other types of accounts. Apart from the fact that the bars on the register appear in a pleasing green color, there's not a whole lot that's different. The first column, Date, is self-explanatory. The second has been relabeled Ref; you can use this field for any reference purpose (for example, you can use it to track ATM

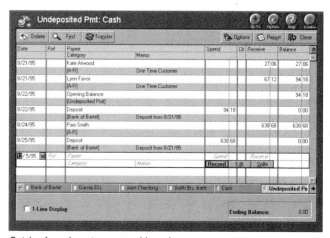

Quicken's cash register resembles other account registers.

transaction codes). The Payee, Category, Memo, and Clr fields are the same as on other types of accounts, while the columns that show incoming and outgoing amounts are relabeled Spend and Receive.

Changing Colors in the Cash (or Other) Register

I enjoyed the green bars on the cash register so much that I decided to investigate how I could change the colors for the other registers. To try this yourself, open a register and click on the Options button at the upper right. The Register Options window will open.

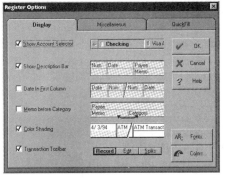

The Register Options window lets you change the appearance of each register.

As you'll see, the Register Options window lets you change a variety of things, such as the font Quicken uses in its registers, whether or not the description bar at the top is shown, whether or not the date appears in the first column (hooray!—this can be toggled to match the layout of a typical checkbook register), and more. Some of these options are especially useful if you're working with a portable computer or other machine whose "screen real estate" is limited.

To change colors, click on the Colors button at the bottom right. Use the drop-down menus to change colors for the six different register types: Bank, Cash, Credit Card, Asset, Liability, and Investment. Then click on OK to return to the Register Options window, and click on OK again to return to the register.

Summary

You may not need to set up a Quicken cash account—it depends on how much cash you actually spend or receive—but for many of us, such accounts are an essential part of compiling an accurate budget. The procedure for setting up a cash account is simple and enjoyable, just as it is for Quicken's other account types.

Investment Tracking and Projection

14

TOM WAS FULLY INVESTED IN COLLECTIBLE TEAPOTS

Before you start using Quicken to track your investments, it's important to decide the level of detail you need. All brokerage houses, banks, and others who manage investment accounts must send you periodic statements that tell you exactly how you're doing. A typical statement will show you the number of shares you own of each stock or mutual fund, the value of each share, and any purchases or redemptions (sales) you have made during the preceding period. A brokerage house will also keep track of your capital gains or losses and will send you an end-of-the-year statement with all the information you'll need for your tax return.

In other words, someone else is already doing your record-keeping for you. However, it's always a good idea to check the investment firm's accuracy. These firms, like banks, have been known to make mistakes. It's also a good idea to keep your own running balance of how you're doing.

But whether you need to have up-to-the-minute information on exactly how your funds are doing depends, in part, on the type of investor you are. If you're "playing the stock market" by buying and selling on a regular basis, then it's very important to have complete knowledge not only of what you own but also of what it's worth. If you're investing for the long term, as we advise in Chapter 22, then chances are you're not keeping a close eye on each of your funds.

If you have a modem, you can let Quicken automatically go online to find out how much each of your securities is worth and, if you have an accurate record of your number of shares, you can let the program update the actual value of your portfolio.

Even if you aren't concerned about the latest value of each account, it's generally a good idea to keep an eye on how your investments are doing—especially if you own stocks or any volatile mutual funds. If a fund or a stock is dropping and shows no likely sign that it will go up in value, it may be a good idea to dump it in favor of something else. One way to find out if that's the case is to check the newspaper periodically for the value of your stocks, bonds, and funds. Another way is to use the Portfolio Price Update service or Mutual Fund Finder to automatically price each of your securities. We'll discuss these later in this chapter.

Quicken lets you have it either way. You can use Quicken to set up accounts for your investments and fastidiously enter each purchase, sale, and new dividend, or you can enter the information once and periodically adjust your share balance from the information on your schedule. Either way, if you have a modem, you can let Quicken automatically go online to find out how much each of your securities is worth and, if you have an accurate record of your number of shares, you can let the program update the actual value of your portfolio.

I use Quicken to automatically track each new purchase in my modest portfolio of mutual funds. I don't, however, methodically update my records on a monthly basis. Instead, from time to time, I'll compare my Quicken records with a statement from a brokerage house and use the Update Balance feature (on the Activities menu) to adjust my share balance in Quicken to match what it says on the statement (more on that later).

I recently made an exception to my generally laissez-faire investment practice because I had to use a good portion of my mutual fund holdings for the down payment on a house. Of course, I wanted to sell my funds at as high a price as possible during a period when the market was relatively unstable. During the three weeks when I was selling off funds to accumulate cash, I kept a very close eye on my positions in each fund, the value of my stock, and the market in general.

Types of Investment Accounts

To recap what you learned in Chapter 8, Quicken has several types of accounts that can be used to track investments.

Investment Accounts

The Investment account is mainly used for stocks and mutual funds. You can use a single Investment account to track a single security (stock, bond, or mutual fund) or several securities. One strategy is to have a separate Investment "account" for each account you have at a brokerage firm, even if that account is used for more than one fund. You can use an Investment account for stocks, bonds, mutual funds, and real estate partnerships in taxable, tax-exempt, and tax-deferred accounts, including IRAs or Keoghs.

It's a good idea to set up separate Investment accounts for your IRA (or other retirement plan) and your spouse's plan. Even if you earn and spend the money together, the IRS requires that you account for it separately.

You can also use a Quicken Investment account to track whatever cash you may have in your investment portfolio. Many brokerage accounts, for example, allow you to invest in a variety of cash accounts where they keep your money that's not invested in a security. If you sell a security, the funds generally go to one of these cash accounts, which serve as a parking spot for money between investments. Quicken automatically tracks the cash in such an account, as we'll cover later in this chapter.

If you plan to take advantage of check-writing privileges from a cash or money market fund that's part of an Investment account, you can use a Quicken Checking or Money Market account to track the cash and record any checks and deposits. If you do that, you'll have to use Quicken's transfer routine (covered later in this chapter) to be sure that you transfer cash between the Investment account and the Money Market or Checking account.

When you set up a new Investment account, you'll be able to indicate if the account contains a single mutual fund. As we said earlier, you can use a single account to track one or several funds.

We'll get back to Investment accounts soon but, just for the record, here are some other types of accounts that you can use to track investment information.

Money Market Accounts

You can track money market accounts that you have at a bank, savings institution, or brokerage firm. You can also track a Money Market (or Cash) account as part of a regular Investment account. A Money Market register looks exactly like a Savings account register, which, in many ways, is similar to a Checking account register.

Savings Accounts

A Savings account should be used to track regular savings accounts or savings-type accounts whether at a bank, savings institution, or brokerage firm. You can record regular deposits and withdrawals in a standard register.

Asset Accounts

An Asset account is used to track the value of a security or other valuable for which you don't know the share price. You can also use an Asset account to track coin and stamp collections, precious metals, real estate, and any other items of value. The Asset account register lets you track the value of assets but does not track share prices or number of shares. For that type of asset, use an Investment account.

Setting Up an Investment Account

Setting up and using a Money Market, Savings, or Asset account is pretty straightforward. You set them up as covered in Chapter 4 and simply use the register to track any deposits, withdrawals, or fluctuations in value.

Setting up an Investment account is covered in detail in Chapter 8. As you set up the account, remember that you need to determine in advance if the account will contain a single mutual fund. If so, check the Account Contains a Single Mutual Fund box in the New Account dialog box; you will be prompted to add information about the specific fund.

Setting Up Securities to Use with Investment Accounts

Regardless of whether you're working with an account tracking a single mutual fund or a group of funds, you have to set up each security that you'll track in the fund. You can do this in advance, by selecting Security from the Lists menu, or you can do it on-the-fly from within any investment account register. If you're using an account with a single mutual fund, you already told the account about the security when you set it up, so there's no need to do it again.

First-Time Use of an Investment Account with a Single Mutual Fund

The first time you open an account tracking a single mutual fund, Quicken will display the Create Opening Share Balance window. This will ask for an "opening balance," which consists of the number of shares and price per share as of the date you're setting up the account. As the dialog box will point out, you should only enter that information if you don't plan to use Quicken to track the historical basis, cost basis, and performance reports of this particular fund. If you do plan to do that, you need to leave the information blank and copy all the information from your statement to the appropriate places on the register.

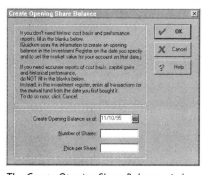

The Create Opening Share Balance window.

Adding Securities to an Investment Account

The actual process of buying and selling securities is the same whether it's a single mutual fund or a grouped securities account. First, you have to tell Quicken about the security (that's already done if it's an account with a single mutual fund) and then you tell it how many shares you've purchased or sold, as well as the price per share. You can tell Quicken about each of your securities by selecting Security from the Lists menu (or by pressing Ctrl-Y), or you can add securities on-the-fly as you enter information into the register. If you choose Security from the Lists menu, you get a list of securities: Clicking on the New button will display the Set Up Security dialog box. If you enter a security from the register that hasn't been set up previously, Quicken will display the Set Up Security dialog box automatically.

The Set Up Security dialog box.

Filling Out the Set Up Security Dialog Box

To fill out the Set Up Security dialog box:

1. Enter the name of the security in the Name field. This is generally the actual name of the company or mutual fund.

2. Enter the ticker Symbol used by the exchange (if any) that tracks the fund or security. This is optional, but you'll definitely need it if you plan to have Quicken automatically track the value of your portfolio via its online links. Even if you don't plan to use such a service, I recommend that you enter the ticker symbol if only to help you find the security in the newspaper.

3. In the Type field, use the drop-down menu to pick a security type. The preset security types include bonds, CDs, mutual funds, and stocks. (You can add a type by selecting Security Type from the Lists menu, then clicking on the New button.)

4. The Goal field is optional and, frankly, probably a little silly. I'm sure you know what your goal is. Just for the record, Quicken's preset goal types are College Fund, Growth, High Risk, Income, International, and Low Risk.

5. Click on <u>A</u>dd to Watch List to add the security to the "Watch List" available in the Portfolio View window. The Watch List is a list of securities you choose to follow that you don't necessarily own.

6. If you know the estimated annual income per share (generally mentioned in the prospectus), enter it here in the <u>E</u>st Annual Income field so that later you can see if the security is doing as well as predicted.

7. Check Tax <u>F</u>ree if you plan to hold this security in an IRA or other tax-free or tax-deferred account.

8. Click on <u>O</u>ther Info to open the Additional Security Information window. This will let you enter your broker's name and phone number, plus other information if desired.

The Additional Security Information window.

Adding in Shares

Every time you add or remove shares from an investment account, you need to tell Quicken what type of transaction you've performed. Unlike other types of accounts, this can get a bit tricky with investment accounts because there are lots of options. You'll be able to see the full list of options if you click on the down arrow in the Action field in the Investment register. (See the sidebar on page 217 for an explanation of all the abbreviations.)

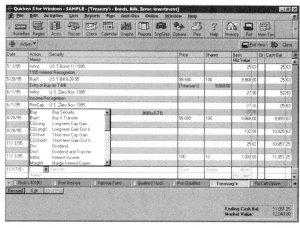

Quicken's Investment register requires you to specify the type of action you're performing.

Understanding Investment Actions

For each action in the Investment register there are usually two entries. One has an "X" after it and the other doesn't. The "X" simply means that the action involves a transfer of funds from one Quicken account to another. "BuyX," for example, means that you are buying a security and paying for it with funds that you're taking from another account. You would use this if you were paying for a security with funds in your Checking or other account.

Rather than entering actions from the drop-down menu in the register's Action field, you're better off using the Action button at the top left of the Investment register. If you don't see any buttons, click on the chevron above the scroll bar, near the upper right corner of the Register window.

The Action button makes it easy to enter an action in the Investment register.

If you select ShrsIn (to add shares to an account), you will see the Add Shares to Account dialog box that will let you enter in the name of the security (you can select it from the drop-down list by pressing the down arrow), the number of shares, and the price per share.

If you don't care to enter the price per share, you can enter the total amount you paid for the stock in the Cost Basis field and Quicken will calculate the price by dividing the total cost basis by the number of shares. Or you can enter the price and the total cost basis and let Quicken calculate the total number of shares. (If you don't have any of this information until you find the right shoebox, fear not—it may all be added in later.)

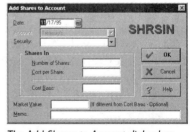

The Add Shares to Account dialog box.

Unless this is, literally, a new account (I'm talking about the actual investment account with your broker, not your new Quicken account) then you've probably already purchased some securities. At this point you need to decide how much detail you want to enter into your register.

The quick and dirty solution (the one that I naturally used) is to simply enter in the total number of shares you own and the current price per share. That will give you an immediate accounting of your position with that security but won't give you any historical information such as average annual total return, capital gains summary, or income and

Abbreviations for Actions in the Investment Register

Action	Description	Meaning
Buy	Buy a security	Buy a security from cash already in your account
BuyX	Buy and transfer	Buy a security with funds transferred from an existing Quicken account
CGLong	Receive long-term capital gains distribution	Receive the profit earned on the sale of a capital asset held for more than one year
CGLongX	Receive long-term capital gains distribution and transfer cash to another account	Transfer the profit earned on the sale of a capital asset held for more than one year to another account
CGShort	Receive short-term capital gains distribution	Receive the profit earned on the sale of a capital asset held for one year or less
Div	Receive dividend income	Receive your share of the profit from a company
DivX	Receive dividend income, then transfer it	Transfer the dividend income as cash to a regular investment or mutual fund account
Intinc	Receive interest income	Receive the fee you earn from the financial institution for the use of your money over time
Margint	Margin interest expense	Pay interest to the brokerage house for money borrowed using stock as collateral
MiscExp	Miscellaneous expense	Pay a miscellaneous expense item that doesn't fit into any other category
Miscinc	Receive miscellaneous income	Receive miscellaneous income that doesn't fit into any other category
ReinvDiv	Reinvest dividend	Use your dividends to buy additional shares of a company's stock without a broker's commission and in some cases at a slight discount
ReinvInt	Reinvest interest	Invest in additional shares of a security with money from interest income (from regular investment accounts and mutual fund accounts)
ReinvLg	Reinvest long-term capital gains distribution	Use long-term capital gains of mutual funds to buy additional shares in the mutual fund
ReinvSh	Reinvest short-term capital gains distribution	Use short-term capital gains of mutual funds to buy additional shares in the mutual fund
Reminder	Reminder	Write a short (30-character) note to yourself
RtrnCap	Return of capital from regular investment accounts	Receive cash from return of capital (earnings divided by capital invested)
RtrnCapX	Return of capital from regular investment accounts and mutual fund accounts	Receive cash from return of capital (earnings divided by capital invested)
Sell	Sell security	Sell a security in your portfolio and receive cash
SellX	Sell a security and transfer the money	Sell a security and transfer the cash to another account
ShrsIn	Add shares to an account	Add shares to an account without transferring any cash
ShrsOut	Remove shares from an account	Remove shares from an account without transferring or recording cash
StkSplit	Stock split	Change the number of shares as the result of a stock split
XIn	Transfer cash in	Transfer cash in from another account
XOut	Transfer cash out	Transfer cash out to another account

expense summary. If you want that type of information, you'll need to go back to your records from the date you opened the account and enter in each trade with the amount of shares purchased (or sold) and the price of the security on the day of each transaction. Be sure to enter the exact date of the transaction as Quicken will use that in its calculations.

Either way, you enter information about old purchases by selecting the ShrsIn option to tell Quicken that you are entering shares into the account. You use the Buy option if you are actually buying shares at this time.

If you make a mistake after you've recorded an item, you can edit it directly in the register by typing over the old number and clicking the Record button.

After you've entered one or more transactions in the register, you'll see one or more numbers in the lower right corner. In the case of a single mutual fund account, the register will show the Ending Share Balance (total number of shares) and the Market Value (number of shares times the value per share). If the account isn't a single mutual fund account, you'll see the Ending Cash Balance and the Market Value. No cash is actually in the account (we'll get to that soon), but the account does have a total market value.

Dealing with Cash

Some investment accounts have a cash component that may be called "cash reserve," "money market funds," or some other name. Whatever it's called, the cash in your account has three basic purposes. First, it's an investment in and of itself. Although interest rates will always be modest compared to the most bullish of stock and mutual fund returns, the cash you have on deposit does earn interest and is usually a very low-risk investment.

Another purpose of cash in an account is to serve as a source of payment if you wish to purchase securities. Many investment firms encourage you to keep some cash in the account so you can use it for trades. If you sell a security, the cash, by default, goes into the cash component of your account. Finally, the cash on hand can be withdrawn and spent—it's your money. Some companies provide customers with a checkbook so that they can use the cash account like any other checking account.

If you're depositing cash from another account, such as your checking or savings account, then you should use the Transfer Cash In function. Click on the Action button at the top left of the register, then select XIn. The Transfer Cash In window will appear. Simply enter an amount in the Amount field, then use the drop-down menu in the Transfer Acct field to show where the money is coming from.

The Transfer Cash In dialog box.

Buying and Selling Shares

Once you have your account up to date, you'll no doubt be buying and selling more shares. The buy and sell process is pretty much the same, except that when you buy, you spend money from your investment account or transfer it from another account. When you sell, you do the reverse, depositing money in either your investment account or another account.

To buy shares:

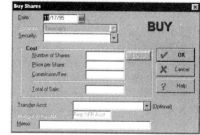

The Buy Shares window.

1. Click on the Action button and select Buy. The Buy Shares window will appear.

2. Select the security from the drop-down list in the Security field. If it's a security that hasn't previously been entered in the list, just type in its name. Since Quicken doesn't find it on its list, it will pop up the Set Up Security window so you can enter the necessary information.

3. Enter the Number of Shares and the Commission/Fee (if any). You don't need to fill in the Total of Sale. If you are using funds from another account (such as Checking) to buy the security, select that account from the Transfer Acct drop-down menu. If you don't select a transfer account, Quicken will automatically debit the cash in the account you're using. If there isn't sufficient cash, it will show a negative balance (in red).

Note: *Enter a commission in the Commission/Fee field only if it is explicitly added to your purchase. Some mutual funds or securities feature a "load" or "front-end load," whereby the commission is built into the purchase price for each share. Such a fund has two share prices:*

A "Buy" or "Offer" price and a "Sell" (Net Asset Value) price. Enter the purchase of a front-end-loaded fund at the "Buy" price with no additional commission. If you want to correct the market value, you may do so later.

Selling is basically the same process in reverse.

1. Click on the Action button and select Sell.

2. Enter the information called for on the screen. Select a transfer account from the Transfer Account field if the money is to be paid into a different account. Quicken will automatically deposit the funds into that account. If the funds are to stay in your investment account, don't select a transfer account: Quicken will credit the proceeds as cash in your investment account.

Recording and Reinvesting Income

The Income entry, which comes just below Sell on the Action menu, lets you record dividends, interest, and both short- and long-term capital gains. Using the statement sent by the company that sold you the securities, you enter information in the Record Income window. Similarly, if you reinvest the dividends from your fund, you can select Reinvest to plow dividend and interest income back into your portfolio.

To record income:

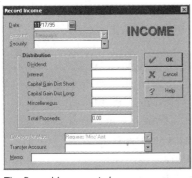

The Record Income window.

1. Click on the Action button and then select the Income entry from the menu. The Record Income window will appear.

2. Check to see if the Date field is correct. If not, change it.

3. Select the Security from the drop-down list. If it's a dividend from a money market account, enter that account name as the security.

4. Enter amounts in the Dividend, Interest, Capital Gain Dist Short, and Capital Gain Dist Long fields.

5. If income is to be transferred to another account, select that account from the drop-down list in the Transfer Account field.

Some securities automatically reinvest any earnings from interest, dividends, or capital gains. The advantage to reinvesting the earnings is that you increase your number of shares. It's similar to compound interest because, over the long run, it increases the value of your account, assuming the security doesn't go down in value. Even if it does go down a little, you may still increase the value of your portfolio since you're buying more shares.

 Quicken handles recording reinvestments similarly to recording income, except there is also a "buy" component to reinvestments since you're adding securities to your account. When you're reinvesting dividends or other income, you enter in the dollar amount and the number of shares you're buying, and Quicken adds those shares to your register. It's the same process regardless of whether it's a dividend, interest, or long- or short-term capital gain.

 To reinvest income:

1. Click on the Action button, and select the Reinvest entry from the menu. The Reinvest Income window will appear.

2. Check to see if the Date field is correct. If not, change it.

The Reinvest Income window.

3. Select the Security from the drop-down list. If it's a dividend from a money market account, enter that account name as the security.

4. Enter the dollar amount and the number of new shares you are receiving using the Dividend, Interest, Cap Gain Short, and Cap Gain Long fields. If a mutual fund doesn't tell you whether a capital gains distribution is short-term or long-term, assume it's long-term.

5. To transfer income to another account, select that account from the drop-down list in the Transfer Account field. If you have no other accounts, none will appear.

Stock Splits

In a stock split, the stock generally goes down in value but you are given more shares, so the total market value remains the same.

Quicken lets you record a split by entering numbers for new shares, old shares, and the price after the split.

The Stock Split window.

To record a stock split:

1. Click on the Action button, and select the StkSplit entry from the menu. You will see the Stock Split window.

2. Check to see if the Date field is correct. If not, change it.

3. Select the Security from the drop-down list.

4. Enter numbers to express the ratio of new shares to old. For example, if the stock split is 2:1, enter 2 in the New Shares field and 1 in the Old Shares field. Enter the new price per share in the Price after Split field.

Savings Bonds, Treasury Bills, and Zero Coupon Bonds

The example I give is for a U.S. Savings Bond, but the process is similar with Zero Coupon Bonds and Treasury Bills:

Recording the purchase of U.S. Savings Bonds via the Set Up Security window.

1. Within the register or portfolio view of an investment account, click on the Action button and select Buy.

2. Enter the name of the bond in the Security field. This is usually something like "U.S. $500 5% 3/09" which means it's a U.S. Savings Bond with a face value of $500 paying 5% interest and maturing in March 2009. Since this is a new security, Quicken will bring up the Set Up Security window with the new bond name automatically entered. Fill in any other relevant information and click OK.

Additional Options

Additional options in the Action menu are, for the most part, fairly self-explanatory. You can use the Reminder option to write yourself a very brief (30-characters) note, which is entered in the Memo field of your register. This is a good place to record transaction control numbers from your brokerage house; you can then refer to them in case there's a problem with the trade. You can also use the Reminder option with Billminder, Quicken's automatic reminder feature.

Portfolio View

So far we've primarily worked with the Investment register. But there is another way to view your investments. You can view your securities in the Portfolio View to get a complete overview of your investments.

The Portfolio View can list all of your securities, or just securities from a specific account. Either way, it presents them alphabetically and shows you how much you own of each security, the current value per share, and the total market value of each stock, your cash, and the account as a whole. Frankly, this is the most useful way to look at your data because it hides detail you generally don't need and provides you with a quick overview of where you stand.

The Portfolio View can also be used to display the prices, over time, of each security; a graph of performance; and a variety of reports that list any transactions for the account or for a specific security.

There are three ways to get to the Portfolio View. You can select Portfolio from the Activities menu, you can type Ctrl-U, or you can click the Port View button from within any investment register.

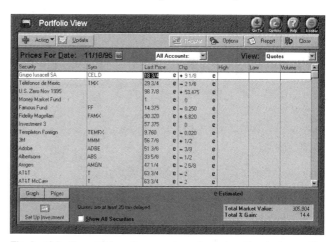

The Portfolio View displays the current market price of each share, tells you whether its value is up or down, and more.

Ways of Looking at Your Investments

In the View drop-down menu, you have the following choices:

View	What You See
Holdings	The "big picture" of your investments
Performance	How well each security is performing (look at the ROI—return on investment—percentage)
Valuation	How much an investment is worth compared to how much it has cost you
Price Update	The dollar gain or loss due to changes in price
Quotes	The latest security price information you've retrieved online with Portfolio Price Update
Custom View 1 and Custom View 2	Specialized views you design

Getting Historical Data

By default, the Portfolio View will show you the situation as of today's date (based, of course, on your computer's system clock). You can move that back or forward by using the pop-up calendar by the Prices for

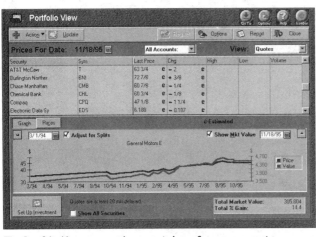

The Portfolio View can graph a security's performance over time.

Date field to select a different date. All the data in the Portfolio View will be adjusted to reflect your account(s) on the day you select.

The screen normally will show you the current value of a security and whether its value most recently went up or down. You can get more information by changing the column headings in the Portfolio View window. Simply click on the down arrow next to View to select one of six different ways of looking at your investments (see the sidebar "Ways of Looking at Your Investments").

If you would like to view historical data about a security graphically, highlight the security in the register with a single mouse click, then click on the Graph button. A window will open to graph the security's performance over time.

You can adjust the end points of the graph by clicking on the drop-down calendars at the left and right of the screen. You can also click on checkboxes to select whether or not to Adjust for Splits or Show Mkt Value.

Creating Custom Views

To create a custom view, click on the Options button at the top of the Portfolio View window. The Portfolio View Options window will appear. Click on the Custom Views tab to bring it to the foreground. You can set both the Custom 1 and Custom 2 views by using the drop-down menus to choose column headings.

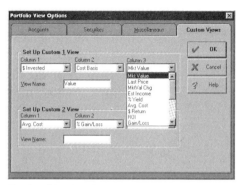

The Portfolio View Options window lets you choose which column headings you want to see. Other tabs in the Portfolio View Options window let you choose which accounts to monitor and which securities to track.

Column Headings in the Portfolio View Window

For six of the Portfolio Views (Holdings, Performance, Valuation, Price Update, Custom View 1, and Custom View 2), the last three column headings are different. (For Quotes, the last five columns are different.) You choose the column headings for the Custom Views (see below under "Creating Custom Views"); Quicken provides preset column headings for the other views.

The meanings of most column headings in the Portfolio View window are pretty apparent, so I won't go into them here. If you're uncertain about any, you'll find full details in Quicken's online help system.

Avg Cost	ROI	% Gain Loss	Chg
Cost basis	Security	% Income	High
Est Income	Shares	% Invested	Last Price
Gain/Loss	Sym	% MktVal	Low
Inv. Yield	Total Market Value	% Yield	Volume
Mkt Price	Total % Gain	$ Income	
Mkt Value	Type	$ Invested	
MktVal Chg	% Cost	$ Return	

Changing Accounts

If you enter Portfolio View from within the register of any account, it will automatically display only the securities in that account. You can select a different account (or All accounts) by clicking the down arrow next to the name of the account. A drop-down list will appear that will let you select any or all of your accounts.

A drop-down list lets you display any or all accounts in the Portfolio View.

Conducting Transactions

As you can see from the presence of the Action button at the left of the window, you can perform the same actions in the Portfolio View window as you can in the Register window. It really doesn't matter which of the two places you are when you buy, sell, or perform some other transaction. A Set Up Investment button at the bottom left gives you access to the EasyStep interface for setting up a new account (see Chapter 8).

Getting Security Price Information

There are many ways to get the prices of your securities into Quicken. The hardest is to look them up in the newspaper and type them in yourself. The easy way is to use Quicken's Portfolio Price Update feature to have Quicken go online and retrieve the information for you.

The software required for Portfolio Price Update is included with all editions of Quicken 5. Quicken Deluxe, whether supplied on floppy disks or CD-ROM, also includes two additional features, Mutual Fund Finder and Investor Insight.

Using Portfolio Price Update

Portfolio Price Update is an online service from Intuit that updates the prices of the stocks, mutual funds, and market indexes in your Quicken investment portfolio. The service can update prices of all stocks and mutual funds traded on the New York Stock Exchange, American Stock Exchange, and NASDAQ.

The Portfolio Price Update service is available 24 hours a day, seven days a week. It includes last price and change information. It also includes high, low, and volume, when available.

There is a 15-to-20-minute lag if you seek a quote while the market is open. In other words, the quote you get will be at least 15 minutes old. Mutual fund prices are quoted at the closing price, which is updated at about 5:30 P.M. EST.

You can use the Portfolio Price Update service three times for free. After that, you'll be charged $2.95 a month, which includes six free updates. Additional updates are around 50 cents each (call Quicken's 24-hour hotline at 800-245-2164 to find out the exact charges).

Remember, the ability to download quote information requires that you have entered valid ticker symbols for each of your securities. If you haven't, go to the Lists menu, select Security, and edit any securities that don't have the ticker symbol. You can usually find the ticker symbol in your newspaper, or call your broker for it.

To use the Portfolio Price Update service:

The Update Portfolio Prices window.

1. Open the Quicken file you want to use with Portfolio Price Update.

2. From the Online menu, choose Portfolio Price Update. (Or, if you already have the Portfolio View open, simply click on the Update button.) You'll see the Update Portfolio Prices window.

This window will appear if you're missing ticker symbols.

3. In the About Portfolio Price Update window, click OK.

4. If some of your stocks do not have ticker symbols, a window will appear alerting you to that fact. Either exit to correct the situation, or click on OK to ignore the problem.

5. Portfolio Price Update will dial a toll-free number automatically and download the quote information without any intervention. Upon completion, a new window will display the updated prices.

Using Mutual Fund Finder

If you are planning to change, add, or monitor your mutual fund investments, you can use the Mutual Fund Finder included with Quicken Deluxe to find all the information you need to make sound investment decisions. You can cre-

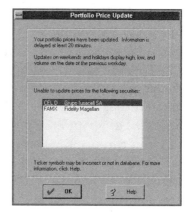

This window is displayed after the Portfolio Price Update has logged off.

ate a list of funds that meet the risk and return limits you have in mind, see a detailed summary of each fund's performance, trace its history, and understand its fee structure.

When you start Mutual Fund Finder for the first time, you will be guided through the selection of criteria. The next time you open the program, Mutual Fund Finder will display the Search Results window with the results from your last search. Mutual Fund Finder will remember your criteria; you will start from where you left off.

To use Mutual Fund Finder:

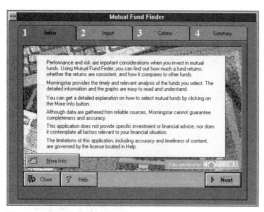

The main Mutual Fund Finder window.

1. Select Mutual Fund Finder from the Quicken Add-Ons menu or click on Mutual Fund Finder from the Quicken Deluxe Gateway. (Mutual Fund Finder may also appear in the Windows 95 Start Menu or the Windows 3.1 Program Manager.)

2. The Mutual Fund Finder window will appear, complete with Morningstar disclaimers. Click on Next to continue.

3. Mutual Fund Finder will ask you if you already own any mutual funds. If so, click on the Import button so that it can read your Quicken data file(s). Either way, click on Next to continue.

4. Mutual Fund Finder will ask what types of funds you want to invest in. Basic asset classes, which are the default, are broad classes of funds that include domestic stocks and bonds, international stocks, and other securities. Extended asset classes are funds with more specific objectives, such as aggressive growth or short-term world income. The complete list of extended asset classes may be viewed by clicking on the Extended Asset Classes radio button. Click on the Next button.

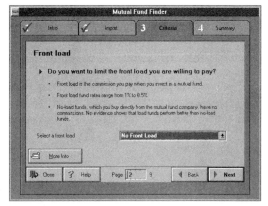

Picking mutual funds by class.

5. Now, Mutual Fund Finder will ask you what front load—the commission you pay when you invest in a mutual fund—you are willing to pay. The drop-down menu lets you pick any front load, no front load, or specific values from 0% to 5%. When you've made a choice, click on the Next button.

6. Mutual Fund Finder will ask you what star rating you are looking for. This is an overall measure of how well a fund has performed in the past compared to other funds in the same asset class. Morningstar bases its rating on the historical profitability of the fund's investments as well as the riskiness. Funds with more stars have higher profitability, less risk, or both. From the drop-down menu, choose Any Star Rating or select values from one to five stars. Then click on Next to continue.

7. The next window, almost identical, will ask you how much risk you are willing to accept. Use the drop-down menu to choose, then click on the Next button.

8. The Manager Tenure screen will ask if you want to be sure a fund's current manager is the one who built its track record. From the drop-down menu, your choices include Any Manager Tenure all the way through to Manager Tenure of at Least Ten Years. Choose one, and then click on Next.

9. Specify a minimum investment amount. Choose from Any, Less than $250, Less than $500, Less than $1000, or Less than $3000. This will eliminate from consideration funds that have a higher minimum investment than you can afford to spend. Click on Next.

The Mutual Fund Finder Summary screen.

10. Specify how much you are willing to accept in the way of fund overhead: Less than 1%, Less than 2%, Less than 3%, or Any. Click on Next.

11. Specify a dividend yield if you require one. (Generally, this is less important than long-term yield, but your needs may vary.) Click on Next to continue.

12. What five-year performance level do you expect? Choose Any, or enter percentages ranging from 5% to 15%. After you have made a choice, click on Next to continue.

13. The Summary screen will show you the choices you have made so far and let you alter any of them. When you are satisfied, click on Search.

14. Mutual Fund Finder will summarize the results via the Search Results screen. You can print the complete list of information by clicking on the Print

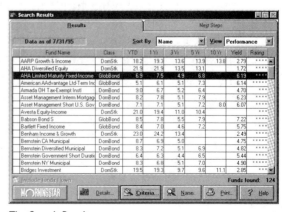

The Search Results screen.

button, view details of any particular fund by clicking on Details, search via fund Name, or specify further Criteria. (The last of these choices takes you back to the series of windows you completed in the above steps.)

15. Select the Next Steps tab in the Search Results screen for general help evaluating

The details of a selected mutual fund.

the funds in your launch list. The Next Steps window will call up advice about selecting a mutual fund.

Now you can shut down the Mutual Fund Finder program. The next time you open it, it will show the Search Results screen you produced in Step 14. Therefore, you will not need to re-enter any information in order to pick mutual funds in the future.

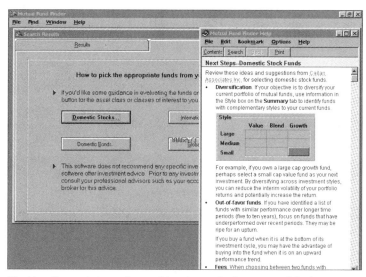

The Next Steps window calls up advice about selecting a mutual fund.

Updating the Mutual Fund Finder Information

You may have been wondering where the Mutual Fund Finder program gets the information it so graciously supplies. The answer is that, initially, it is supplied on your Quicken Deluxe CD-ROM. However, you may want to order updated information when you need it, or even subscribe to a quarterly update available on floppy disk. To do so, call Morningstar at 800-224-0873, extension 810354.

Using Investor Insight

Investor Insight is a service that lets you keep track of your stocks and mutual funds and analyze your investments in meaningful ways. Investor Insight brings you up-to-date stock and mutual fund quotations, along with the latest news stories on stocks you're interested in. You can capture data automatically or schedule a session to download data at any time. You can also generate and print some reports automatically so you have the information when you need it.

With Investor Insight you can:

- Display a variety of charts and reports that let you evaluate and compare your investments.
- Create a personal report that summarizes the latest investment activity in a newsletter-style format.
- Group stocks in portfolios and set up custom indexes for analyzing market trends.
- Use hot spots in charts and reports to link directly to related information.
- Use memorized windows to display commonly used charts or reports.

The EasyStep interface for Investor Insight.

To use Investor Insight, select Investor Insight from the Online menu. If this is the first time you have used the program, a series of EasyStep windows will appear to help introduce you to it. After you have read all of these, you will see the Investor Insight desktop.

Your work in Investor Insight is based on the Watch List, which appears at the desktop's left. This is a list of the stocks and mutual funds you want to track. (You need not own

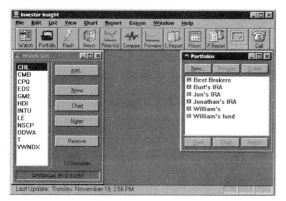
The Investor Insight desktop.

any of these; the Watch List is not linked to any other Quicken files.) Investor Insight uses the Watch List, or a subset of your choosing, to capture price information and news, generate charts and reports, and create portfolios and custom indexes.

You begin by adding a security to the Watch List. Investor Insight is preprogrammed with a list of over 16,000 securities (those listed on the NYSE, AMEX, or NASDAQ exchanges). To add a security, click on the Watch List window to activate it, then select Add. You will see the Add Securities to Watch List window.

If you know the symbol of the security you're interested in, click on the Symbol button and then enter it in the Type field. If you only know

The Add Securities to Watch List window.

the company name, click on the Name button and then type the first four letters of the name. Either way, Investor Insight will find the company for you when you click on the Search button. If the result is what you desired, click on Add to add it to the Watch List. When you are through adding securities, click on Close.

A dialog box will warn you that you will not receive quotes and news for the security you just entered until you call the Investor Insight service via modem. You may call now or defer the online session.

Instead of going online immediately, let's examine some of the information already stored in the Watch List (this is sample data provided with Investor Insight, but it could also be data you retrieved in a previous online session). To get news about a security, click on its symbol in the Watch List and then select the News button.

To get information on a new security, you will need to go online.

The News window will show you recent news headlines about the selected security. To view any article, just click on its headline; you'll see the contents in the window below. To see news articles about a different security, you do not need to close the News window—just click on a different symbol in the list at the upper left.

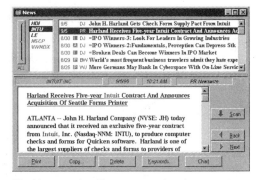

The News window shows you articles about securities in your Watch List.

If you want to view a price/volume graph for any security, select an article pertaining to the security in the News window and then double-click. A graph like the Price/Volume Graph will open. You can change the year displayed, overlay the Dow Jones Industrial Average and Standard and Poor 500, and otherwise change the graph by using the drop-down menu and Options button at the bottom of the graph.

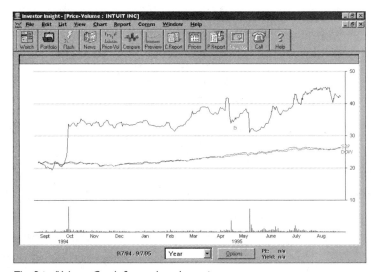

The Price/Volume Graph for a selected security.

At the right of the Investor Insight desktop is the Portfolios window. Once you have added stocks or mutual funds to the Watch List, you're ready to create a portfolio. Although you can include any number of stocks and mutual funds in a portfolio, groups of 30 or fewer are easier to view in chart form.

You can create three kinds of portfolios:
- Simple
- Advanced
- Quicken

To create a portfolio, choose Portfolio List, or click the Portfolio icon on the icon bar. Any existing portfolios are listed by name, along with a symbol showing whether each portfolio is simple (S), advanced (A), or from Quicken (Q).

Creating a Simple Portfolio

Create a Simple portfolio when you want a quick and easy way to analyze the performance of a group of stocks or mutual funds. A Simple portfolio is based solely on your current holdings and does not include transactions and cash adjustments. A report generated from this data can show current portfolio value, the aggregate cost of the portfolio, and dollar and percent gains for each individual stock or mutual fund. Charts can show historical values of the current holdings, which is adequate for long-term investors who do not trade often.

Although the value of a Simple portfolio can be calculated in charts and reports for any day, it is based on current holdings, not necessarily on holdings for that day. Because you can only enter one purchase lot of a security, you must edit the holdings in the portfolio when you buy or sell the security after the starting date of the portfolio so that the revised number of shares becomes the current holdings. (To create a portfolio that calculates true value on any given day and performance figures for any period, see "Creating an Advanced Portfolio" below.)

To create a Simple portfolio:

1. In the Portfolios window, click <u>N</u>ew. The Create Portfolio window will appear.

2. Type a name for the portfolio, and then select <u>S</u>imple.

3. Click OK. The Add To Portfolio window will appear (if this is empty, it's because you haven't yet placed any securities in your Watch List).

4. Select a stock or mutual fund by symbol.

5. To add the selected stock or mutual fund to the portfolio, click Add. The Enter Holdings window will appear, showing the full name of the company or mutual fund. Enter the number of shares you own or want to track and the purchase price per share, and then click OK.

6. To continue adding stocks and mutual funds, repeat Steps 4 and 5. When you're finished, click Close. Your portfolio will be displayed in a window showing the portfolio's name, a list of the stocks and mutual funds you added, and the number of shares and price per share you entered.

Creating an Advanced Portfolio

Unlike a Simple portfolio, which is based solely on current stock and mutual fund holdings, an Advanced portfolio includes transactions and cash adjustments. It contains a full accounting of all transactions related to a group of stocks or mutual funds, including buy and sell transactions (with broker commissions), contributions, withdrawals, income (such as dividends and interest), split transactions, and cash adjustments. (You can't include short sales, bonds, options, or commodities.)

In charts and reports, Investor Insight uses this data to calculate true portfolio value on any day and to calculate performance figures (internal rate of return and time-weighted return) for any period after the portfolio's starting date. You can display the transactions you enter on a price/volume chart for the stock or mutual fund.

To create an Advanced portfolio:

1. In the Portfolios window, click <u>N</u>ew. The Create Portfolio window will appear.

2. Enter a name for the portfolio and then select <u>A</u>dvanced.

3. Click OK. A Start Date window will appear.

4. Set the starting date of the portfolio by using the scroll arrows beside the date (or the plus (+) or minus (–) keys) to change it one day at a time, or by typing a new date in the box.

5. Click OK. The Initial Cash window will appear.

6. Enter the Cash Balance as of the end of the day for the portfolio's start date, and then click OK. Your portfolio will open in a window displaying the portfolio's name.

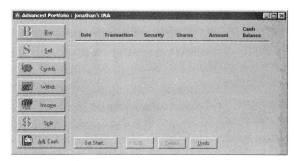

The Advanced Portfolio window.

7. The window will not show any securities. You enter these by recording their purchase using the Buy button. To enter transactions, click the icon of the transaction you want from the list on the left.

Other transaction icons include Sell, for entering sell transactions; Contrib, for entering contributions; Withdr, for entering withdrawals; Income, for entering income; Split, for entering a stock split; and Adj Cash, for making cash adjustments. I will not explain these further here since, frankly, relatively few among us are "serious investors" who really need to use an Advanced portfolio. If you are one, you'll find complete documentation in the online help system.

Creating a Quicken Portfolio

You can export information from either of the above portfolios to a variety of file types, including Excel and Quicken. However, the best way to use Investor Insight if you have already set up a Quicken investment account is to create a Quicken portfolio.

You can import Quicken investment account information so you can analyze it using Investor Insight's features. When you import a Quicken investment account, it appears in the Portfolios window, marked with a Q. A Quicken portfolio is similar to an Advanced portfolio; however, you can't rename the portfolio or add, edit, or delete transactions from within Investor Insight (obviously, you do this using Quicken itself).

Investor Insight works best with securities with ticker symbols. Before you import Quicken investment accounts, make sure each security has a valid ticker symbol associated with it. (Add ticker symbols using the Quicken Security list.) If some of the securities in your Quicken investment account have invalid or missing ticker symbols,

Investor Insight can't add them to the Watch List, and the transactions will appear differently in Investor Insight.

To import a Quicken investment account:

1. From Investor Insight's File menu, choose <u>G</u>et Quicken Investments. Investor Insight uses the currently open Quicken file, or if Quicken isn't running, it uses the last Quicken file you opened.

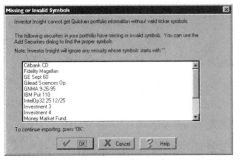

Investor Insight warns you of missing ticker symbols.

2. Investor Insight will warn you if a Quicken account has securities with missing or invalid ticker symbols. Investor Insight will still create a portfolio, but the transactions will be converted differently. Click OK to continue importing.

3. In the Get Quicken Accounts window, select the Quicken account(s) you want to import to Investor Insight. All the investment accounts will be listed. Click <u>C</u>lear All to deselect all the accounts or <u>M</u>ark All to select all the accounts.

4. Click <u>G</u>et Data, and then click OK. Investor Insight will create a new portfolio for each specified Quicken account. The portfolio will have the same name as the Quicken account. Its start date will be the date of the earliest transaction in the Quicken account, with a starting cash balance of zero.

Each Quicken transaction will be converted to a corresponding Investor Insight transaction or transactions. Investor Insight will also add each Quicken security with a valid ticker symbol (and with at least one associated transaction) to the Watch List.

After you import a Quicken investment account to Investor Insight, you can update the portfolio any time you've added, edited, or deleted transactions in the Quicken account.

To update a Quicken portfolio:

In the Quicken portfolio window, click Update. Investor Insight will update the Quicken portfolio by importing the current Quicken investment account.

Investor Insight Conversions

Because Quicken's transactions are slightly different from Investor Insight's transactions, Investor Insight will convert Quicken transactions as described below (the conversion will differ if a security doesn't have a valid ticker symbol):

Quicken Action	Investor Insight Transaction (With Valid Ticker Symbol)	Investor Insight Transaction (Without Valid Ticker Symbol)
Buy	Buy	Withdrawal
Buy/Transfer	Contribution + Buy	<None>
Sell	Sell	Contribution
Sell/Transfer	Sell + Withdrawal	<None>
Dividend Income	Dividend	Dividend (General)
Dividend/Transfer	Dividend + Withdrawal	Dividend (General) + Withdrawal
Interest Income	Interest	Interest (General)
Capital Gain Short	Capital Gain Short-Term	Capital Gain Short-Term (General)
Capital Gain Short/Transfer	Capital Gain Short-Term + Withdrawal	Capital Gain Short-Term (General) + Withdrawal
Capital Gain Long	Capital Gain Long-Term	Capital Gain Long-Term (General)
Capital Gain Long/Transfer	Capital Gain Long-Term + Withdrawal	Capital Gain Long-Term (General) + Withdrawal
Reinvest Dividend	Dividend + Buy	Dividend (General) + Withdrawal
Reinvest Interest	Interest + Buy	Interest (General) + Withdrawal
Reinvest Capital Gain Short	Capital Gain Short -Term + Buy	Capital Gain Short -Term (General) + Withdrawal
Reinvest Capital Gain Long	Capital Gain Long-Term + Buy	Capital Gain Long-Term (General) + Withdrawal
Stock Split	Split	<None>
Misc. Income	Interest	Interest (General)
Misc. Expense	Interest (Negative Amount)	Interest (General, Negative Amount)
ShrsIn (Add Shares)	Contribution + Buy	<None>
ShrsOut (Remove Shares)	Sell + Withdrawal	<None>
Return of Capital	Interest	Interest (General)
Margin Interest Expense	<Not Applicable>	Withdrawal
Transfer In	<Not Applicable>	Contribution
Transfer Out	<Not Applicable>	Withdrawal
Check	<Not Applicable>	Withdrawal
Reminder	<Not Applicable>	<None>

Going Online

To obtain up-to-date price information and news stories and receive company reports, you need to communicate online with Investor Insight. By using e-mail (electronic mail), you can also communicate online with technical support.

Before you can capture data from Investor Insight, you need to set up your account and provide information about your modem and telephone service. It only takes a few minutes and you only have to do it once. Your first month of service is free, and you can order one company report during the trial period at no charge.

To sign up for Investor Insight:

I. Click the Call icon on the icon bar, choose <u>D</u>ial from the Comm menu, or choose Call Now from the Changed Watch List window. Investor Insight will set up your modem automatically and display the Set Up Modem window so you can make any necessary changes.

You shouldn't have to make any changes in the Set Up Modem window. If the settings aren't correct, you'll see an error message when Investor Insight tries to make the connection. You can change this information later if necessary.

2. Click OK.

3. Click No when you're asked if you're already registered, read the subscription agreement, and click Accept if you agree to the terms.

4. Enter the requested information in the User Registration window. Investor Insight will assign you a user name; you specify a password. Store your password in a safe place.

5. Click Register Now. Investor Insight will make a call to register you (using a local number if

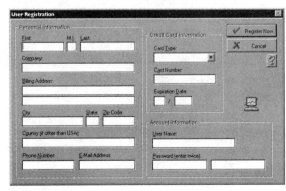

The User Registration window for Investor Insight.

Investor Insight displays this dialog box while downloading information.

possible, a toll-free number if necessary), will disconnect automatically, and will display a confirmation in your Inbox. If you have trouble making a modem connection, see Troubleshooting.

6. Click OK to confirm your registration. The Download window will appear.

The Investor Insight Download window.

7. Click on Full to download quotes and news stories for all the securities on your Watch List. Click on Quotes Only to download just the quotes. Click Custom to download news stories for selected companies. (If you pick the latter, a Custom Download window will open to let you select the securities for which you want news stories.)

8. Click on Call to begin the download. Progress gauges will let you know how long each portion of the download will last. After the data is captured, Investor Insight will automatically disconnect you. Click OK to confirm that the download is complete.

   Note: *Intuit suggests you avoid using other programs that would write to the hard drive while you're capturing data. Since just about every Windows program writes to the hard drive while it's in operation—whether or not you are explicitly saving a file—that means it's time to take a break. Since Investor Insight automatically disconnects when it's through downloading, you've got plenty of time to search the refrigerator. And if this is ruining your diet, be advised that Investor Insight also includes a timer that you can set for automatic, unattended dialing at any time.*

9. After your download is complete, a Flash Report will appear to summarize the changes since your last call.

   The first time you make an online connection, Investor Insight

Investor Insight's Flash Report.

updates daily price quotes for securities on your Watch List, plus captures related news stories from the past 90 days (up to a maximum of 50 stories). Only price information is captured for mutual funds. The Quicken CD already contains security quotes going back five years, which shortens the first online session considerably. After that, Investor Insight captures only the price information and news stories since your last online session.

You'll probably want to begin each Investor Insight session by capturing up-to-date information. Prices (high, low, and closing prices; trading volume; and splits) are available on a 15-minute delayed feed from S&P ComStock. News stories are available from Dow Jones News Service, including *Wall Street Journal* articles. Press releases are available from PR Newswire and Business Wire.

A nice bonus of Investor Insight is its integrated e-mail feature. From the Comm menu, you can select Write E-mail to enter a message for Investor Insight customer service. You can also select Get Billing Information to automatically receive the latest billing information about your account.

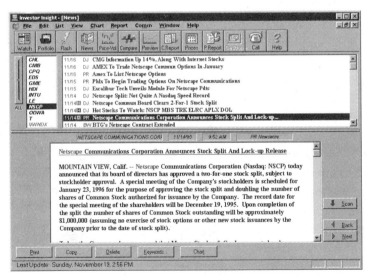

"Trendy" stock information that was just downloaded by Investor Insight.

Using Quicken Quotes

Quicken 5 for Windows is compatible with Quicken Quotes (Versions 2 and 3) with the following limitation. Quicken Quotes Version 3's Automated Download feature is no longer supported with a Quicken data file with a password. You must either remove the password on the Quicken data file or change the Automated Download setting to Save To File, then import the file into Quicken during your next Quicken session.

To bring high, low, and volume information into Quicken from Quotes, use Save As in Quotes to make a QQUOTE.CSV file, then import this file into a Portfolio View in Quicken.

To use Tradeline with Quicken 5, you need to manually install a special file that has been created to let the two applications work together. It is located on the Quicken Deluxe CD in the \support\qrpc folder (subdirectory). Copy this file, QRPC.DLL, to the folder where you previously installed Tradeline.

Other Information Available Online

If you are curious about investments, but don't really feel it's worth your time and money to subscribe to one of Intuit's services, you may want to investigate the securities information that's available via the major online services. This may interest you particularly if you have invested in only one "pet stock" and just want to see how it's doing day by day.

In Chapter 15, we discuss the Internet in the context of Intuit's own Web page—and the Netscape Web browser that was included with your copy of Quicken. More established alternatives include the major online services such as Delphi, Interchange, Microsoft Network (as this book went to press, it now has about 800,000 subscribers), and more. Unquestionably, the "Big Three" in the online industry are:

- CompuServe
- Prodigy
- America Online

I'm not going to recommend a particular online service, since their content changes all the time. My columns currently appear on Prodigy, so I can't pretend to be impartial in any case. The important thing to remember is that you don't have to pay anything to try an online service. Most offer free startup kits (odds are that one fell into your lap the last time you picked up a computer magazine) and free 30-day trial periods. Your best bet is to take them all up on the offer, try each service for a month, and then decide which one(s) best meet your needs.

CompuServe

A few years back, CompuServe used to be accessible only through a stark terminal interface. Strictly speaking, it still can be used that way, but if you have a startup kit, you'll be using the Windows interface, WinCIM.

The list of financial services available via CompuServe would take up pages: It's probably more comprehensive than a similar list for any other online service. You can find some of CompuServe's financial services by clicking on the Basic Services button in WinCIM's main window.

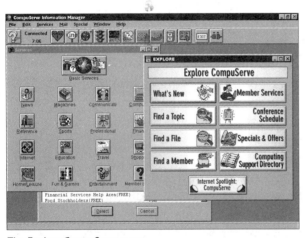

The Explore CompuServe menu.

dow. WinCIM will log on to CompuServe using your previously defined account settings, then show you the Explore CompuServe menu.

Click on the Find a Topic button and you can search via keywords such as "stocks." You'll then see a scrolling list of "forums" related to your topic. "FREE" next to their names indicates that you will pay nothing to access them. The others will be billed at your standard rate for connect time (usually $2.95 per hour), except for the ones with dollar signs by them, which are premium services that carry additional surcharges. You can go directly to any of these forums by pressing Ctrl-G and then typing in the name.

Relatively few of the financially related forums are free of connect time. (Yes, it takes money to make money.) However, some of them are a bargain, especially if you're using the free connect hours that CompuServe gives you every month.

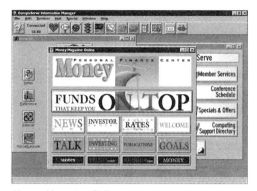

Money Magazine Online.

One very interesting area is Money Magazine Online, accessible by clicking the Finances button in WinCIM's main window. Among other things, Money Magazine Online gives you access to an easy-to-use, fast stock-quote service. You can look up your stocks via ticker symbol, retrieve their values, and export the data to Quicken.

Money magazine's Fund Watch Online allows you to search quickly through more than 1,500 funds that are consistent with your goals and investment philosophy. You can also use this service to obtain a report on any fund by entering its ticker symbol. The database, which is updated monthly, is very comprehensive and easy to use.

Dun's Market Identifiers—a premium forum—is another CompuServe feature. It offers directory information on more than 7.8 million public and private U.S. establishments. Information includes the name, address, and telephone number, as well as company characteristics such as sales figures,

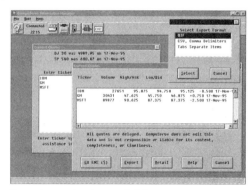

Exporting stock values to Quicken.

number of employees, net worth, date and state of incorporation, corporate family relationships, and chief executive's name. Records can be retrieved by company name, geographic location, product, or service.

Prodigy

Prodigy also has a number of areas to interest the investor, with the advantage that any area that comes with your basic subscription at no extra cost is clearly labeled "free" in the lower right corner of the screen. Prodigy's opening menu makes it easy to access the service's Business and Finance area.

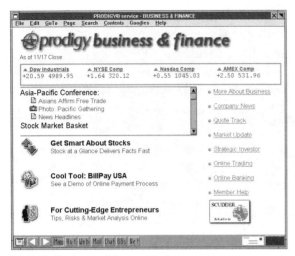

Prodigy's Business and Finance window.

One of the most useful areas for Quicken users is the Tradeline Performance History, which allows you to download price history files in a form that can be imported into Quicken. The process can be a bit cumbersome, but the results are gratifying.

You can access the area anywhere on Prodigy by typing Ctrl-J and then entering the "jump" word Tradeline. Select Download and then enter in a ticker symbol. Prodigy will ask if you want one-year-daily, one-year-weekly, or specific dates. In most situations, one-year-weekly should do the trick. Make your selection. Then, on the next screen, Prodigy will ask what form you want the data in. Click on Quicken and then let the service download the data to the folder of your choice. Afterwards, load Quicken and select Portfolio View from the Activities menu. Then select Import Prices from the File menu and enter the file name you saved the data to while you were in Prodigy.

Prodigy's Strategic Investor area is an extra-cost service that provides detailed information on thousands of mutual funds and individual companies. It also has charts and the opinions of analysts and

Prodigy's Quote Track window.

Prodigy's Tradeline window.

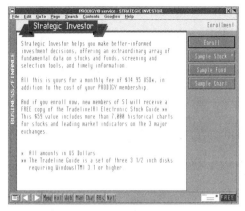

Prodigy's Strategic Investor window.

newsletter writers, making it more or less one-stop shopping for all your financial information needs.

You can get to Strategic Investor from anywhere in Prodigy by typing Ctrl-J and then keying in Strategic Investor to the jump word box. Once there, you can select Company Reports for details on any public company, Stock Hunter to help you select stocks based on some professional research models, and—my favorite—Fund Reports for information on mutual funds.

America Online

You enter America Online's financial area simply by clicking on the Personal Finance button on the main menu. There, you'll find Morningstar Mutual Funds, which, like the service available through Quicken itself, provides data on thousands of funds. You'll also find a number of other useful research tools, including Hoover's Company Profiles; the latest issue of Business Week magazine; and Top Advisors' Corner, where you'll get samples of advice from some of the country's best-known financial gurus.

With America Online's Quotes and Portfolio system, you can track prices and yields of stocks and funds listed on the NYSE, AMEX, and NASDAQ exchanges (with a 15-to-20-minute delay), maintain an updated portfolio, and more.

The main window for America Online's financial area.

America Online's Financial Newsstand.

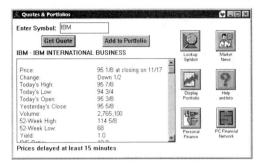

America Online's Quotes and Portfolios window.

If you know the stock or fund symbol for the company you're interested in, you can select Get Quote to receive a delayed quote for that stock or fund. If you would like to add this stock or fund to your portfolio, select Add to Portfolio.

Once you have added various stocks and funds to your portfolio, you can check on their progress by selecting Display Portfolio. You will see the total current value of your portfolio, delayed by about 15 minutes. If you would like detailed information on one of the stocks in your portfolio, highlight it and then select Details. You may also delete stocks in your portfolio by selecting Remove. An America Online portfolio can handle up to 100 stocks and funds.

You can save an America Online stock portfolio to disk. When you select the Save Portfolio option from the portfolio screen, the Quotes and Portfolios system saves an ASCII copy of your portfolio. This copy can then be printed out, or it can be used in Quicken, with some massaging.

Hoover's Company Profiles section is just one of the tools within America Online's Financial Research window.

Summary

Even without the Mutual Fund Finder or Investor Insight features that come with the Deluxe version, Quicken offers an overwhelming number of possibilities for tracking your investments. The Portfolio Price Update service is easy to use and extremely effective. If you choose not to register with Intuit's new online options, however, you can continue to use Quicken as you have in the past—with the Quicken Quotes software, perhaps, or in conjunction with quotes via one of the major online services.

Online Banking

LOOKS EASY ENOUGH FOR A 40-YEAR-OLD.

AL-MOST

1ST DIGITAL BANK

15

When applied to previous versions of Quicken, the term "online banking" meant just one thing: a few brave, pioneering souls using their modems to order up payments via CheckFree. With Quicken 5 and Quicken Deluxe 5 for Windows, online banking takes many different forms.

Using Intuit's online services and a modem, you can now:
- reconcile your bank account online
- pay your bills electronically
- get mutual fund information
- find out the current prices of stocks in your portfolio
- trade e-mail with your bank
- download the latest updates to the Quicken program
- cruise Intuit's Web pages
- order blank checks and other supplies

With Quicken, there is no single online link that does everything. This surprises some people who expect Intuit to let customers use its Internet site—the "Quicken Financial Network"—to handle financial transactions. Intuit instead built a private network for online banking that is completely separate from the Internet. When you use Quicken to pay bills and access your bank accounts, all your information is transmitted over that private network, secured by state-of-the-art encryption technology.

Quicken's Online Services

Service	For More Information
Online banking	See "Setting Up" in this chapter.
Online bill payment	See "Online Bill Payment" in this chapter.
Investor Insight	See Chapter 14, "Investment Tracking and Projection."
Portfolio Price Update	See Chapter 14, "Investment Tracking and Projection."
Quicken Financial Network	See "Quicken Financial Network" in this chapter.
Intuit Marketplace	See Chapter 16, "Protecting Your Work and Getting Help."

The sidebar "Quicken's Online Services" lists all the functions Quicken can perform via modem and tells you where you'll find more information. For a different kind of overview regarding this topic, you can take Quicken's own QuickTour. From the Help menu, select QuickTours, then click on the Using Quicken with a Modem button.

Setting Up

Before you can start banking online with Quicken, you must first have a properly set up modem connected to your computer. Next, you need to establish an "Intuit Membership," a master account that creates an online relationship between you and Intuit. (The Intuit Membership is exclusive of any bank fees and does not cost anything to set up.)

Of course, you also need to contact your financial institution to activate online banking features for your bank account(s). A partial list of participating banks appears in the Quicken user manual; for a more up-to-date listing, you can call Intuit's online banking hotline at 800-224-1047 or visit Intuit's World Wide Web site at **http://www.intuit.com/int-fin-parts/**. If all goes well, getting your present account converted to online access will take a week or two, after which time you'll receive a routing number and a personal identification number (PIN).

It's possible, however, that your bank or credit union does not plan to offer online banking. In that case, you'll have to decide whether or not to switch. In their efforts to attract Quicken customers, some banks are offering online banking for free, even providing blandishments such as $50 rebates or free checking. In other words, if you're open to changing banks, it's a buyer's market.

You may, however, have some very good reasons not to change banks: the general hassle factor, a good working relationship with your current bank's staff, your bank's convenient location, and so on. Or, you may be a credit union member, with the option of below-market interest rates on car loans, and other benefits.

If you do not want to switch banks and your bank has no plans to introduce online banking, you can still pay your bills electronically. Do this by signing up with Intuit Services Corporation (708-585-8500). The cost of the service is competitive with the banks' (at least after their introductory offers expire) and, in any case, compares favorably with the cost of a stamp and an envelope.

Setting Up Your Modem

If you recently installed Windows 95, you've probably set up your modem once or twice already and are mightily sick of it. Never mind. Quicken does need you to set up your modem *again* for online banking—and also when you sign up for Investor Insight or the Quicken Financial Network—but the process is very automatic.

To set up your modem:

1. If you have an external modem, make sure it is turned on.

2. From Quicken's Online menu, choose Set Up Modem.

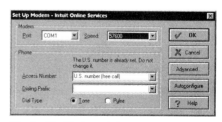

The Set Up Modem window.

3. Quicken will configure your modem automatically and display a dialog box. If for some reason Quicken is unable to configure your modem—or if you have configured your modem previously within Quicken—the Set Up Modem window will appear so that you can make changes manually.

You should not need to make changes to the Port or Speed entries in the Set Up Modem window. The Access Number for U.S. calls, represented by the text "U.S. number (free call)" is already set in the software.

Do not change this. In the Dialing Prefix box, you can use the drop-down list to enter a prefix such as "9," if that's needed to access an outside line. You can also enter "*70" to prevent interruptions that might otherwise be caused by call-waiting services.

If you change any of the automatic modem settings and then wish to restore them, you can do so with Autoconfigure, which will run the automatic modem setup again. (Use Autoconfigure if you install a new modem, too.) To run Autoconfigure, choose Set Up Modem from the Online menu, then click on the Autoconfigure button.

Quicken displays this message when your modem has been configured.

Creating an Intuit Membership

To use any online services with Quicken, you need to create an "Intuit Membership." This sets up a relationship between you and Intuit that costs you nothing, yet ensures that you can keep using Quicken for online banking even if you switch banks in the future.

To set up an Intuit Membership:

1. From the Online menu, select Intuit Membership and then choose Set Up (if this menu choice is grayed out, someone has already set up a membership for this copy of Quicken).

The Intuit Membership Setup window.

2. Click on the Set Up New Membership button in the dialog box that will appear.

3. The Intuit Membership Setup window will appear. Enter your name, address, and phone number, and then click on OK.

4. Set your Intuit Membership password. Be sure to write it down, in case you forget it later.

5. Click on Connect.

The Set Intuit Membership Password window.

Quicken will now dial Intuit, establish an online connection, and set up your Intuit Membership.

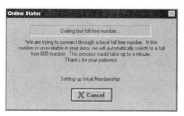

Quicken displays this message when going online for the first time.

Once your membership is set up, Quicken will end the online session and display a confirmation message with your new Intuit Membership number. You may need to provide this number if you call Intuit for technical support. You don't need to write the number down, however, because you can always view it later (from the Online menu, select Intuit Membership, and then choose View Detail).

Confirmation that your Quicken membership has been set up.

Storing Your Password

Online banking, online bill payment, and Portfolio Price Update all require the Intuit Membership password for access. However, you can store the password so that you don't have to enter it again.

To store your password:

1. From the Online Menu, select Membership Password and then choose Store.

2. The Store Password for Online Service dialog box will appear. Place a check mark by the service or services for which you want to store your password, and then click OK.

3. Enter your password to confirm the choice, and then click OK again.

Quicken does *not* let you store the personal identification number (PIN) supplied by your bank, which is required for online banking and online bill payment. Obviously, this is a prudent precaution: You should treat this PIN with the same caution you'd treat the one for your ATM card or other financial instrument.

The Store Password for Online Service dialog box.

Note: *If you wish to change your Intuit Membership Password or the name and address Intuit has on file for you, you can do so via the Online*

The Change Intuit Membership Password dialog box.

menu. Select *Intuit Membership* or *Membership Password* and then choose *Change*. New name and address information will be sent to Intuit only. If you want to let your bank, credit card company, or other institution know about you new name or address, you must contact them directly.

Going Online for the First Time

Assuming you've already contacted your financial institution to set up an online account, you'll need to watch your mail for two items. Your bank will send you an 8.5-by-11-inch packet containing the "routing number" you'll need, plus an "Intuit Online Services Guide" produced especially for Quicken users. Under separate cover, you'll also receive the all-important personal identification number (PIN), which you'll need to access your account.

Turning on Online Banking

When you have received your routing number and your PIN, the first thing you need to do is to turn on online banking within Quicken.

To set up a new Quicken account with online banking:

1. From the Lists menu, choose Account.

2. In the Account List window that appears, click on New.

3. Select an account type from the Create New Account dialog box.

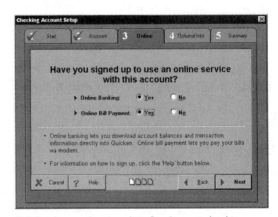

Tell Quicken you've signed up for electronic banking.

4. Work through the Easy-Step dialog boxes, which help you set up a new account (see Chapter 4).

5. Choose Yes in the window that asks if you have signed up for electronic banking.

6. Enter your account information. You can select the bank from the Financial Institution drop-down menu, and enter the routing number in the Routing Number field. On the next screen, enter the Account Number and Account Type. Finally, enter your Social Security number.

Enter information supplied by your financial institution on this screen ...

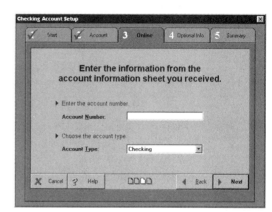

... and this one.

Yet another of life's opportunities to enter your Social Security number.

Making the First Call

Now that you've entered all the background information, going online is simple:

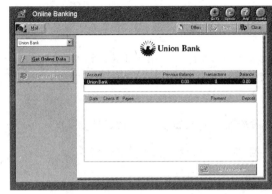

This window lets you select which online account to call.

1. From the Online menu, choose Online Banking.

2. If you have an online account at more than one financial institution, choose the institution you wish to contact. Quicken will retrieve data for all the accounts (checking, savings, etc.) at that particular institution.

3. Click on the Get online data button and then enter your PIN. If this is the first time you have called the financial institution, Quicken will ask for the PIN that was sent to you, then request that you change it.

Quicken makes you change the default PIN before proceeding.

4. Quicken will now go online to retrieve your account information and will inform you of its progress. When it is finished, review the Transmission Summary window if it appears, and then click on Close.

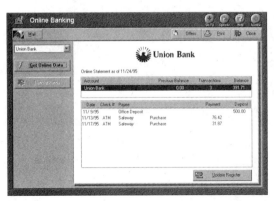

The Online Banking window displays your recent transactions.

5. In the Online Banking window, select an account from the list to see the transactions for that account. (If you have only one account with the institution, that account will appear by default.) The list will show the current balance and the transactions that have occurred since the last time you retrieved data.

Updating Your Register

When you choose to update your register, Quicken will take the new transactions from this online statement and enter them into your Quicken register. Then, it will mark all the items as cleared, meaning they've been posted at your financial institution.

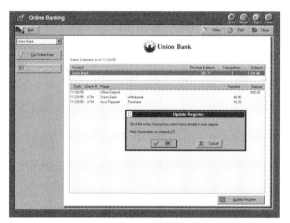

If you've been diligent, your Quicken register will match the online statement.

To update your register, select an account from the Online Banking window and click on the Update Register button. Quicken will compare the online statement data to the information already in your register. If there are no new transactions—meaning that you already have entered them in your register manually, paragon of virtue that you are—Quicken will automatically mark these as cleared in your register. If Quicken finds new transactions, or transactions it cannot match up (perhaps because you entered the payee information differently) it will display the Update Register window. This will let you edit payee information or delete a duplicate transaction before the register is updated.

Note: *One example of a duplicate transaction can arise during your first session. You probably entered your new account's starting balance as the amount of money you deposited in the bank. The online statement, however, sometimes considers the "starting balance" to be 0, treating your initial deposit of funds as a subsequent transaction. The difference in nomenclature calls for some minor manual editing.*

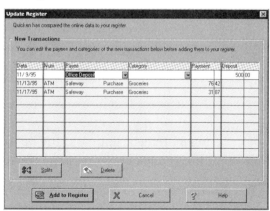

Usually it doesn't, though, and you will see this Update Register window.

Reconciling Your Account

As I hope the above section has made clear, when you use online banking with Quicken, you are not updating your register directly. (However, the converse *is* true, as we shall see: When you pay bills in your Quicken register and enter Send in the Num field, you're setting up an automatic electronic transaction.) You are merely receiving a bank statement electronically instead of on paper: You still need to make your register match the statement.

Since online banking is merely a way of receiving a convenient, up-to-date statement, you have to make a decision. You can either:

- update your register throughout the month with the aid of online banking, then reconcile to your bank's paper statement
  – or –
- reconcile throughout the month to your online balance

Why can't you do both? Because Quicken presents your statement's opening balance based on the balance to which you last reconciled. If you reconcile to your online balance during the month, then the Quicken opening balance will always disagree with the opening balance on the paper statement. In addition, if you reconciled during the month, Quicken will have removed all the reconciled transactions from the Reconcile window. Therefore all these transactions will appear to be totally missing when you try to reconcile to your paper statement.

To choose which way to reconcile:

1. From the Activities menu, choose Reconcile.

2. Choose a balance to reconcile to, either Paper Statement or Online Balance. If you choose Paper Statement, you will need to enter the ending statement date and the balances. If you choose Online Banking, simply click on OK to begin reconciling.

Sending Mail

Do you have questions about bank charges or other financial information? Instead of wading through your bank's voice mail system, you can use Quicken's integral e-mail system to send inquiries to your bank.

To send mail:

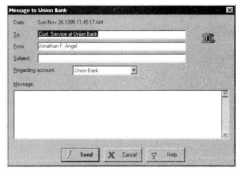

This window lets you send messages to your bank's customer service department.

1. Choose Online Banking from the Online menu.

2. The Online Banking window will appear. Click on Mail.

3. Click on the Create button at the bottom of the window.

4. Enter your name, a subject, and a message, and then click on Send.

The message will be sent automatically to the customer service department at your bank. While sending the message, Quicken will also take the time to check for any new financial data.

Any time you connect to Intuit for online banking or bill payment, Quicken will check for mail addressed to you. If you have mail, Quicken will notify you in the Transmission Summary window.

Note: *If you think your account data contains an error, you should contact your financial institution directly using the instructions that appear on the back of your paper statements. Similarly, for an urgent matter such as loss or theft of an ATM card or credit card, you should contact your bank by telephone. The Quicken e-mail service is not intended for these urgent matters, but rather for questions specifically about the online banking process.*

Online Bill Payment

While getting bank statements whenever you want them is pretty spiffy, the best thing about online banking is online bill payment. It makes paying bills as close to painless as it will ever be. By entering a payment in your Quicken register just as you would if you'd written a check, you can instruct your bank to make a payment to anyone you wish. No more stuffing and licking envelopes, hunting for stamps, or driving to the post office.

I think of "online banking" and "online bill payment" as synonymous, but the Quicken manuals and menu structure make a distinction between the two because if your financial institution doesn't offer online banking, you can still use an online bill payment service. You can enroll in the online bill payment service offered by Intuit Services Corporation, whose phone number was mentioned above in "Setting Up" on page 250.

Turning on Online Bill Payment

Because of this distinction between online banking and online bill payment, you need to take an extra step to set up both of them.

To turn on online bill payment for an existing account:

1. Choose Account from the Lists menu.

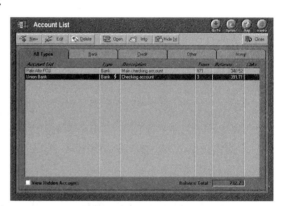

2. From the Account List, select the account from which you want to pay bills, and then click on the Edit button.

To enable online bill payment, select the account from which you want to pay bills.

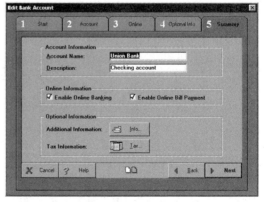

3. Click on the Enable Online Bill Payment checkbox.

4. Continue through the EasyStep windows to enter the rest of the information about your new account.

You can edit account details to turn on online banking and online bill payment together or separately.

To create a new account with online bill payment:

1. From the Lists menu, choose Account.

2. In the Account List window that will appear, click on New.

3. Select an account type from the Create New Account dialog box.

4. Work through the EasyStep dialog boxes, which help you set up a new account (see Chapter 4).

5. Choose Yes in the window that asks if you have signed up for an online service, then make sure that Online Bill Payment (along with Online Banking, if applicable) is selected.

6. Enter other information about your account. Select your bank from the Financial Institution drop-down menu, and enter the routing number in the Routing Number field. On the next screen, enter the Account Number and Account Type. Finally, enter your Social Security number.

Setting Up Payees

The first time you connect to online bill payment, Quicken will download a list of possible payees for you to use. This list is specific to you and to the region where you live. It can include local utility companies, department stores, and other retailers. It also can include your credit card companies.

You have sent paper checks to some of these companies in the past. To convert them to online payees:

1. Select Online Payees from the Lists menu. The Online Payee List will appear.

2. Click on New. The Set Up Online Payee window will appear.

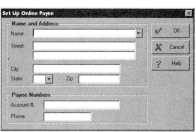

Enter online payee details in this window.

3. Enter the payee's name. If there is a matching payee already in the list, which is likely, Quicken's QuickFill feature will

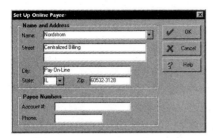

Quicken comes programmed with payees relevant to your geographic location.

fill in the complete name. As you move to the subsequent fields, QuickFill will fill in any other information that is available about the payee.

You'll notice that address information may already appear: Don't worry if you didn't put it there or if it's not the same as that shown on your bill. A completed address means that the payee has an agreement with the payment center that enables your bill to be paid sooner. Or, the address may be for reference only, with the actual payment made by electronic funds transfer (EFT).

If the payee is set up to receive EFTs, the payment center will transfer funds directly from your account to that of your payee. If the payee cannot receive EFTs—which is obviously the case today with most individuals and small businesses, though for how long—the payment center will print a check and mail it to your payee.

If the payee cannot receive electronic funds transfer, the payment center will print a check and mail it.

4. Enter the account number the payee uses to identify you. If you're sending a check to a private individual, you can leave this field blank or perhaps squeeze in a very short memo.

5. Click on OK. The new payee will now appear on your Online Payee List.

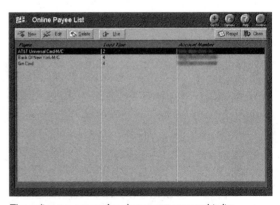

The online payees you've chosen appear on this list.

Lead Times

The Online Payee List shows the current lead time—the number of business days it takes from when you give a payment instruction to when payment is actually received—for each payee. (Quicken occasionally modifies these lead times as new payees accept EFTs.) Intuit claims that the lead time when checks have to be printed and mailed is about four days, and this seems to be true. It was certainly how long it took for me to mail checks to myself! By comparison, the lead time for EFTs is supposed to be about one or two days.

You may get a better feel for lead times as your experience with online bill payment grows. Sadly, given today's state of the art it's probably best to consider EFT as a stamp-saving convenience rather than as a magical way to keep money in your own account longer.

When you create an online payment in the register, Quicken automatically enters as the date the earliest possible day on which payment could be made. If you wish to create a delayed payment, just change that default date to any date within the next year.

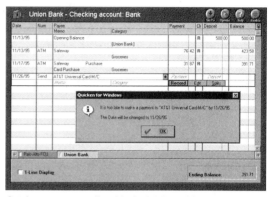

Quicken automatically adds the lead time for online bill payments.

Making Payments

Once you have entered payees in the Online Payee List, you're set to make payments more easily than ever before. To make payments from the register, just open the account for which online bill paying is active. Instead of entering a check number in the Num field, type Send.

Quicken's QuickFill feature will limit the drop-down list of payees to those on the Online Payee List. Once you have chosen one, specify the payment amount. As noted above, the date will be filled in automatically (although you can choose a different date manually). Finish entering the transaction information and then click on Record.

To make an online payment from the Write Checks window, choose Write Checks from the Activities menu. Select an account that is set up for online bill payment, and then select the Online Payment checkbox. Enter a payee. The date will be filled in automatically, as explained above. Click on Record to finish.

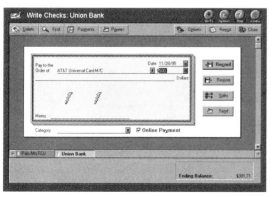

From the Write Checks window you can select the Online Payment checkbox.

Repeating Payments

Online bill payment is a good way to make payments that are the same amount each time and that take place at regular intervals. These can include your mortgage, rent, or car payments.

With repeating payments, the online bill payment center will take your instructions and generate payments for you. When you go online, it will send you check numbers for the payments it has created and make the appropriate entries in your register, saving you substantial drudgery. (All *you* have to do now is make sure you earn the money.) You may stop any single payment in the sequence or change its amount without disrupting the rest.

Payments will be made whether or not you go online to do other business, which is advantageous in that it's a "set and forget" function. However, you *should* make it a habit to go online at least every few days so that your Quicken register will be debited to show the current state of your account. You may also use Quicken's Reminders function to be notified of an impending payment in advance.

To set up a repeating payment, first make sure the payee is already on the Online Payee List. Then:

1. From the Lists menu, select Scheduled Transaction (or just press Ctrl-J).

2. The Scheduled Transaction list will appear. Click on New.

3. Click on the Online Repeating Payments radio button, then on the OK button.

4. If necessary, select the account from which to make payments from the drop-down menu, choose the payee, enter the amount, and so on. Enter the interval at which payments need to be made using the drop-down menu near the Frequency field. You can also set payments to stop automatically after a preset number of installments—ideal for a car loan.

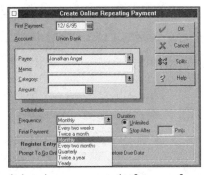

A drop-down menu sets the frequency for repeating payments.

Changing Instructions After the Fact

Once you've set up a repeating payment, you can always change the amount or the number of payments later.

To change instructions, do the following:

1. From the Lists menu, select Scheduled Transaction (or just press Ctrl-J).

2. The Scheduled Transaction list will appear. Click on the Online Repeating tab. Select the transaction you want to change, then click Edit.

3. Change the amount, duration, memo, category or splits in the Edit Online Repeating Payment window that will appear. If the repeating payment is tied to a loan, you can also click the Loan Info button to edit the loan.

4. Click OK. Then, from the Online menu, choose Online Bill Payment, and click on Send. Quicken will make a connection to Intuit to issue the instructions, then change the pending payments in your register to reflect the new conditions.

Deleting Payments

To delete a repeating payment permanently—which will both delete any pending payments that have been generated and stop creating new ones—follow these steps:

1. From the Lists menu, select Scheduled Transaction (or just press Ctrl-J).

2. The Scheduled Transaction list will appear. Click on the Online Repeating tab. Select the transaction you want to change, then click Delete.

3. Click on OK to confirm which payments you are deleting.

4. From the Online menu, choose Online Bill Payment, and click on Send. Quicken will make a connection to Intuit to issue the instructions, then change the pending payments in your register to reflect the new conditions.

Note: You can also stop a single repeating payment if you want to do so without disturbing other payments in the sequence. Select the payment in the register, then choose Stop Payment from the Edit menu. Click OK to confirm. To enact the change, choose Online Bill Payment from the Online menu and click on Send. Quicken will warn you if it is too late to stop the payment; in that case, you may still be able to halt it by calling your bank to stop the check.

For CheckFree Users

If you have been using CheckFree as your online bill payment service, you can continue to do so. You can even move back and forth between CheckFree and the Intuit online bill payment service until you have decided which to stick with. However, Intuit has made it difficult, maybe impossible, for *new* customers to enroll in CheckFree.

If you are using CheckFree and would like to try Intuit's online bill payment service, create an Intuit Membership as described earlier in this chapter. Send any outstanding CheckFree payments. Then, from the Online menu, select Online Bill Payment. Click on OK to use the Intuit system and temporarily disable CheckFree.

Note: When switching from CheckFree to Intuit's online bill payment service, remember that you'll be entering Send instead of Xmit in the Num field of the register. Also remember that you'll continue to be charged for CheckFree unless you call to cancel the service.

To switch back to CheckFree, make any outstanding online bill payments, then select CheckFree from the Activities menu. Click on OK to use CheckFree again and temporarily discontinue Intuit's online bill payment. (If you never had a CheckFree account, the choice to enable CheckFree will not appear on the Activities menu. New customers apparently *must* use the Intuit service, a development that I think is a shame because I've been using CheckFree for years and am very happy with it.)

Transferring Funds

You can use online banking to move money between two accounts at the same financial institution. Once you transfer funds in the Online Banking window, Quicken will go online to issue a transfer request to your bank; the money will usually be transferred the next business day.

To transfer funds:

1. Select Online Banking from the Online menu.

2. Select the institution where the two accounts are located and click on the Transfer Funds button. A Transfer Funds Between Accounts window will appear.

3. Select the source and target accounts using the Transfer Money From and To drop-down menus.

4. Click on Send, and Quicken will make an online connection and perform the transfer.

Note: If you do not have enough funds to cover the transfer, your financial institution will inform you. You must then adjust the records in the Quicken registers so they show the correct balances and try again later.

Transferring funds from one institution to another can be done electronically if you set up your account at the other bank as a payee. However, this could be to your disadvantage. Since the target bank would know nothing of the deposit until it actually received the funds, you would not receive the float. (In other words, if you have an existing bank account and you deposit a check via teller or ATM, your bank will usually let you withdraw some or all of the money deposited without waiting for the check to clear.)

Credit Card Accounts

Credit card accounts work the same way as other online accounts in Quicken, with several exceptions. For example, Quicken will remind you to pay your credit card bill when it is due. It will also add categories to your credit card transactions based on merchant codes (you can, of course, alter these categories manually if you wish).

To check your credit card balance and recent transactions, go online to retrieve financial information as previously described in this chapter. Then select your credit card from the account list. If the balance appears in red, you owe money on your credit card; if it appears in black, you have a credit. After you have downloaded your first monthly statement, a Payment Info button will appear that will let you view information such as the minimum payment and payment due date. To pay your credit card bill:

1. Select the credit card account from the Online Banking window.

2. Click on the Payment Info button. The Credit Card Payment Information window will appear.

3. Click on Make Payment. The Make Credit Card Payment window will appear.

4. Select an amount to pay and the account from which to pay it.
　　Note: If your credit card account is at the same bank as your checking account, you can also make a credit card payment by using the Transfer Funds Between Accounts window described above. Any transfer of funds into a credit card account is considered a payment. Don't overpay and then decide to transfer money out: Any transfer of funds out of a credit card account is considered a cash advance, liable to any fees or interest charges your credit card issuer normally charges.

The Quicken Financial Network

Quicken's World Wide Web server, confusingly known as the Quicken Financial Network—it has nothing directly to do with the network of computers that handles financial transactions for Quicken—is accessible free of charge to every Quicken user with a modem.

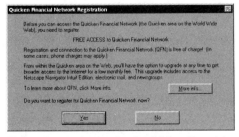

The registration window for the Quicken Financial Network.

　　To use the Quicken Financial Network:

1. Click on Quicken Financial Network from the Online menu.

2. If you have used this service before, skip to Step 6 below. Otherwise, the first time you select this option, the Quicken Financial Network

The Netscape Navigator introductory screen.

Registration window will appear. To get more information on the Quicken Financial Network or the World Wide Web, click on the More info button. To register for the Quicken Financial Network, click on Yes, then click on Accept to accept the license agreement.

3. The Netscape Navigator Intuit Edition introductory screen will appear. Click on Continue.

4. The Netscape Registration Wizard will appear. Click on User Information to enter your name, address, and phone number. Then click on Modem Setup to specify your modem, or let the Registration Wizard select it automatically.

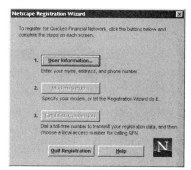

The Registration Wizard lets you connect without entering IP addresses and the like.

5. Click on Establish Connection. The Netscape Navigator Dialer will now dial a toll-free number to transmit your registration data. Then, it will ascertain the local access number you'll use for future calls.

6. Netscape Navigator will dial the local access number for you and log on to the Quicken Financial Network home page.

The Quicken Financial Network home page offers a variety of financial resources. As on any other World Wide Web page, hypertext links are indicated either by underlined text or by "hot" areas in the graphic. To select one of these, just double-click with your mouse. For example, double-clicking on the light bulb will take you to Intuit's "What's New" page. To return to the previous menu,

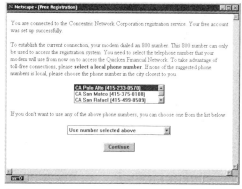

Selecting a local telephone number.

The home page of the Quicken Financial Network World Wide Web site.

either click on the Back arrow at the left of the menu bar or press Alt and the left arrow key. You can also return to the Quicken main menu by clicking on the Home button. To print any page, click on the Print button or select <u>P</u>rint from the <u>F</u>ile menu.

Intuit changes its Web pages on a regular basis to provide up-to-date information. As this book was going to press, for example, the Quicken Financial Network alerted users to a minor bug in Quicken 5 and provided "patches" for downloading.

The Quicken Financial Network uses Internet protocols to connect you to its site and resides on a standard Internet server. Therefore, you can use any other Internet account you may have (or an online service with a browser) to call up the Quicken Financial Network, by typing in the address **http://www.intuit.com**. However, if you access the Quicken pages using one of these methods, you will incur connect-time charges (if any) payable to your service provider. Access is free only via the browser supplied with Quicken.

If you have previously set up an Internet browser (perhaps Trumpet Winsock, or the Serial Line Internet Protocol software included with Windows 95), you probably found the process convoluted and difficult (that's because it is). In contrast, the procedure for connecting to the Quicken Financial Network is consummately simple—as well as free. However, it does not provide complete Internet access.

Internet Access

Your Quicken Financial Network connection lets you visit only the Quicken area on the World Wide Web. If you want to get access to the entire World Wide Web—including electronic mail, newsgroups, and more—you will need to upgrade to a full Internet account. To make this process easy and relatively inexpensive, Intuit has partnered with the Internet service provider Concentric Network Corporation (CNC) to offer full Internet accounts.

Concentric's Starter Plan costs $1.95 a month and offers one free hour of connect time. Each subsequent hour costs an additional $1.95. Concentric's Frequent User Plan costs $9.95 per month, with seven free hours of connect time (each additional hour costs $1.95). The Frequent User Plan also provides access to 5MB of online storage for your own Web pages. These were the prices at press time but prices are always subject to change, especially in this competitive area.

To activate one of these plans, click on the Upgrade icon in the Netscape Navigator Intuit edition browser. The Concentric service will

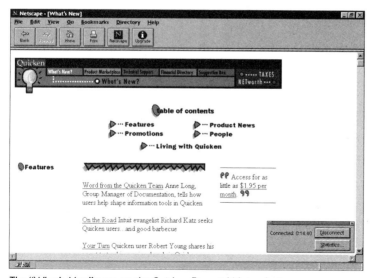

The "What's New" page on the Quicken Financial Network site.

help you download any additional software necessary (such as Eudora Light, for which there isn't room on floppy-disk editions of Quicken), unlock access to the full World Wide Web, and assign you a user ID for sending and receiving e-mail.

Should you choose Concentric for Internet access just because you're a Quicken customer? Maybe. The company's rates are competitive and, as we've seen, the ease of setup is unparalleled. On the other hand, you may already belong to an online service that provides all the access you need, or you may plan more intensive use. (Some Internet service providers permit unlimited Web use for a monthly flat fee.) Check around before settling on Concentric. Other Internet service providers that offer national service include Netcom (800-353-6600), PSI (800-827-7482), and CompuServe (800-848-8199).

Summary

You'd never believe it from all the media hype about going online, but some computer users still don't have modems. If you're one of them and you use Quicken seriously, it looks as though you're going to have to join the crowd and get a modem. Quicken's online features can sometimes be confusing (because of the different ways you must dial in), but all in all, they are comprehensive and enjoyable to use.

Protecting Your Work/ Getting Help

16

RITA WAS HAVING ONE OF THOSE BAD MONEY DAYS.

If you use Quicken regularly, it's probably going to become one of the most important software products you own. Your Quicken data files, which you've compiled just by spending a few minutes here and there entering information in the register, now represent hours of work. It would probably take you days, if not weeks, to replace them.

Unfortunately, being binary devices, computers don't work in the slow, painstaking way you do. They prefer to work with 1s and 0s—*all* or *nothing.* Given the wrong set of circumstances—a disk failure, a virus that scrambles your file allocation table, pressing the delete key at the wrong time—all your financial data could easily disappear.

The good news is that if you take the right precautions, you don't have to worry about this. Remember when you tried to make a copy of that valuable audiotape or old LP? Even if you were careful, it was never the same as the original: Tape hiss, wow, and flutter meant you were bound to lose information somewhere along the line. But digital information storage means that when you make copies of your Quicken data, you won't miss so much as a decimal point.

Backing up your data is always going to be the high-tech equivalent of flossing. Quicken makes it so simple and pleasant that you've at least got your choice of mint or cinnamon flavor.

Protecting Windows

Remember when you could store the system files necessary to start up a computer, in addition to a software program and some data, on a single floppy disk? Then you really *do* need to floss every day, if not stock up on Grecian Formula (sorry!).

Most of us don't miss the days of yore all that much. Simple software often meant software that was also simpleminded or hard to use. But underneath the pretty face of today's Windows computer lies DOS (yes, even if you're running Windows 95), plus dozens of program modules and configuration files. (It's said that just loading the Windows desktop requires your computer to execute more than 15 million instructions.) If Windows is partially erased or mangled, it might refuse to load; and if you have to reinstall Windows to make your system run, you might lose some settings you previously customized.

Since Windows is the "platform" for Quicken, the first thing you need to do to make sure you can always run Quicken is to make sure you can always run Windows. I hate to sound like a cheerleader for the tape drive industry, but with the size of today's hard drives and program files, a tape backup is really your only way to do this. You should back up your entire hard disk to tape, paying most particular attention to the Windows subdirectories. As suggested above, these contain information customized to your particular system that may *not* be restored if you have to reinstall Windows from floppies or a CD-ROM.

Although most cars today come with air bags, few computers come with tape drives. Fortunately, you can purchase a tape drive that holds about 800MB per cartridge for around $150. Simple to install, it connects either to one of your computer's floppy disk data cables or directly to the IDE hard disk controller. (SCSI tape drives are also available; they can transfer data faster, though setup is almost always more complicated.) If you are loath to open up your computer, or if you have a portable computer with no room for a tape drive, you should purchase a tape drive that connects to the machine's parallel printer port to transfer data.

Tape backup software lets you make two different types of backup. A *full* backup stores everything on your hard disk. An *incremental* backup stores everything that has been changed since the last full backup. If you combine a full backup every week or so with an incremental backup at the end of each day, you'll always be able to reconstruct the contents of your hard drive. While I haven't yet (touch wood) had a hard drive fail on me, there have been many times when I deleted something on purpose or by accident and was glad that I could retrieve a copy of it from my tape.

Since Windows is the "platform" for Quicken, the first thing you need to do to make sure you can always run Quicken is to make sure you can always run Windows.

MIS professionals use even more arcane backup strategies, designed to protect against the failure of any individual tape cartridge. They also use offsite backup, which is something you can do yourself: Send your tapes to a friend or relative who lives in another area, and you can be sure that the fire, flood, or earthquake that destroys your computer won't zap your backup too.

If you are using Windows 3.1, you can use either DOS tape backup software or Windows tape backup software. Indeed, the DOS backup software may be the best way to go, since it doesn't require that you have Windows up and working in order to restore files. Some software vendors give you the best of both worlds, offering a Windows program you can use to backup files, and a compatible DOS program you can use to restore the files if necessary.

Windows 95 has presented particular problems for both users and authors of backup software. Because of the system's long file names feature—and because it stores many essential settings in the "registry," a special type of file—it isn't possible to back up Windows 95 successfully from the DOS command line. (Strictly speaking, there are ways to back up the long file name information and then save most of the data you need—but they're so complicated you don't want to know about them.) Instead, you need a backup program that has been written especially for Windows 95.

Incredibly, when Windows 95 first came out, the only compatible backup program was one supplied by Microsoft—which didn't support any of the popular 800MB Travan-type tape drives. This problem has been solved. If you purchased a tape drive recently, it probably came with a compatible program. If you have an older tape drive from a company such as Iomega or Conner, you'll find Windows 95-specific software upgrades free on online services or the World Wide Web.

In the (happily unlikely) event that your hard drive fails totally, you will need to reinstall Windows 95 from the floppies or CD-ROM, reinstall the backup software, and *then* retrieve data from your tape drive. It won't be fun, but it sure beats the alternative.

Viruses

Computer viruses are still an emotional subject. Some people claim the topic is overblown, while others refuse to work on a computer that isn't completely protected by memory-resident antiviral software.

I wouldn't say that I've encountered a deluge of viruses in my years of working with personal computers, but I have come across them often enough that I think you will, too. It used to be said that "you'll never get a virus if you don't download software from bulletin boards," but this is patronizing and incorrect. My computers have contracted viruses from promiscuous floppy disk shuffling, but also (on occasion) from shrink-wrapped disks direct from the manufacturer.

Undoubtedly, you should scan your computer regularly for viruses using whatever antiviral software you may have. A good time to scan is, in fact, right before you do a backup. Otherwise, you risk backing the virus up on tape and unwittingly restoring it later.

Antiviral programs exist that scan files each time you stick in a new floppy or decompress a file you've downloaded. I don't use one of these—for me, faster speed is worth the small amount of safety I'm trading away—but I do use a program that checks my computer's memory and hard disk boot sector for viruses every time I start up my machine. (Boot sector viruses are some of the most common and insidious, spreading themselves from machine to machine every time a disk is accessed.)

You should update your antiviral software regularly so it is aware of the latest viruses. You don't need to pay much to do this, since the companies in the industry (such as Symantec, McAfee, and S&S International) distribute their updates via online services. McAfee, a long-time leader in the field, distributes fully functional evaluation copies of its products via its bulletin board and via the World Wide Web.

Saving Quicken Data

Once you've made sure that your Windows platform is secure, you're ready to worry about saving Quicken data specifically. Fortunately, Quicken is a true pussycat in this regard. Unlike many Windows programs, it can be quickly reinstalled from its floppies or CD-ROM without losing extensive customization.

Better still, the data files Quicken creates—your financial information—are compact enough to fit on a single floppy (when's the last time you heard that?). I found that even the sample data files supplied with Quicken, bloated to show all possible program features, took up only about half of a standard 1.44MB diskette.

You may have already discovered that Quicken thoughtfully prompts you to make a backup after every few uses. By making a choice from the dialog box that appears, you can have Quicken copy all data files to a different subdirectory on your hard drive or to a floppy disk. This automatic backup may be all the Quicken-specific data protection you need. However, I'll explain below how to call up Quicken's data protection features manually.

File Management

Unlike a word processor or spreadsheet, Quicken does not keep all the data you enter in a single disk file. Instead, it keeps the data in six or seven different files, all of whose names begin the same but end with a different extension (the three letters after the period). This fact led Intuit to build in file management functions that have, in Quicken 5, become quite comprehensive.

You access Quicken file management functions, logically enough, from the File menu.

To copy a Quicken file:

1. Select File Operations from the File menu. Then select Copy from the submenu that will appear.

2. Enter a name (limited to eight characters) for the new Quicken file. Then enter a Location (drive and subdirectory), and click OK.

To copy just part of a file:

1. Select File Operations from the File menu. Then select Copy from the submenu that will appear.

2. Enter a name (limited to eight characters) for the new Quicken file. Then enter a Location (drive and subdirectory).

3. Use the From and To drop-down calendars to select a date range, and clear one or both of the "Prior Transactions" checkboxes. Click OK.

You can also delete a file permanently. To delete a file:

1. Select File Operations from the File menu. Then select Delete from the submenu that will appear.

2. Select the name of the main Quicken file (ending in .QDB) you want to delete. Remember, Quicken will delete not only the .QDB file but also all the other files beginning with the same prefix. Include the directory path if the file is not in the directory where you installed Quicken. To display the files in a particular directory, double-click the directory name in the Directories list. To select a particular file, click its name in the list under the File Name box.

The Deleting File window.

3. Click OK. The Deleting File window will appear.

4. To cancel the delete, click Cancel. To confirm that you want to delete the file, type Yes in the box, and then click OK.

To rename a file:

1. Select File Operations from the File menu. Then select Rename from the submenu that will appear. The Rename Quicken File window will appear.

The Rename Quicken File window.

2. Double-click a directory name in the Directories list to display the files in a particular directory. Click the file's name in the list under the File Name box. If you already know the name and location of the file, you can type the path and file name in directly.

3. Enter the new name in the box at right under New Name for Quicken File. The new name must be eight characters or fewer. Do not include a file name extension.

4. Click OK.

The Validate Quicken File function can check the integrity of your data and rebuild your data file, if necessary. This can be worth a try if you're experiencing problems with your Quicken data.

To validate a file:

1. Select File Operations from the File menu. Then select Validate from the submenu that will appear. The Validate Quicken File window will appear.

2. Double-click a directory name in the Directories list to display the files in a particular directory. Click the file's name in the list under the File Name box. If you already know the name and location of the file, you can type the path and file name in directly.

3. A bar graph will appear while Quicken checks your file for errors and, if necessary, repairs them.

Year-End Copy

Below the File Operations choice in the File menu, you will see an option for Year-End Copy. This is where you save an archive file containing last year's transactions, or create a new file with last year's transactions removed.

Many people like to "close out accounts" before continuing to the new year, and some accounting packages require it. It means you save all the information about completed transactions from the previous year in an archive file, and continue to the new year with only those transactions that are still not cleared.

Quicken does not require you to close out an account at the end of the year, or at the close of any fiscal period. In fact, if you do close out a Quicken file, you give up easy access to reports spanning several years. If you still want to close out a file, however, Quicken offers two options, depending on how you want to organize your historical files: Archive and Start New Year.

Archiving a Quicken file after the end of the year saves a copy of earlier records for safekeeping. However, it also leaves last year's transactions in your current file, so your reports can include them.

To archive a Quicken file:

1. From the File menu, choose Year-End Copy.

2. Click on Archive, and then click OK.

3. If desired, change the Quicken-generated file name for the archive file.

4. If you want the archive file to be in a different directory than the directory where you installed Quicken, change the directory path shown in the window.

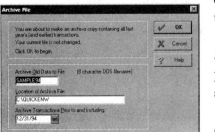

The Archive File window.

5. If you want to archive transactions from only part of last year, change the Prior to date shown in the window.

6. Click OK. Quicken will create the archive file and copy the historical transactions to it.

When it finishes, Quicken will ask you which file you would like to use: the current file or the archive file.

Note: *You should never need to make changes to the archived file. To ensure that changes are not made inadvertently, you can set either a file or transaction password for the file.*

Your other option is to start a new file, which will contain only the new year's transactions, all uncleared transactions, and all investment transactions. The Start New Year option saves a copy of your current file and then deletes any transactions in the current file that are not for the current year.

To create a new file:

1. From the File menu, choose Year-End Copy.

2. Click on Start New Year, and then click OK. The Start New Year window will open.

3. Enter a new file name in the Copy All Transactions to File field. If you want your current file moved to another subdirectory, enter that subdirectory in the Move Current File to field. By default, the cutoff date before which transactions will be deleted is January 1 of the current year. If you want to change this, use the drop-down calendar in the Delete Transactions From Current File Older Than field.

The Start New Year window.

Note: *This procedure will work properly only if you reconcile your accounts faithfully. If Start New Year didn't work as you expected, it could be because you haven't reconciled your previous year's transactions. Since Quicken made a complete copy of your data file, load that file, reconcile your accounts, and then create another new file.*

4. Click on OK. Quicken will create the new file and then ask whether you want to use the new or the old file.

Setting Up a Password

You can apply a password to control access to any Quicken data file. This is a good idea especially if you have a portable computer: It would be bad enough if someone stole your portable, but horrible if they then gained access to your financial information.

To apply a password to a data file, make it the current file, then select Passwords from the File menu. Select File from the submenu that will appear, and you will see a box with two blanks in it. Enter your desired password in the first blank, then confirm it by entering it again in the second blank. Click OK and your password is set.

To remove or change a password, use the same procedure as above. A box with three blanks (instead of two) will appear. You must type the current password in the top blank to enable any changes. Then type the new password you want in the second two boxes, or leave them both blank if you want to remove password protection.

You can also apply a transaction password to any file. To do this, make the file the current file, then select Passwords from the File menu. Select Transaction from the submenu that will appear. As above, you will see a box with two blanks in it for entering and confirming a password. However, this window will also contain a drop-down calendar, which lets you select a date before which transactions will become read-only. In other words, the password will be requested before changes can be made to any transaction dated on or before this date. You might want to apply this type of password to protect the data from the first half of a year from accidental changes later in the year—even if you're sure you're the only person who will ever be opening the file.

Backing up a File

While it's true that the archiving operations outlined previously in this chapter back up all or part of a Quicken data file, the program also has built-in file backup abilities. To back up a file, select Backup from the File menu or press Ctrl-B. You will see the same menu that occasionally appears at the end of a Quicken session.

The Select Backup Drive window.

You can either back up the Current File or Select from a List of your Quicken data files. Select a drive by using the drop-down menu in the Backup Drive field. You can back up to a floppy by inserting a formatted diskette in drive A and hitting enter. Or you can back up to another subdirectory on your hard drive by selecting drive C. Quicken will then prompt you for a target subdirectory.

Note: Even if you don't store tape backups for your computer offsite, why not back up your Quicken data files to a floppy and store them somewhere else? You might be glad you did.

Restoring a File

Restoring a file is simply the reverse of the above. To restore a file, select Restore from the File menu, then double-click a directory name in the Directories list to display the files in a particular directory. Click the file's name in the list under the File Name box. If you already know the name and location of the file, you can type the path and file name directly into the File Name box. Then click OK and you're done.

Changing Backup Settings

There's no mystery as to when Quicken will prompt you to make a backup. It simply counts the number of times you've used the program and then prompts you every third time. If you want to be prompted more or less often, you can change this setting manually. To do so:

1. Quit Quicken.

2. In Windows 3.1, start the Windows Notepad by double-clicking its icon in the Program Manager. In Windows 95, start the Notepad applet by clicking Start on the taskbar and choosing Programs from the Start menu, then Accessories, and finally, Notepad.

3. From the File menu, choose Open.

4. Select QUICKEN.INI in the File Name box. You may need to change the directory to \WINDOWS, \WIN95, or whatever your Windows subdirectory is called.

5. Click OK. Notepad will display the QUICKEN.INI file.

6. Locate the AutoBackup line in the QUICKEN.INI file. The number following the equal (=) sign indicates how often Quicken will prompt you to backup your data.

7. Change the AutoBackup number to whatever you would like. If you change the number to 1, Quicken will prompt you to back up every time you exit the program; if you change the number to 0, Quicken will never prompt you to back up.

8. From the Notepad File menu, choose Save.

9. Quit Notepad, and then restart Quicken.

When Quicken makes a copy of your current file, it places the copy in a subdirectory named BACKUP in the directory where you keep your Quicken data files. If the BACKUP directory doesn't exist, Quicken will create it. Normally, Quicken keeps two historical copies of your data in the BACKUP directory.

If you want to change the number of copies Quicken keeps in the BACKUP directory, or turn the feature off completely, do the following:

1. Quit Quicken.

2. In Windows 3.1, start the Windows Notepad by double-clicking its icon in the Program Manager. In Windows 95, start the Notepad applet by clicking Start on the taskbar and choosing Programs from the Start menu, then Accessories, and finally, Notepad.

3. From the File menu, choose Open.

4. Select QUICKEN.INI in the File Name box, specifying the path to your Windows subdirectory if necessary.

5. Click OK. Notepad will display the QUICKEN.INI file.

6. Locate the AutoCopy line in the QUICKEN.INI file. The number following the equal (=) sign indicates how many copies of your data Quicken will keep in the BACKUP directory.

7. Change the AutoCopy number to a value from 0 to 9. If you change the number to 0, Quicken will never copy your data to the BACKUP directory.

8. From the Notepad File menu, choose Save.

9. Quit Notepad, and then restart Quicken.

Getting Help

Quicken 5, especially in the Deluxe and Deluxe CD-ROM versions, is loaded with online help features—so many that it can be difficult deciding exactly which ones to use. It seems ironic that anyone should need *help* understanding an online help system, but this is a benign legacy of the way Quicken is designed.

Intuit's help begins with a basic system—similar to the one supplied with most other Windows applications—that you'll find on both Quicken and Quicken Deluxe. Quicken Deluxe for CD-ROM adds Finance 101 and Ask the Experts, covered in Chapter 19. There is also a Video QuickTours feature, in which Intuit employees appear in multimedia clips that introduce many Quicken features.

In a mostly successful attempt to unify the various help features, Intuit has added two more systems to Quicken Deluxe for CD-ROM. First is the Onscreen Manual, an enhanced help system that leads you through Quicken. The Onscreen Manual has a large amount of new material; however, it also contains hyperlinks in its documents that take you to the *standard* Help system. This can be confusing, although only in a minor sort of way.

The second system Intuit has added is the Quicken Deluxe Index. This is an index similar to the one you find in the standard help system, yet it is more attractive and is "aware" of all the features in Quicken Deluxe for CD-ROM. In other words, if you ask about using

Finance 101, for example, the Deluxe Index can tell you about it and even run the program. The Deluxe Index calls up the standard Help Index at times.

All versions of Quicken include QuickTours, windows that you can open to be guided through program features. They also include "flyover help," meaning that if you hold your mouse cursor over any Quicken icon for a few seconds, you will get a message about what that icon does.

Since all these help systems lend themselves to browsing and exploration, there's no need to delve into each in detail here. However, I'd like to tour each quickly to help give you an idea of their structure.

Getting Help Online

As in any other Windows program, you can get context-sensitive help from within Quicken by pressing F1. This takes you into the standard help system for Quicken. Using Windows' standard help engine, this lets you view a table of contents about Quicken, search for a particular phrase, print a topic or save it to the clipboard, and define a bookmark if desired.

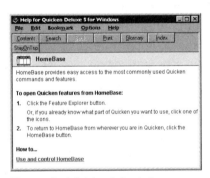

The standard Quicken help window.

The help window shown here is probably familiar to you from other Windows software. If not, play around with it and check your Windows documentation (assuming your machine came with any). If this help system doesn't answer your questions, you'll want to explore further using the Quicken Help menu.

The Help Menu

To access Quicken's special help facilities, go to the Help menu (at the far right in Quicken's main program window). The first choice on this menu is Quicken Help, which pops up the same window that pressing F1 does. If you select it now, you'll see help about HomeBase because that's where you are. However, it's easy to locate other topics. If you want more information about using this help system, click on the next menu choice, How to Use Help.

QuickTours

Quicken's QuickTours give short, screen-based introductions to Quicken as a whole and then to specific features. To start one, select QuickTours from the Help menu; the QuickTours window will appear.

The QuickTours window.

To select one of the eight specific topics shown, just click on its button. Or click on the Quicken Overview button at the bottom of the screen. Then use the Back and Next buttons to step through the lessons. (With all due respect, it has to be said that the QuickTours are pretty basic; you won't learn much that's new if you've worked through this book so far. However, they might help introduce other family members to what Quicken can do.)

Video QuickTours

If you have Quicken Deluxe for Windows on CD-ROM, you have access to Video QuickTours. Start it by selecting Video QuickTours from the Help menu. Provided your computer is wired for sound, you can see and hear any of the Video QuickTours by clicking on one of the seven buttons.

The Video QuickTours mimic the look of various Quicken windows, but also use animation, movies, and other media. Although I'm no video critic, I'd say these displays are lively and fast-paced—enough so

The Video QuickTours window.

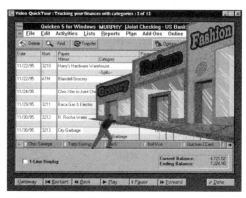

A Video QuickTour in progress.

that you may want to use the buttons at the bottom of the screen to pause and return to previous screens.

After each Video QuickTour is concluded, a window will appear that helps you explore the subject further in any of Quicken's other online help systems.

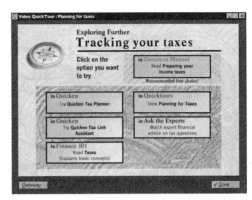

This window appears at the end of a Video QuickTour.

The Deluxe Index

If you have Quicken Deluxe for Windows on CD-ROM, you have access to the Quicken Deluxe Index. Start it by selecting Deluxe Index from the Help menu. The Deluxe Index operates similarly to the standard Help Index, except that it is aware of all the add-ons that come with Quicken Deluxe. Clicking on a help topic may open an item in the standard Help system, run the Onscreen Manual, or start up one of the supplementary programs such as Finance 101.

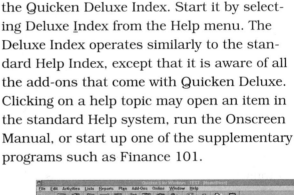

The Quicken Deluxe Index.

Onscreen Manual

The Onscreen Manual for Quicken Deluxe is the substitute for the paper manual you *don't* get with the program. To open it, select Onscreen Manual from the Quicken Help menu. It is divided into three sections, accessible via the "coins" interface on the main screen: Using Quicken, Life Events, and Business Uses.

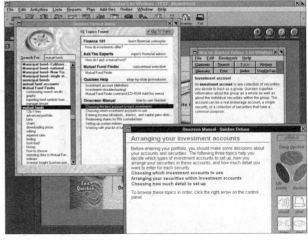

The Quicken Deluxe Index can open any of Quicken's other modules. Here, it has launched the Onscreen Manual and the standard Help system.

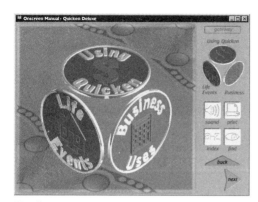
The Onscreen Manual.

Within the text of the manual, clicking on phrases displayed in green type will jump you to related topics in this manual. Clicking on underlined phrases in green type will jump you to related topics in other applications on the Quicken Deluxe for Windows CD-ROM. You can print any of the sections by clicking on the Printer icon, and you can consult the Deluxe Index by clicking on the Index icon. For better or worse, it is not possible to copy any of the manual's sections to the clipboard for pasting into any other applications. (An exception to this is if you open an entry in the *standard* Help Index, which does work with the clipboard like any other Windows help file.)

The Business section of the Onscreen Manual.

The Life Events section of the Onscreen Manual

Getting Help from Humans

If you can't find the answers you're looking for in the online help system, perhaps you will want to talk to Intuit's support staff. You can do this either online or via one of the company's online forums.

Intuit does not offer toll-free telephone support, but, on the other hand, it doesn't charge for technical assistance (something that all too many other companies do these days). The telephone numbers to use are different depending on the aspect of Quicken for which you'd like help. The sidebar "Intuit Support Numbers" shows Intuit's telephone numbers by subject, along with claimed hours of operation.

Intuit Support Numbers

If You Want	Call	Hours
Quicken Deluxe help	505-896-7221	6 AM–6 PM PST, Monday–Friday
Intuit Online Service troubleshooting	708-585-8500	7 AM–11 PM CST, Monday–Friday; 8 AM–5 PM CST, Saturday–Sunday
Answers via fax	800-644-3198	Anytime
Tax Update hotline	505-896-7259	Anytime
Mutual Fund Finder	800-224-0873, extension 810354	Anytime

Other numbers, including those for ordering Quicken supplies, are in the manuals that came with your copy of the program. Remember that if you have a question about online banking that deals with a specific account, you need to call the financial institution for information, not Intuit. (For more information, see Chapter 15.)

In addition to its Financial Network (covered in Chapter 15), Intuit maintains forums on America Online, CompuServe, and Prodigy. If you're a member of one of these services, you'll find the Intuit forum useful. You can pose questions to Intuit support staff, download lists of frequently asked questions, and learn from the experiences of other users.

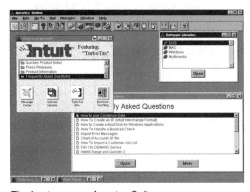

The Intuit area on America Online.

Intuit on CompuServe.

To access the Quicken area on America Online, log on as you normally do, then go to the keyword Intuit. To go to the similar area on CompuServe, log on and then enter go Intuit. Finally, to access the Intuit area on Prodigy, log on and then enter jump Intuit.

Summary

To back up Windows itself properly, you really need to use a tape drive regularly. Once Windows *is* backed up, preserving your Quicken software and data is simple. Just use the commands available in Quicken's File menu to back up the several files on your hard drive that make up a single Quicken data file.

As for getting help, you're spoiled with a wealth of choices. Quicken has several interlinked help systems, and Intuit forums—staffed by the company's support representatives—are available on most major online services.

Budgeting and Planning

Why Budget?

This is, by far, the hardest chapter that I had to write. It's not that setting up a budget is so difficult. It's just that it's always my last priority. When I hear the word "budget," I think of having to live a spartan life, pinching every penny and denying myself all of life's pleasures, or at least those that cost money.

But using Quicken's budgeting features doesn't necessarily mean that you have to put yourself on a severe spending diet. Budgeting is simply a way of creating a plan of how much you will spend. And you don't have to be in the poorhouse to need a budget.

Just about all businesses, nonprofit organizations, and, believe it or not, government agencies, operate on a budget. I spent the first half of my career running nonprofit organizations, and I can assure you that every dime we spent came from one line item or another. That doesn't mean that we didn't sometimes overspend in one category and underspend in another. A budget's purpose is to facilitate your goals, not become a goal in itself.

As an individual or head of a family, you can use Quicken's budgeting tools to make a plan for how you want to spend your money. And, by using Quicken to track what you spend you can find out how you're doing. You might find that you've budgeted too much for some categories and not enough for others, or you might be right on track. In the end, you might increase or decrease your budget allocations, or you might decide to abandon the budget feature altogether. It's your money and your choice.

Setting Up a Budget

You can create your Quicken budget in two ways: You can set one up from scratch, or you can let Quicken automatically create a budget for you, based on the data you've already entered into your account registers. Letting Quicken set up your budget automatically is definitely easier because the program enters the amounts for you (assuming that you have been recording your expenses and assigning each expense to a category).

The budget Quicken will create is based on what you have spent in the past. It isn't necessarily what you should be spending, although, for items such as housing or car payments, you probably have little choice but to continue to spend at that rate. To make this an actual budget, rather than just a report on what you're spending, you have to take a look at each category to decide whether the amount is too high, too low, or just right.

Setting Up a New Budget

To set up a new budget:

1. Select Budgeting from the Plan menu; you can then go directly to the default budget. Or, click on the Budgets icon on the Budget button bar to create a new budget.

2. Either use the default budget (called "Budget") or click on the Create icon to create a new budget (if you wish, you can have more than one budget).

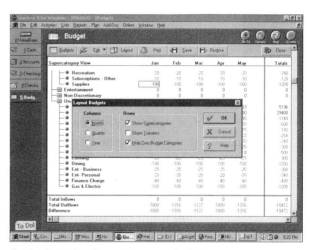

Quicken's window for creating a new budget.

If you create a new budget:

3. Type in the name of the new budget, such as "Family Budget." If you wish to use numbers based on your previous spending, be sure that "Autocreate Budget" is checked. If you wish to start out with a zero in each category, check "Zero-Filled Budget." Click OK.

4. Check to see that the date range is appropriate. You may wish to change it by using the calendar or by typing in new dates. You also need to decide whether to round off to the nearest dollar (a good idea) and whether to create your budget with details for each month (month by detail) or to use averages for the period. If you go with the default (averages), Quicken will report the average you spend for the period rather than breaking it down by month. Click OK.

5. The budget you create will automatically include all categories, but you can select which categories to include or exclude by clicking the Categories button.

Regardless of whether you selected Zero-Filled Budget or let Quicken automatically fill your budget, now is (almost) the time to look at each category to decide how much you want to spend. But, before you do that, there are a few options you need to consider. These options are selected from the Layout tab on the Budget button bar.

Supercategories

One important layout option lets you show supercategories. Supercategories allow you to group categories so you can view data in multiple categories at once. This sometimes can help you analyze your financial data. Let's say, for example, that you have separate categories for meals, movies, professional sporting events, and golf greens fees. For budgeting purposes, you're only interested in what you spend on the sum of these categories, so you could create a supercategory called "Entertainment" that would lump together these categories. You could still enter your data in each separate category, and you could still find out how much you spend on golf as opposed to going out to eat, but for budgeting purposes, you could use the supercategory as if it were one category.

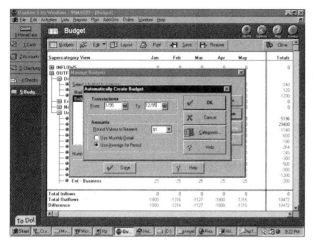

Layout options help you control your budget.

I recommend that you check Display Supercategories as there really isn't any downside to seeing the information, and it can help you get a better overview of your financial situation.

Creating and editing supercategories is covered in Chapter 5.

Show Transfers

The Show Transfer layout option lets you show transfers between accounts. If your budget includes transferring money from your checking account to your savings or investment accounts (as it should), this will let you include those savings or investments as budget items. If you don't want to show transfers, leave the box unchecked.

Hide Zero Budget Categories

As its name suggests, Hide Zero Budget Categories lets you suppress the display of any categories that have no dollar amounts.

Columns

The Columns option on the Layout tab allows you to display data by month, quarter, or year. The default (by month) is the way most people analyze their spending, but you can always go back to the Layout tab to switch between month, quarter, and year.

Entering or Modifying Budget Data

To enter or modify budget data:

1. Go to the Plan menu and select Budgeting.

2. Enter a budget amount for each category. If Quicken has already filled in an amount based on past spending, review it to see that it makes sense. If it doesn't, change it. If it's a recurring monthly (or quarterly) expense, you don't have to enter it each time. Just enter it once in January and click on the Edit button in the Budget button bar to select Fill Row Right. Click OK and Quicken will automatically carry the January amount through to December.

Hint: If you have an annual expense that you wish to look at on a monthly basis, you can use the Layout tab to temporarily switch into yearly view, enter the data, and then switch back to monthly view. Quicken will automatically allocate ¹⁄₁₂ of the amount to each month. For example, if your car insurance is $1,500 a year, you could click Layout, change the Columns option to Year, and enter $1,500 once; when you go back to monthly view, Quicken will show the expense as $125 each month.

3. You can easily collapse categories if you wish to avoid seeing too much detail. You may have several sources of income, for example, but might not necessarily need to see each income item separately in your budget.

4. Click Save on the Budget button bar to save your budget. Unless you entered a new budget, it will automatically be named "Budget."

It's a good idea to take a serious look at each category in your budget and think about what you really spend in that area. Don't forget to include money that you might not be tracking within Quicken. I don't, for example, bother to use Quicken to keep track of my non-business-related meal expenses, but I do spend money on restaurants, so when I did my budget, I estimated how much I spend and entered that data. Don't forget to review these amounts with your partner, as he or she may be aware of spending that you don't know about.

Savings Goals

When I was a kid, I had a piggy bank in my room; every week when I got my allowance, the first thing I did was put a quarter in the jar so I could buy myself a transistor radio (they were expensive back then). Well, this is a nice story, but it's not true. I never did save for that radio, though my parents eventually gave me one as a present. But if I had put a quarter into my piggy bank each month to save for a radio, I would have established and then funded a savings goal.

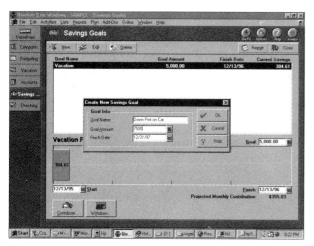

Creating a new savings goal.

Quicken lets you establish goals and squirrel away money by, essentially, hiding it so you can't use it for other purposes. It does this by creating an "account" where money is tracked. It isn't a real account such as a savings account at a bank because, in this scenario, the money is never transferred out of your checking account. Your balance is reduced by the money you put into this so-called "savings goal," but it remains in your account. Once you've established a savings goal, you can then "contribute" to it by having the money "deducted" from whichever account you want to use to fund that goal. Remember, this is basically like playing a trick on yourself, and, frankly, it's not my favorite Quicken feature. For big-ticket savings, such as retirement or my kids' college education, I have real accounts at banks and investment firms. For smaller savings goals, I simply move money into a savings account and spend from there. Yet, if this savings goal feature is a good way for you to allocate money, by all means use it. The good thing about Quicken is that it's flexible enough to suit different people's needs.

To set up a savings goal:

1. Go to the Plan menu, and select Savings Goals.

2. Click New.

3. Enter a name for the goal, the goal amount, and the date when you plan to finish funding the goal.

4. Click OK.

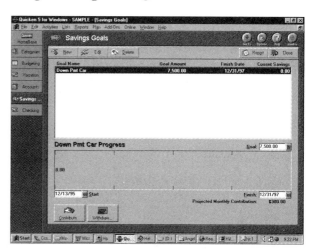

Naming your new savings goal.

Contributing to a new savings goal.

Quicken will then display the name of your goal, the total amount, the projected finish date, and the amount you have saved so far.

To contribute to your goal, click on the Contribute button in the lower left corner of your screen.

Quicken wil let you select the account from which to take the money and will suggest an amount equal to the total amount of the goal divided by the number of months between now and the finish date. You can override that amount. When you're done, the amount will be deducted from the account, recorded in that account's register, and added to the "current savings" line of the savings goal. Your progress will be automatically charted in a Progress bar on the screen.

When you're ready to actually spend all or part of the money, you can click on the Withdraw button.

You can print out a report of your savings goal just as if it were a real account.

Creating a Budget Report and a Budget Variance Graph

Now for the tough part. You've got a budget, and you're spending money. But are your budget and your spending in sync? Assuming you're tracking all of your spending, you can find out in a flash by creating a budget report or a budget variance graph.

To create a budget report:

1. Go to the Reports Menu, and select <u>O</u>ther and then <u>B</u>udget.

2. Quicken will search your transactions and then display a report that includes your budget and expenses for each category.

To create a monthly budget report:

1. Go to the Reports Menu, and select <u>H</u>ome and then Monthly <u>B</u>udget.

2. Quicken will search your transactions and then display a report that includes your budget and expenses for each category broken down by month.

To create a budget variance graph:

1. Go to the Reports menu, and select Graphs and then Budget Variance.

2. Enter the dates you wish to see displayed.

3. Be sure that Budget Variance Graph is checked.

4. Select any accounts, categories, or classes from the buttons at the bottom of the form.

5. Click Create.

Planning for Big-Ticket Expenses

If you're like me, this section on big-ticket expenses, such as college or retirement, will probably depress you. But before you completely give up on ever sending your kids to college or enjoying your retirement, remember that you may have resources available to you that you aren't anticipating. And, as my co-author Louis Fortis shows in Chapter 21, the earlier you start to plan and save, the easier it is.

Let's start by looking at saving for a college education. My son William, who is now 9 years old, wants to go to Stanford. That doesn't mean that he's necessarily going to go there. First he has to make the grades in middle school and high school, second we have to be able to afford to send him there, and, perhaps most importantly, he has to want to go to Stanford 9 years from now. Fortunately, for me at least, 9-year-olds don't routinely get into college.

I checked Stanford's World Wide Web site (**http://www.stanford.edu**) and found out that it cost about $29,000 a year to send a student to Stanford during the 1995 school year. By the year 2004 it will cost more, and though no one knows exactly how much, Quicken has the ability to come up with a pretty good guess.

The other data you need to have is the amount you've already saved, your guess of the annual yield on your savings or investments, and the annual rate of inflation. Quicken defaults to an 8% yield and a 4% inflation. The real numbers may be better or worse, but don't let a wild year or two on Wall Street lure you into a false sense of security as to the growth rate of your savings. Over the years, 8% has been a pretty good estimate.

Let's say, for argument's sake, that I already have $20,000 put aside for William's college education. Let's start planning.

1. Go to the Plan menu, and select Financial Planners and then College.

2. Enter today's annual college costs. You can get that information from a variety of sources, including the admissions office or World Wide Web site of most colleges.

3. Enter the number of years until enrollment.

4. Enter your current college savings.

5. Enter the annual yield or leave it at 8%.

6. Click Schedule (don't click Done).

Now you'll see the bad news. But play around with some figures. Change the annual yield to 12%, and notice how much better the situation is. Try reducing the inflation rate. Then select Inflate Contributions on the assumption that your income will go up as your kids get older.

Finally, remember that things may not be as bad as they seem. Scholarships exist, as do lots of cheaper colleges (Stanford is one of the most expensive), and you may be able to draw on other resources such as equity in your house. And don't forget financial aid, part-time jobs, and other sources of income.

Planning for Retirement

Retirement planning uses the same principles as planning for college, but requires that you enter different types of data. Let's use a more optimistic scenario for this one. Let's say you're 30 years old and for the past 6 years have been putting $2,000 a year into an IRA account that has been generating a 10% annual yield. That means you now have $22,871 in your IRA account—not bad considering that you only put in $16,000.

Let's see what happens if you continue at this rate until age 65.

1. Go to the Plan menu, and select Financial Planners and then Retirement.

2. Enter the data, and then click Schedule. Notice how the savings grow each year until, at age 65, you have nearly $1.2 million. Seems like a lot of money, but click Close and notice (just under where you entered the data) that your income in today's dollars is only $20,643. Now uncheck the Annual Income in Today's Dollars box near the bottom of the window. The amount jumps to $81,462, which would be great if it weren't for the fact that inflation will eat away at most of it.

Now make a very simple change by checking Inflate Contributions, which assumes that the amount you're contributing will grow over the years. This will help a little. If you really want to

The Retirement Planner shows how your money can grow over 35 years.

see a big change, adjust the amount you're putting in each year. As you can see, a little extra savings, over the years, goes a long way. And remember, retired people don't necessarily need as much money to live on as young families, although I know some retirees who are spending a lot and enjoying every penny of it.

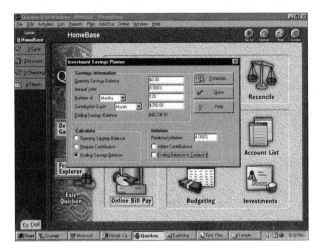

Sock away $250 a month for 10 years (120 months) at 8% interest and you'll have almost $46,000 by the time you're done.

Savings Calculator

The Savings Calculator is fairly straightforward. You access it from the Plan menu by selecting Financial Planners. Enter the data the calculator requests. Click Schedule, and you'll see how your savings can grow.

Refinance Calculator

Deciding whether to refinance a loan—especially a home mortgage—can be a tough decision. In most cases, it's only a serious option when rates have fallen below the rate that you got when you last financed your home, or when you have an adjustable rate and want to take advantage of reasonable fixed rates to avoid the uncertainty of the adjustable rate's increase.

The Refinance Calculator is amazingly easy to use. All you have to know is your current monthly payment, the amount you wish to refinance, the interest rate of the proposed loan, and any points or closing costs. Enter that information, and you will immediately find out what your new monthly payment will be. Most importantly, you'll also find out how

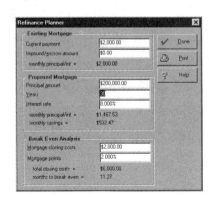

Quicken's Refinance Calculator makes a big decision a lot easier.

many months (if any) it will take to recover the cost (if any) of refinancing. In some cases, your monthly payments will be higher, so you'll get a negative number in the months-to-break-even analysis. This doesn't necessarily mean that it's a bad idea to refinance if you're in a situation where you're getting rid of an adjustable-rate loan that could go up in interest in the future, or if you're changing from a 30-year to a 15-year loan that has higher payments but pays off the debt faster (resulting in lower total interest payments over the life of the loan).

Note: *The Impound/Escrow Amount box should only be filled in if your current mortgage payments include taxes, insurance, or other payments that are not related to the loan itself.*

Summary

Learning to budget and plan isn't exactly a lot of fun, but it does help you get a better handle on what's in store for you. You can also use Quicken to organize your savings program to plan for retirement, your children's education, or other goals. Finally, Quicken offers a number of financial planning tools to help you calculate payments on a loan, determine whether it makes sense to refinance your home, and see how various savings programs might grow. Armed with that information, you can face the world a wiser, and perhaps happier, person.

Tax Planning and Preparation

18

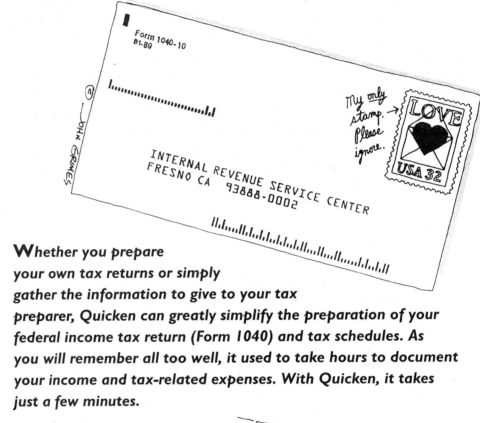

Whether you prepare your own tax returns or simply gather the information to give to your tax preparer, Quicken can greatly simplify the preparation of your federal income tax return (Form 1040) and tax schedules. As you will remember all too well, it used to take hours to document your income and tax-related expenses. With Quicken, it takes just a few minutes.

The secret is categorizing your transactions throughout the year so you can generate reports with the tax information you need. If you have categorized faithfully, Quicken can produce useful Tax Summary and Tax Schedule reports. It can also transfer its data directly to Windows or DOS tax software programs, so you don't have to re-enter financial information when you prepare your taxes. Intuit's TurboTax program even allows you to file your return electronically.

Setting Up Categories for Easy Tax Preparation

As noted in Chapter 5, you use categories in Quicken to group transactions into related areas of income or expense. Many of those categories are not tax-related. For example, assigning the category Clothing
or Telephone to a transaction usually makes no difference to your
taxes. But some categories (such as Charity, Dividend Income, Medical,
and Mortgage Interest) are tax-related. Contributions to charity, for
example, are reported on Schedule A; income from dividends is
reported on Schedule B; and so on. If you are using Quicken to manage
your small business, all of your business expenses are tax-related.

In the sidebars "Quicken's Standard Home Categories" and
"Quicken's Standard Business Categories," you can see that many of
the categories are already flagged as tax-related. For U.S. readers, the
applicable tax schedule is listed in the right column. The forms are
obviously different for Canadian readers and are documented in
Quicken's online help.

Note: *If you live in Canada, you can use Quicken not only to track
income tax, but also to track GST (Goods and Services Tax) and Provin-
cial Sales Tax. See the "Using Quicken in Canada" section of Quicken's
online manual.*

Quicken's Standard Home Categories

Category	Type	Tax-related	Description	Tax Schedules
Bonus	Income	Tax	Bonus Income	1040: Other Income
Div Income	Income	Tax	Dividend Income	B: Dividend Income
Gift Received	Income		Gift Received	
Int Inc	Income	Tax	Interest Income	B: Interest Income
Invest Inc	Income	Tax	Investment Income	B: Interest Income
Other Inc	Income	Tax	Other Income	1040: Other Income —Miscellaneous
Salary	Income	Tax	Salary Income	W-2: Salary
Salary Spouse	Income	Tax	Spouse's Salary Income	W-2: Salary, Spouse
Auto	Expense		Automobile Expenses	
Fuel	Subcategory		Auto Fuel	
Insurance	Subcategory		Auto Insurance	
Loan	Subcategory		Auto Loan Payment	
Service	Subcategory		Auto Service	
Bank Chrg	Expense		Bank Charge	
Charity	Expense	Tax	Charitable Donations	
Cash Contrib.	Subcategory	Tax	Cash Contributions	A: Cash Charity
Non-Cash	Subcategory	Tax	Non-Cash Contributions	A: Non-Cash Charity

(Continued on next page.)

Quicken's Standard Home Categories (Continued from previous page.)

Category	Type	Tax-related	Description	Tax Schedules
Childcare	Expense	Tax	Childcare Expense	2441: Child Care—Daytime
Clothing	Expense		Clothing	
Dining	Expense		Dining Out	
Education	Expense		Education	
Entertain	Expense		Entertainment	
Gifts	Expense		Gift Expenses	
Groceries	Expense		Groceries	
Home Repair	Expense		Home Repair and Maintenance	
Housing	Expense		Housing	
Insurance	Expense		Insurance	
Int Exp	Expense	Tax	Interest Expense	
Invest Exp	Expense	Tax	Investment Expense	A: Investment Management Fees
IRA Contrib	Expense	Tax	IRA Contribution	1040: IRA Contribution
IRA Contrib Spouse	Expense	Tax	IRA Contribution Spouse	1040: IRA Contribution, Working Spouse
Medical	Expense	Tax	Medical Expense	
Doctor	Subcategory	Tax	Doctor and Dental Visits	A: Doctors, Dentists, Hospital
Medicine	Subcategory	Tax	Medicine and Drugs	A: Medicine and Drugs
Misc	Expense		Miscellaneous	
Mort Int	Expense	Tax	Mortgage Interest Expenses	A: Home Mortgage Interest
Other Exp	Expense		Other Expenses	
Recreation	Expense		Recreation Expense	
Subscriptions	Expense		Subscriptions	
Supplies	Expense		Supplies	
Tax	Expense	Tax	Taxes	
Fed	Subcategory	Tax	Federal Tax	W-2: Federal Withholding
Medicare	Subcategory	Tax	Medicare Tax	W-2: Medicare tax Withholding
Other	Subcategory	Tax	Miscellaneous Taxes	
Property	Subcategory	Tax	Property Tax	A: Real Estate Tax
Soc Sec	Subcategory	Tax	Social Security Tax	W-2: Social Security Tax Withholding
State	Subcategory	Tax	State Tax	W-2: State Withholding
Tax Spouse	Expense	Tax	Spouse's Taxes	
Fed	Subcategory	Tax	Federal Tax	W-2: Federal Withholding, Spouse
Medicare	Subcategory	Tax	Medicare Tax	W-2: Medicare Tax Withholding, Spouse
Soc Sec	Subcategory	Tax	Social Security Tax	W-2: Social Security Tax Withholding, Spouse
State	Subcategory	Tax	State Tax	W-2: State Withholding, Spouse
Telephone	Expense		Telephone Expense	
Utilities	Expense		Water, Gas, Electric	
Gas and Electric	Subcategory		Gas and Electricity	
Water	Subcategory		Water	

Quicken's Standard Business Categories

Category	Type	Tax	Description	Schedules
Gr Sales	Income	Tax	Gross Sales	C: Gross Receipts
Other Income	Income	Tax	Other Income	C: Other Business Income
Ads	Expense	Tax	Advertising	C: Advertising
Car	Expense	Tax	Car and Truck	C: Car and Truck
Commission	Expense	Tax	Commissions	C: Commissions and Fees
Insurance, Bus.	Expense	Tax	Insurance (not health)	C: Insurance
Int Paid	Expense	Tax	Interest Paid	C: Interest Paid Expense, Other
L&P Fees	Expense	Tax	Legal and Professional Fees	C: Legal and Professional
Late Fees	Expense	Tax	Late Payment Fees	C: Other Business Expense
Meals & Enter	Expense	Tax	Meals and Entertainment	C: Meals and Entertainment
Office	Expense	Tax	Office Expenses	C: Office Expense
Rent on Equip	Expense	Tax	Rent: Vehicles, Machinery, Equipment	C: Rent on Vehicles, Machinery, Equipment
Rent Paid	Expense	Tax	Rent Paid	C: Rent on Other Business Property
Repairs	Expense	Tax	Repairs	C: Repairs
Returns	Expense	Tax	Returns and Allowances	C: Returns and Allowances
Supplies, Bus.	Expense	Tax	Supplies	C: Supplies
Taxes	Expense	Tax	Taxes and Licenses	C: Taxes and Licenses
Fed	Subcategory	Tax	Federal Tax	C: Taxes and Licenses
Local	Subcategory	Tax	Local Tax	C: Taxes and Licenses
Property	Subcategory	Tax	Property Tax	C: Taxes and Licenses
State	Subcategory	Tax	State Tax	C: Taxes and Licenses
Telephone, Bus	Expense	Tax	Telephone Expense	C: Utilities
Travel	Expense	Tax	Travel Expenses	C: Travel
Utilities, Bus	Expense	Tax	Water, Gas, Electric	C: Utilities
Wages	Expense	Tax	Wages and Job Credits	C: Wages Paid

Adding New Categories

If your taxes are fairly straightforward and you don't want to use tax preparation software, all you may need are Tax Summary reports that group transactions in your accounts by tax-related category. Therefore, if you add any new categories, simply mark than as tax-related by clicking the Tax-Related box in the Set Up Category window.

On the other hand, if you want Tax Schedule and Capital Gains reports that group and subtotal your transactions by tax schedule line item, you need to make sure you're set up to use tax schedules. Then you need to assign the category to the correct tax schedule line item. Finally, if you want both simple Tax Summary reports and detailed Tax Schedule reports, you need to both mark the category as tax-related *and* assign it to a tax schedule line item.

To assign tax form line items to any new categories:

1. From the <u>L</u>ists menu, choose <u>C</u>ategory & Transfer.

2. Click Tax Lin<u>k</u> on the Category & Transfer List button bar. (Or, from HomeBase, click the Investing/Taxes tab, then the Tax Link Assistant button.) The Tax Link Assistant window will open.

The Tax Link Assistant window.

3. In the Category box, select the category or categories you want to assign a tax form line item to. Use the scroll bar to see categories that may not be visible in the list.

4. In the Tax Form Line Items box, select the tax form or tax schedule line item you want to use. The Tax Link Assistant window will display information about the line item you've highlighted.

5. Click the Assign Line Item to Category button to assign the line item to the selected category or categories.

6. When you've completed assigning tax forms to categories, click OK.

The tax schedule line items Quicken uses include these forms and schedules:

- Form 1040
- Form 2106
- Form 2119
- Form 2441
- Form 3903
- Form 4137
- Form 4684

- Form 4952
- Form 6252
- Form 8815
- Form 8829
- Schedule A
- Schedule B
- Schedule C

- Schedule D
- Schedule E
- Schedule F
- Schedule K-1
- W-2 Form
- 1099R Form

Quicken does not include tax forms and schedules that require special calculations or tables. If you need to use a form or schedule that is not listed here, you will need to enter the amounts reported on those forms directly into your tax software. In Quicken, you can mark the appropriate categories as tax-related and then use the figures from the Tax Summary report.

Setting Up Accounts for Tax Preparation

In addition to creating tax-related categories, you can set up entire accounts as tax-related and link them so transfers in or out of the account are assigned to specific tax schedules. You can also mark an account as tax-deferred.

For example, set up a 401(k) account so that it is marked "Tax-deferred," and assign transfers to the line item "W-2-Salary." When you enter your paycheck in Quicken, your taxable wages will be reduced by the 401(k) contribution and your 401(k) account balance will be increased. (For more information on entering your paycheck, see the next section.)

Entering Your Pay

If you work for someone else, the most important transaction you'll be entering is your pay. There are several different ways of handling this in Quicken. The simplest way is to enter each paycheck as a deposit of your net take-home pay in your checking account. When you get your W-2 at the end of the year, you can then enter one Quicken transaction with splits that contain the total deductions for federal and state tax, medical insurance, 401(k) contributions, local withholding, and state disability insurance. Or you can simply enter the W-2 totals in your tax software and ignore them in Quicken.

This simple way to enter a paycheck saves time because you don't have to check your paycheck stub each time to be sure you have the exact amounts for these deductions. However, it does mean you can't get complete early Tax Summary reports and you can't use the Quicken Tax Planner to see exactly where you stand.

After you've entered your paycheck deposit, you can either memorize it or set it up as a scheduled transaction. Sometimes paychecks vary by a few cents. You can ignore the variation or change the amount when you recall the transaction. Or you can memorize your paycheck twice and choose the appropriate memorized transaction to recall.

Entering your paycheck with deductions isn't actually all that difficult. After you've done it once, you can memorize the transaction and use it again and again, or simply schedule it so that Quicken enters it for you automatically. You can edit the individual transactions if your paycheck varies slightly each pay period.

To enter your paycheck:

1. Using a blank transaction in your bank account register, type Paycheck in the Payee field. Do not fill in an amount.

2. Click Splits.

3. In the first split, choose Salary from the drop-down list in the first Category field and enter the gross amount of the paycheck in the Amount field. The gross amount is your pay before any deductions are made.

4. Enter the various tax deductions from your pay on the following lines as negative amounts. Assign them to the expense categories Tax:Fed, Tax:State, and Tax:FICA.

Enter one deduction on each line. You may also have deductions for items such as local withholding, medical insurance contributions, and state disability insurance. Set up new expense categories for these as needed. Be sure to assign each new category to a tax form line item.

If this is your spouse's paycheck, use the categories Tax Spouse:Fed, Tax Spouse:State, and so on.

Note: *If you are Canadian, your tax categories are Tax:Fed, Tax:UIC, and Tax:CPP. You may also have deductions for pension contributions, union dues, and charitable donations. Set up new expense categories for these as needed. If you track your pension plan in a separate asset or investment account, enter the account name instead of a category.*

5. Check the amount in the Splits Total field at the bottom of the window. It should equal the net amount of your paycheck.

6. Click OK to close the split, and then click Record.

7. Memorize your paycheck transaction and set it up as a scheduled transaction (optional).

If You Have More Than One Job

If you have more than one job and therefore receive more than one W-2, you can use classes to assign paycheck transactions to appropriate W-2 forms. Just set up a class for each job. Then assign the splits in your paycheck transactions to the appropriate category and class.

For example, if you used the standard Quicken home categories, you have a category and subcategory named Tax: Fed for your salary. The subcategory is set up so it is linked to the tax form W-2. Suppose you set up classes for a day job and a moonlighting job (for example, teaching and freelance writing). When you enter a paycheck, you can then assign the transaction to both the category and the class: for example, Tax: Fed/Teaching for the day job and Tax: Fed/Writing for the moonlighting job.

As a result, you can customize Quicken's Tax Summary report to show these classes so you can see separate totals for each W-2. If you use TurboTax to prepare your income taxes, it will correctly assign salary transactions to the appropriate W-2.

Note: *Do not use classes to distinguish between your W-2 and your spouse's W-2. Quicken expects you to use the two separate categories designed for tax withholdings from your salary and your spouse's. See the sidebar "Quicken's Standard Home Categories" earlier in this chapter for a list of these categories.*

Entering Year-to-Date Information

If you want to keep track of your paycheck deductions for the entire year, but didn't buy Quicken until June or July, Intuit suggests that you enter one transaction that summarizes your year-to-date deductions. Follow the instructions in the "Entering Your Pay" section, but make these changes:

1. Type Paycheck to Date in the Payee field.

2. For the amounts assigned to gross salary and deductions, use the year-to-date figures listed on your paycheck stub.

3. Because this is a one-time-only transaction, you don't need to memorize or schedule it.

After you save the year-to-date paycheck transaction, enter a balance adjustment transaction, so your current balance isn't affected. (For example, if your year-to-date paycheck transaction put a $46,000 deposit in the register, enter a $46,000 payment transaction to keep your current balance the same.) Categorize this transaction with the name of the account in which you're entering it. Using the account name as a category keeps the entry from affecting your reports or graphs.

Finding Out How Much Tax You've Paid

To see how much you've paid in income taxes from your paycheck so far this year:

1. From the Lists menu, choose Memorized Transaction.

2. Select your paycheck transaction in the Memorized Transaction list.

3. Click Report.

Quicken will show all the deductions subtracted from your gross salary amount.

Tracking Your Business Income

Normally, you track the gross sales or receipts for your business by assigning them to a category such as Gr Sales (see the sidebar "Quicken's Standard Business Categories" earlier in this chapter). Gr Sales is marked as tax-related and is linked to Schedule C: Gross Receipts.

However, at the end of the tax year you may receive a 1099-MISC statement from someone who paid you for services during the year. Therefore, you need to be sure you don't duplicate any amounts in the tax software, which can happen if you import receipts to the Schedule C, Gross Receipts line and also complete a 1099-MISC for the same income. After importing, view your Schedule C. You may need to manually reduce gross receipts by any amount that's reported on a 1099-MISC.

Multiple Businesses

Quicken 5 for Windows allows you to track taxes for multiple businesses. You can have one copy of any tax form for each business. When you transfer your Quicken data to tax software, you will be able to generate separate copies of Schedule C for your different businesses.

To do this, follow a procedure similar to the one in the "If You Have More Than One Job" section above. Set up a class for each business that is linked to a unique copy number of the Schedule C. As you enter transactions, assign them both to categories and to the appropriate class. For example, suppose you have two businesses: a programming business and a gardening business. You must file a copy of Schedule C for each business. Set up two classes, such as Programming and Gardening. In the Set Up Class window, assign Copy 1 to Programming and Copy 2 to Gardening.

When you enter a deposit from your programming business, assign the transaction to the category and the class, such as Gr Sales/Programming. When you enter a deposit from your gardening business, enter it as Gr Sales/Gardening.

Quicken 5 for Windows lets you follow a similar procedure to track tax-related items for multiple rental properties reported on your federal Schedule E: Supplemental Income and Loss. When you transfer your Quicken data to tax software, you will be able to import each rental property to a separate column on Schedule E. To do so, set up a class for each property that is linked to a unique copy number of Schedule E.

When It's Time to Pay

When it's time to pay your taxes, you'll need to create a new category, called something like "Fed Tax Paid." When you set it up, remember not to check the Tax-Related checkbox and to leave the Form box empty. This check isn't tax-deductible, so this category must not be linked to any tax schedule.

State income taxes, of course, *are* deductible. If you pay additional state income taxes at the time you file your state return, these taxes are deductible in the year paid. Set up a new category named "State Taxes." Mark the Tax-Related checkbox and assign the category to Schedule A: State and Local Taxes.

State income taxes withheld from your salary are also deductible, but should be tracked differently than the state taxes you might pay with your state tax return. Classify them as Tax:State or Tax Spouse:State, categories that are assigned to W-2:State Withholding and W-2:State Withholding, Spouse.

Estimated Tax Payments

Some people have to make estimated federal tax payments quarterly, to avoid tax penalties. If you are one of them, create a category named "Fed Est Tax." Mark the new category as tax-related and assign it to Schedule 1040:Federal Estimated Tax.

When you make an estimated tax payment, assign the transaction to this category. Your Tax Schedule report will display all the payments you've made to date. When you transfer your Quicken data to Turbo-Tax, these estimated payments will be transferred to the Tax Payments Worksheet. (After importing into TurboTax, you must verify that each quarterly payment imported to the correct quarter of the Tax Payment Worksheet. You may need to enter your fourth-quarter installment directly into TurboTax if you made the payment after the end of the calendar year.)

Follow a similar procedure if you need to make estimated state tax payments quarterly. Create a category named "State Est Tax." Mark the new category as tax-related and assign it to Schedule A:State Estimated Tax.

Tax Refunds

When you receive a tax refund, you need to create a new income category, called something like "Tax Refund." When you set up this category, remember not to check the Tax-Related checkbox and to leave the Form box empty. Since the federal refund isn't taxable, it must not be linked to any tax schedule or even marked as tax-related.

Your state tax refund, however, usually *is* taxable if you took an itemized deduction for state income taxes in the prior year. When you receive the refund from your state, create a new income category called "State Tax Refund." Mark the Tax-Related checkbox and assign it to Form 1040:State and Local Refunds.

IRA Contributions

If you are tracking your Individual Retirement Account contributions in order to import them into tax preparation software, remember that importing is usually done on a calendar year (January to December) basis. Since most of us postpone making the IRA contribution until right before the filing date of the tax return—naturally, April 15 of the *follow-ing* year—that transaction will not be imported into the tax software properly. (In fact, the amount that gets imported might be the IRA contribution for the previous year.) Therefore, be sure to review the amount that gets imported to the IRA worksheets to make sure it is the amount for the correct year. Also check the figures against any IRS limits.

Creating Reports

Whether you are filling out your tax forms by hand, exporting information to a tax program, or passing the data on to a paid tax preparer, you'll appreciate the variety of reports available in Quicken. The first type of report is the Tax Summary report, a report that lists all tax-related transactions from all of your accounts (except IRAs or 401(k) accounts).

In other words, this type of report shows the total amount of tax-related income and expenses. (If you have set up classes to track multiple tax forms for separate businesses or multiple W-2 forms, be sure to customize the Tax Summary report to include these classes.)

To create a Tax Summary report, just click on the Reports button at the top of the Quicken screen. When the Create Report window appears, select the <u>H</u>ome tab to bring it to the top, then click on the Tax Summary button and the <u>C</u>reate button. (For more information on reports, see Chapter 11.)

The second type of report is the Tax Schedule report, which lists the exact figures you need to fill in on

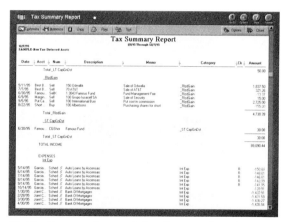

The Tax Summary Report window: To see it all at once, you need to print it out.

your 1040 tax form and schedules (with the qualifications listed below). To create a Tax Schedule report, click on the Reports button at the top of the Quicken screen. When the Create Report window appears, select the <u>H</u>ome tab to bring it to the top, then click on the Tax Schedule button and the <u>C</u>reate button.

As you can see, the Tax Schedule report lists transactions assigned to the corresponding tax schedule line items, grouped and subtotaled. You can export Tax Schedule reports to tax preparation software. If you use TurboTax, there's an easier way to transfer information directly

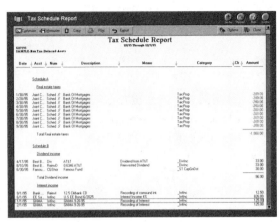

The Tax Schedule Report window.

(see the section "Transferring Quicken Data to Tax Preparation Software," below). However, it's still a good idea to print out the Tax Schedule report to check things over before you proceed.

The Tax Schedule report gathers figures from all accounts in the current file except tax-deferred investment accounts (for example, 401(k) and IRA accounts) and from all categories that have been assigned to a tax form and line. Several categories or accounts can be totaled to the same figure in the report. For example, the Salary line on Form W-2 can include both regular salary and bonuses. Use QuickZoom to see the transactions that make up any figure in the report.

Quicken's Tax Schedule report simply gives you your personal totals. You'll need to check the figures against any limits defined by the IRS—for example, the maximum deduction allowed for IRA contributions. If you import into TurboTax, however, it will limit the deduction and warn you about excess contributions.

If you have investment accounts with realized capital gains (following buy and sell transactions), the Tax Schedule report won't show these realized gains. To get figures for your realized gains, run a Capital Gains report. To get income by security, run an Investment Income report. The Capital Gains report lists your long-term and short-term capital gains transactions in a format suitable for Schedule D. You can export Capital Gains reports to tax preparation software. (There's an easier way to transfer your Quicken data directly to TurboTax. See the section "Transferring Quicken Data to Tax Preparation Software," below. But it's a good idea to run this report and use it for reference even when you transfer your data directly.)

Transferring Quicken Data to Tax Preparation Software

If you use Windows or DOS tax software (including DOS TurboTax) to prepare your Form 1040, you can use data from Quicken's Tax Schedule or Capital Gains reports. Quicken will write your tax data to a TXF (Tax Exchange Format) file in a standard format compatible with several major tax preparation programs.

To export your Quicken Tax Schedule report or Capital Gains report to a TXF file:

1. Display the Tax Schedule or Capital Gains report.

2. Click the Export button on the Report button bar.

3. The Create Tax Export File dialog box will appear. Enter a file name for the Tax Schedule or Capital Gains report in the File Name field.

A sample Capital Gains report ready for export.

The Create Tax Export File dialog box.

Note: *If you created both a Tax Schedule report and a Capital Gains report, you must print each report to disk so you have a separate TXF file for each report.*

4. Click OK.

Quicken will write the data to the file and close the Report window. See the instructions that accompany your tax preparation program to use the data file.

If you use TurboTax for Windows, you don't need to do anything special within Quicken to transfer the data. TurboTax for Windows can read and import Quicken for Windows data files without any work on your part. However, it's a good idea to print the Tax Schedule report and the Capital Gains report for reference as you do your taxes.

Updating Your Tax Form Information

Periodically the IRS changes the information required on IRS tax forms and schedules. Most changes occur in January and affect only specialized forms that you probably don't need to file. If the IRS makes any changes to the forms you file, however, you will need to get a new copy of a file from Intuit to update your Quicken software so it can transfer your data smoothly.

You can get this file, an updated list of tax form assignments (the TAX.SCD file), in several ways. Intuit provides it to the manufacturers of tax preparation software, who put it in their packages for your use. If you are a TurboTax for Windows user, your Final Edition will include an updated TAX.SCD file in time for you to file your annual returns. This file will be installed automatically when you install TurboTax. If you aren't a TurboTax for Windows user, you can obtain an updated version of the TAX.SCD file from Intuit. (Traditionally, a call to customer support has been necessary. In the future, however, TAX.SCD files will probably be available for download via Intuit's Web site.)

Note: *The TAX.SCD file for Canada includes Canadian tax forms and links to Win Tax.*

Quicken Tax Planner

With Quicken's Tax Planner, you're no longer limited to waiting until the end of the year to find out what your tax situation will be. This exciting feature lets you: estimate the amount of tax you will owe at year-end; evaluate the impact of a major decision such as buying a house; and create "what-if" scenarios (for example, to see if you should file taxes jointly with your spouse or separately). Using data you may have already entered into Quicken, the Tax Planner also helps determine if you are withholding the correct amount of tax during the year and whether you should be filing quarterly estimated taxes.

Wisely, Intuit does not try to claim that the Tax Planner is a substitute for a professional adviser. Unlike an accountant, the program cannot possibly stay current with recent changes in tax law, especially since Quicken 5 was shipped in August 1995. Intuit maintains a hotline from which you can obtain prerecorded information about using the Tax Planner and about tax law changes. Available 24 hours a day, the hotline's number is 505-896-7259.

Disclaimers aside, the Tax Planner program is a great resource. Before you start any serious work with it, you'll need to marshal your other tax-related information so you can be sure your tax estimation is comprehensive. (Yes, we're still a long way from the paperless office when it comes to taxes!) These include:

- **Income records**

  Paycheck stubs are usually your best source of income information, particularly in midyear, since they show both current and year-to-date earnings and deductions. If you're estimating at year-end, you can use your W-2, W-2G, and 1099 wage forms.

- **Itemized deduction and tax credit records**

  These include medical and dental payment records, tax receipts for real estate, records of interest payments for your home mortgage, dependent expenses, charitable contributions and more. (If you haven't entered all of these in your Quicken file, you're probably starting to realize how useful it would have been.)

- **Tax publications and previous tax returns**

  Available from public libraries, bookstores, or your file cabinet— as the case may be.

Intuit also recommends running a Tax Schedule report and Capital Gains report (see earlier in this chapter) to help check whether all your tax-related financial information is included in your Quicken files. Otherwise, you'll need to enter some or all information into the Tax Planner manually—and there are few things more annoying than getting halfway through an analysis and then realizing you don't have all the information you need.

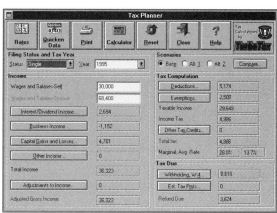

Starting Quicken Tax Planner

To start Quicken Tax Planner, select Tax Planner from the Plan menu. The Tax Planner window will appear.

Enter your filing status and the tax year before you make any other entries. This information will affect automatic calculations throughout the Tax Planner, since your tax rate is based on your filing status.

The Tax Planner window.

From the Status drop-down list, choose the appropriate status. From the Year drop-down list, choose the appropriate year option.

The Tax Planner includes the best information about tax rates, regulations, and information available as of August 1995. At that time, the rates, exemption amounts, and standard deduction amounts for 1996 had not yet been released by the government. While some copies of Quicken now on store shelves may have been updated, others have not. Therefore, as you use the Tax Planner for 1996, you should update the tax information as soon as it becomes available. Call the hotline mentioned above for further details.

Before you change tax rates, choose the filing status for which you want to make changes. Any changes you make to tax rates, exemption amounts, and so on, apply only for the selected filing status. Unless you are comparing the effects of filing jointly versus filing individually, you probably will not need to change rates for more than one filing status.

To change tax rates:

1. From the Plan menu, choose Tax Planner.

2. Set the filing status and tax year options as detailed above.

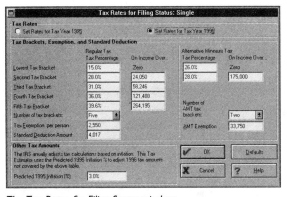

3. Click the Rates button at top left. The Tax Rates for Filing Status window will appear.

4. Choose a Tax Rate year (1996 or 1997).

5. Update any of the rates that have changed.

6. Click OK.

The Tax Rates for Filing Status window.

To change the tax rates back to their original values, click on the Defaults button.

To get tax information from the current file, click on the Quicken Data button. A message will tell you the period for which data is being imported.

The Tax Planner imports year-to-date data through the end of the previous month. For example, if you import on August 4, 1996, the Tax Planner will import data from January 1, 1996, through July 31, 1996. If there is no data for the year you have selected as tax year, you will see a message telling you "No items found to import." For example, if you select Tax Year 1997 in the Tax Planner, and then try to import Quicken data during 1996, you will see the message (unless you have future transactions dated 1997 in your Quicken file).

If you have not assigned tax schedules to Quicken categories, a message will appear telling you "No items found to report. You may need to set up tax schedules for your Quicken categories." Click OK to clear the message. For details on assigning tax schedules to categories, read the "Setting Up Categories for Easy Tax Preparation" section earlier in this chapter.

When the Tax Planner completes the preliminary import, the Preview Quicken Tax Data window will display all information to be imported into the Tax Planner.

The Preview Quicken Tax Data window.

After you have imported data, you should review all your information in the Tax Planner. Select each of the buttons, such as Interest/Dividend Income, Deductions, and Exemptions, and review the information in each of these windows. If you need more information about a window, click its Help button.

Depending on how much of your financial information you track in Quicken, you might need to add information to one or more of these categories using the paper records you collected earlier. (But if you track all your financial information in Quicken—bravo! You may not need to enter any information manually at all.)

To estimate your taxes for a full year, be sure that all information entered into the Tax Planner reflects your best projection of annual amounts. For example, enter the salary you expect to have earned over the course of the entire year, rather than the amount you have earned so far. If you are importing Quicken data, the Tax Planner will automatically "annualize" the information for you to project full-year amounts. After you have entered all your financial information, projected for the year, the Tax Planner will calculate your total tax and show whether you will owe money or have a refund due.

Remaining Tax Due, which may be shown at the lower right of the Tax Planner window, is the projected amount of tax you could owe at year-end. If this amount is more than $500, you may need to make quarterly estimated tax payments or increase withholdings to avoid penalties and interest when you file your return. (The regulations about who needs to file quarterly estimated tax payments are complicated, and you should consult IRS publications or a tax accountant to make a final determination, but a Remaining Tax Due amount of more than $500 is a warning that you need to investigate further.)

Or perhaps you are luckier and see Refund Due listed instead. If the projected Refund Due is significant, you may want to consider reducing your planned estimated tax payments or withholdings.

Creating Multiple Tax Scenarios

The Tax Planner provides three tax scenarios so you can play "what-if" games. They are a Base Scenario, Alternative 1 (Alt 1), and Alternative 2 (Alt 2). You can easily copy information from one to another so you don't have to enter all your information multiple times.

To create multiple tax scenarios:

1. From the Plan menu, choose Tax Planner.

2. Under Scenarios at the upper right of the screen (just below the TurboTax logo) click the scenario you want to use: Base, Alt 1, or Alt 2.

3. If your current scenario contains information but the alternate scenario you choose is blank, Quicken will ask if you want to copy the current scenario.

4. Click Yes if you want to copy all the information in your current scenario to the alternate scenario. Most of the time, you'll want to answer Yes, as this lets you make a few changes on the alternate scenario and then compare scenarios. Click on No only if you want to start with a fresh scenario (with all values set to zero). You can switch between scenarios and make changes at any time.

5. Click the Compare button to display the Tax Scenario Comparisons window. Click OK when you have finished viewing the comparison.

The Tax Scenario Comparisons window.

6. To print your tax data (including the scenarios and their comparison), click on the Print button.

Summary

If you categorize transactions and enter tax-related data throughout the year, Quicken can make your tax preparation (almost) simple. It will export data to TurboTax and other tax preparation software, which can then fill in the tax forms for you. Once upon a time, you would have had to use the tax preparation software to get an idea of whether you were going to get a refund or not. Now, thanks to its Tax Planner module, Quicken can give you a pretty reliable answer to this question all on its own.

Unraveling the Money Mystery:
A Quick Guide to Personal Finance

two

WITH MOST OF HIS NEST EGG IN DAIRY STOCKS,
BILL COULDN'T SEE THE FOREST FOR THE CHEESE.

Introduction to Personal Finance

19

This section of the book is a bit different from first section, because it focuses not just on the mechanics of using Quicken but the larger questions of how you earn, spend, and plan your money. But don't walk away from Quicken as you read through this section. Quicken has a number of financial tools that can help you plan, save, and spend wisely. Whether it's forecasting cash flow, planning for a college education, or establishing a life-long savings plan, Quicken has the tools you need to help reach your goals.

If you bought Quicken Deluxe on CD-ROM, you have two new financial advice programs, *Finance 101* and *Ask The Experts.* These are detailed later in the section "Using Quicken Deluxe's Advice Features" In addition, Quicken's online help system is well worth exploring for information, so see chapter 16. While it's true that these software guides cover similar ground to the rest of this book, we don't see that as a problem. When you're dealing with a complex new subject—especially one as emotionally fraught as saving money for the future—it is very helpful to have it explained twice in slightly different ways.

Just remember that if the Quicken CD-ROM says one thing, and this book says another, we're right and they're wrong. (Only joking.) Seriously, it's not that often that you get financial advice that's truly disinterested. Neither Intuit nor Peachpit Press has any vested interest in whether you save money or where you make your investments. Not as long as you have enough money left over for your annual software updates and your quota of computer books.

Is This You?

Many bright, hardworking people live from paycheck to paycheck, believing that they have little control over their personal financial situation. They don't think they are earning enough money to save and invest, or that they have the time, energy, or knowledge to do any long-term personal financial planning. Despite that they might be successful teachers, mechanics, lawyers, nurses, or computer programmers, they become helpless when it comes to planning their financial futures.

Money is an odd thing in our society. We've all heard the adage that money can't buy happiness—but an inadequate supply of money can certainly bring *unhappiness*. We must all deal with the role of money in our lives, no matter how much or how little we have. And there's no question that money is important.

It is not only necessary to buy food and shelter, it enables us to invest for the future. Most people want a financial sense of well being. They would like to know that they could retire tomorrow whether they wanted to or not. Also, money can enable a person to live more creatively and more expansively: to travel, to study abroad, or to work for causes they support.

But what price must we pay for this freedom? Must we spend 30 or 40 years at a job we don't like so we can accumulate enough wealth to be "free"? If so, are we freer than the person who works at a loved job but can't retire until age 70 on little more than Social Security?

The first question we must answer is: How much of our lives are we willing to trade for money? Are we willing to live on a half-time salary and wear used clothing to pursue our passion for yoga, acting, or tinkering with a computer? Or do we want to work an extra job selling real estate in the evening in order to drive a luxury sports car and have a closet full of new clothes? We may never frame these questions consciously but all of us answer them by the lifestyles we choose and the way we relate to money.

What type of life do we want for our children? Paying for your kids' college education isn't a mandated part of parenting, but most parents want to give their kids as many advantages as possible. Do your kids need to attend Harvard or will the local community college be just fine? Do you need to pay the entire bill or can they get scholarships or, perish the thought, work their way through school? Even when your kids are little, you have to face questions. Sure, you'll pay for their food, medicine and clothes. But do your little ones need the latest fad toys and must your teenagers wear designer clothes? It's up to you.

In this section of the book, we are going to attempt to unravel the money mystery. We will provide some basic knowledge and helpful tools to enable you to more effectively pursue your chosen lifestyle. We will help you minimize your taxes, consume wisely, and choose the best way to invest your savings. The advice works the same, whether you are saving $1,000 a week or $50 a month.

Where Your Money Goes

Your income goes to three places: taxes, consumption of goods and services, and savings. It is a zero-sum situation: if one increases, the others must decrease by an equal amount. If your taxes and consumption are greater than your income, you have a negative cash flow, which means you must either draw down your savings or borrow money. Hopefully this is a short-term phenomena. If, however, you must borrow money, there are wise and not-so-wise ways to do it.

Using Quicken Deluxe's Advice Features

Quicken Deluxe's advice features, *Finance 101* and *Ask The Experts*, load from Quicken's Deluxe Gateway. You can access the Quicken Deluxe Gateway several different ways. If you are not already running Quicken, you can start the Deluxe Gateway by selecting it from the Start Menu (or, if you are running Windows 3.1, the Program Manager). If you are already running Quicken, you can access the Deluxe Gateway by clicking on the Deluxe Gateway area of HomeBase.

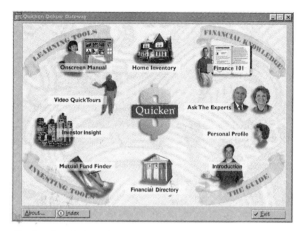

The Quicken Deluxe Gateway.

Note: *If you have a computer with less than 16MB of RAM, it's best to exit Quicken and other software applications before starting one of Quicken Deluxe's financial advice features. Otherwise, you might encounter poor performance when playing some of the video clips.*

Filling out the Personal Profile

Personal Profile is a way for you to tell Quicken information about your financial situation. Quicken uses this data to tailor the way *Ask The Experts* and *Finance 101* offer you advice.

To enter information into Personal Profile:

1. Open the Quicken Deluxe Gateway.

2. Click on the Personal Profile.

3. Enter information in the fields on the General page. Obviously, this includes your name, birthdate, whether you are married, whether your partner works, the ages of your children, and whether you have an employer-sponsored retirement plan (such as a 401(k) plan, a 403(b) plan, or a pension plan).

The Personal Profile General information tab.

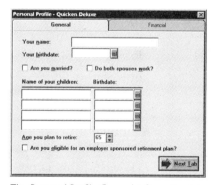

The Personal Profile Financial tab.

4. Click the Next Tab button or the Financial tab to switch to the Financial page. Then enter information in the fields on that page regarding your Annual Gross Income, Adjusted Gross Income, Annual Expenses, etc. To fill in the fields using TurboTax or Quicken data, click Update Data From Quicken and TurboTax. Click the update option you want in the window that opens, and click OK.

5. Click Save from the Personal Profile window.

If your personal data changes, you can repeat these steps and enter new data. The worksheets in *Finance 101* and the questions in *Ask The Experts* will reflect the changes you make.

Hearing Sound

Both *Finance 101* and *Ask The Experts* make extensive use of sound, especially if you choose to play their video clips. Therefore, this is a good time to verify the audio capabilities of your computer, perhaps by running the Windows Media Player (MPLAYER) desk accessory and loading a sample .WAV file to hear how it sounds.

If your computer does not have audio capabilities, consider Quicken Deluxe a good excuse to add them. Sound cards are available for about $50 to $300 for every desktop computer. If you have a portable or a desktop computer without an expansion slot, you can add sound via an external device that connects to your parallel port or via a PCM card adapter.

Microsoft offers a PC speaker driver that can play .WAV files using your PC's built-in speaker. It is available via some online services. However, this is not really a solution we recommend, because the speaker driver is not designed for Windows 95, usually offers very poor quality, and places a great deal of overhead on your CPU.

Finance 101

To start *Finance 101*:

1. Open the Quicken Deluxe Gateway:

2. Click on *Finance 101*.

3. If your Quicken CD-ROM is not in the drive, an error message appears. Insert the Quicken Deluxe disc and click on OK to continue.

This error message appears if you try to run Finance 101 *or* Ask The Experts *without loading the Quicken CD.*

4. You now see the *Finance 101* main window, which mimics the appearance of a book.

You can access information in *Finance 101* several ways. To move through the book, you start by using the introduction and table of contents page. Here, you'll learn what's in *Finance 101* and all about its author, Eric Tyson. You can start there, or choose a topic to review or a worksheet to fill in. You'll also find these work-

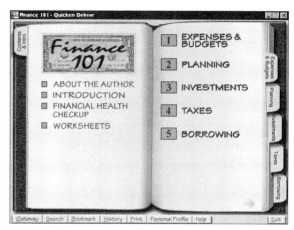

The Finance 101 *window.*

sheets interspersed throughout *Finance 101*.

The items in the Table of Contents correspond to the tabs you see on the edges of the book. Each chapter has a Table of Contents, so you can easily go to a particular topic. You can also go through the book page by page by clicking the arrows at the bottom of the page.

Finance 101 uses various icons to let you know that there's more information on a page for you to review.

Finance 101 has gathered information from the Personal Profile and your Quicken data and pre-filled some information.

When you pass the cursor over a graphic with a purplish cast or outline, notice that the cursor changes to a hand. Click on the graphic and *Finance 101* will display a related topic or play an audio clip. Click on red underlined text for additional information. You'll also find a video at the beginning of every chapter.

Click Chart to see a relevant pie chart or bar graph.

Click Example to review an example of a particular point.

Click Worksheet to display a worksheet related to the topic at hand.

We could say more about the content of *Finance 101*, but you'll discover it soon enough for yourself. If you're biased toward having information in print—which is probably why you bought the Little Quicken Book in the first place—you can print out a *Finance 101* section or even the entire book. Just click on the <u>P</u>rint button at the bottom of the screen. The resulting output won't put any graphic designers out of business, but it is readable.

Ask The Experts

To start *Ask The Experts*:

1. Open the Quicken Deluxe Gateway:

2. Click on *Ask The Experts*.

The Ask The Experts *window.*

3. If your Quicken CD-ROM is not in the drive, the error message appears asking you to insert the CD. Insert the Quicken Deluxe CD and click on OK to continue.

4. You now see the *Ask The Experts* main window.

Click on the <u>H</u>elp button at the lower right and you'll hear an audio introduction. As you listen, you can select topics by choosing one of the tabs along the left edge of the window. *Ask The Experts* uses audio and simple animation to guide you through advice from Jane Bryant Quinn and Marshall Loeb. At the end of each segment, a dialog box pops up offering to take you directly to the relevant section of Quicken Deluxe, such as making a budget.

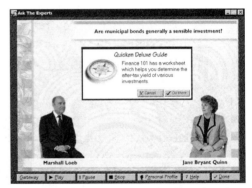

Ask The Experts *can send you directly to the relevant Quicken Deluxe section.*

Summary

If you purchased Quicken Deluxe version 5, you'll get advice not only from this book section, but also from the attractively designed new multimedia features. One way or another, you're going to find out more about personal finance than you ever dreamed possible. In the following chapters, we're going to look at how you earn, spend, and plan your money.

Taxes—How to Plan and Save Money

20

Though Americans constantly complain about their taxes and every politician promises to lower them, we pay fewer taxes than people living in other advanced industrial countries. Knowing this doesn't make paying them any easier for most people, so this chapter will provide you with some ways to lower your tax burden—increasing the money available for you to spend or save.

Basic Concepts of Taxation

Before we discuss tax strategies, let's review some basic taxation concepts. The four fundamental tax-reduction strategies are tax *exclusions*, *deductions*, *credits*, and *deferrals*.

A tax *exclusion* is money you receive that is not subject to taxation. Proceeds from a life insurance policy, recovery in a personal injury lawsuit, fringe benefits like health insurance coverage, or interest from tax-exempt municipal bonds (see Chapter 23) need not be declared as income to the IRS.

A tax *deduction* is subtracted from your taxable income. Your taxable income consists of such items as wages, salaries, interest, and dividends. Assume, for example, that you have a taxable income of $30,000. After you buy a house and pay mortgage interest of $7,000 a year, your taxable income is only $23,000. This is because mortgage interest is a deductible expense. If you are in a 28 percent tax bracket, this $7,000 deduction saves you $1,960 in taxes.

A tax *credit* is a dollar-for-dollar subtraction from your tax liability. If, for example, your tax obligation is $2,000 and you are entitled to a $500 child care tax credit, your taxes due the government are only $1,500.

A tax *deferral* enables you to put off part of your taxable income to some future year. This lowers your current taxable income and, consequently, your income tax. A good example of a tax deferral is a tax-deferred retirement program such as an individual retirement account (IRA). The tax code allows some people to invest $2,000 per year in an IRA (see Chapter 23) and defer any taxes on the $2,000 and its interest, until retirement. Presumably after retirement, your income will be less and, likewise, your tax bracket.

When you use a tax deduction or tax deferral provision, the amount you save in taxes depends on your tax bracket or *marginal* tax rate. The marginal tax rate is the amount of tax that you pay on the last dollar earned. There are now five tax brackets in the federal tax code: 15 percent, 28 percent, 31 percent, 36 percent, and 39.6 percent.

For a single person filing in 1994, the income tax broke down like this: 15 percent on taxable income of up to $22,750; 28 percent on taxable income between $22,750 and $55,100; 31 percent on taxable income between $55,100 and $115,000; 36 percent on taxable income between $115,000 and $250,000; and 39.6 percent on taxable income over $250,000.

Quicken Tip: To get a better picture of your own tax situation, try using the Quicken Tax Planner (explained in Chapter 18). Unlike a tax-preparation program, this tool won't fill out your return but it will give you a pretty good idea. Best of all, it lets you play "what if" games with your tax scenario. You can change the amount of your IRA or other variables and see its impact on your personal taxes. You can even use this planner to help determine how much your employer should withhold from your paycheck.

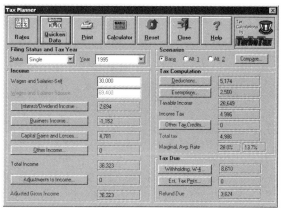

Quicken's Tax Planner gives you a sense of what you'll owe Uncle Sam.

The IRS has a comprehensive book that explains all the various tax items and gives numerous examples. It is called Publication 17 and it is free of charge.

Tax Strategies

The best strategy for lowering your tax obligation is to convert as many ordinary non-deductible expenditures into deductible ones. This lowers your taxable income and, subsequently, your tax bill.

There are many ways to convert non-deductible expenses into deductible ones. For example: As a renter, your rent payments are non-deductible expenses. As a homeowner, however, the mortgage interest and property taxes are tax-deductible. This makes a compelling argument for saving your money for a down payment and buying your own home.

Buying a $100,000 home with a 20 percent down payment can easily provide you with a $10,000 deduction for the mortgage interest and property taxes. If you are in the 28 percent marginal tax bracket, that represents a $2,800 tax savings at the federal level and hundreds of dollars in state taxes, depending on your state's income tax rates. If you buy a duplex and rent the other unit, you can also deduct the expenses associated with the half of the building that you rent, which includes half of the costs of any repairs that affect both units. A good example of a repair that affects both units is a new roof.

If you are saving money each year for your retirement, take advantage of the various tax deferred retirement programs (see Chapter 23). When you use an IRA, a 401(k), a Keogh, or Simplified Employee Pension Plan (SEPP), your annual savings become tax-deferred.

If you are paying high non-tax-deductible interest payments on your credit card balances, furniture loans, or auto loan and you have some equity built up in your home, you may want to get a home equity loan. A home equity loan will invariably be at a lower interest rate than these other loans. In addition, this interest is tax-deductible. The downside is that there are some costs, such as paying for an appraisal, associated with getting a home equity loan. With a home equity loan, you also are putting your house at some risk since the provider of the home equity loan now holds a mortgage on your property.

If the current interest rate is significantly lower than the rate on your first mortgage, you may want to refinance for a larger amount to get money to pay off your debts.

Beyond this fundamental strategy of converting non-deductible expenses into deductible ones, there are other things you can do to lower your tax bite and improve your overall financial planning.

Don't be thrilled about a big tax refund. It only means that you overpaid the government or, in essence, gave the government a tax-free loan.

Don't be thrilled about a big tax refund. It only means that you overpaid the government or, in essence, gave the government a tax-free loan. One study estimates that the average tax refund is about $900. If this money were invested rather than lent to Uncle Sam, the interest earned could really add up over the years. If you are getting large refunds, you need to adjust the amount withheld from your paycheck. On the other hand, you do not want to have too little withheld. This can result in owing the government a large amount at tax time and if it's too large, you may also be assessed a penalty. Quicken's Tax Planner can help you determine how much should be withheld from your check each pay period.

Keep good records and save your receipts. The best way to be sure you capture all your tax-deductible expenses is to use Quicken's category feature for every tax-deductible check, credit card, and cash payment you make. Don't forget to enter charitable contributions and any tax-deductible out-of-pocket expenses in the appropriate Quicken register.

You are more likely to benefit from all of the deductions you are legally entitled to if you are well organized. It's often better to donate items you no longer need to a charity rather than having a garage sale. You are entitled to deduct the "fair market value" of the item and usually end up better off than selling the item for rummage. Be sure you get a receipt for the donation. Also, you can deduct your expenses for charitable work. Mileage can be deducted at 12 cents per mile.

You are more likely to benefit from all of the deductions you are legally entitled to if you are well organized. It's often better to donate items you no longer need to a charity rather than having a garage sale.

If you regularly donate to a particular charity, you may want to contribute an appreciated asset. You get the fair market value of the asset, and neither you nor the charity has to pay the capital gains tax. For example, let's assume that you bought 50 shares of stock at $5 a share, held the stock for more than a year (the IRS-required minimum) while it appreciated in value to $20 a share. Your initial $250 investment is now worth $1,000. If you donate the stock to a charity, they receive $1,000 in value, you receive a $1,000 deduction, and neither you nor the charity pay taxes on the $750 in capital gains. Again, be sure to record all your donations in your Quicken register. If you put $5 a week in a church collection plate, be sure to record it in a Quicken "cash" account!

If you sell your home and have a capital gain, you can defer the taxes on the gain if you buy another home of equal or greater value within two years of the sale. You can continue to defer the capital gains until you are over 55 years old. After you turn 55, you are entitled to a one-time exclusion from capital gains of up to $125,000 from the sale of your primary residence. You must have owned and lived in the residence for three of the past five years.

Finally, if you are working, you may be eligible for the Earned Income Tax Credit. To qualify for a credit of up to $2,038, you must be earning less than $23,755 per year and have one child. If you have two or more children, you must be earning less than $25,296 to qualify for a credit of up to $2,528.

Who Should Prepare Your Taxes

Because you're using Quicken, it's relatively easy to prepare your own taxes using TurboTax, TaxCut, or one of the other tax preparation software programs. TurboTax and Quicken, which are both from Intuit, are specifically designed to work with each other because TurboTax will automatically import a Quicken file. The process of using Quicken files for tax preparation is covered in Chapter 18.

There are a lot of advantages to preparing your own tax returns, though there are some drawbacks. You'll save a little money by not having to pay a tax professional, though part of that will be reduced because of the cost of the tax preparation program (usually about $40). The big advantage is that, by doing your own returns, you'll learn how the system works. What is and is not deductible will start to make more sense to you.

The downside of doing your own taxes is that you don't get the advice of a CPA or tax professional. While tax preparation programs do a good job, they may not be as crafty as a good tax preparer when it comes to gray areas or strategic planning.

Another option: do both. Use a tax preparation program to create a "rough draft" of your return, and then have it examined by a tax professional to be sure you've taken advantage of every possible deduction.

Saving

21

While minimizing your tax burden, covered in the previous chapter, can be almost fun, the same, unfortunately, can't be said of saving money. Your precious after-tax income can be spent today for food, clothing, rent, or to buy a new car; or you can put part of your income aside and spend it in the future for your children's education, your retirement, or a down payment on a home. However, to buy the bigger things in life, like a home, a vacation to Japan, or a secure retirement, you must postpone some of your consumption now and save some of that money for the future.

Americans are not great savers. We typically save less than five percent of our after-tax income. The Germans and the Japanese, for example, are much better savers than Americans. On average, the Japanese save 18 to 19 percent of their income.

The amount you should save depends on your current situation and your goals for the future. Unless you're independently wealthy or have a winning lottery ticket in your pocket, you ought to seriously consider a savings program, regardless of your age. And you need to reevaluate your situation at each stage of life. For example, if you're in your twenties and plan to raise a family, you'll soon need money for a house and a head start on your children's education. Ideally, you should be putting some money into a retirement program as soon as you start working, but retirement planning becomes paramount once you reach your forties.

Saving, which requires you to "live on less," is very difficult for many people. It's like dieting. We know we should eat less, but it is just difficult to do. Crash savings plans, like crash diets, usually fail miserably. You need to develop a reasonable and realistic savings plan that you can maintain, even if it means gradually building up to your goal of 8 percent, 10 percent or even 15 percent of your income.

Analyzing Your Situation

The first step is to analyze your current financial situation. This is similar to the way a business analyzes its financial situation. You need to develop a balance sheet and an income statement for your household.

Quicken Tip: Quicken can create a number of financial statements (Quicken calls them "reports") that give you a picture of your financial

Quicken's Create Report menu lets you examine your cash flow, budget, and net worth.

condition. These are available from the Report Menu and covered in detail in Chapter 11. It's an especially good idea to have a sense of your net worth: your assets minus your liabilities.

To determine your assets, be sure to include all items of value including bank accounts, stocks, bonds, mutual funds, the cash value of any insurance, pension plans, automobiles, and real estate. Also, include anything else of value, such as a coin collection, art, or valuable jewelry. For each item put the estimated value (what it would sell for today, not its replacement value). Collectively, these are your assets. As we discussed in Chapter 4, Quicken lets you create "accounts" for all types of assets, including personal possessions.

Quicken Tip: Quicken also lets you create "accounts" for your liabilities—what you owe. Include your mortgage, the balance you owe on your car, and any other debts that you might have, including any credit card balances. The program will automatically subtract your liabilities from your assets and report your net worth. You will probably find that you have a greater net worth than you realized.

Quicken's Create New Account window lets you create a variety of account types, including liability.

The income statement is simply a record of your after-tax income, minus your expenditures. Although we don't expect you to do this constantly (we don't) it's a great idea, for a month or so, to use Quicken to keep track of *everything* you spend, down to the cost of your morning coffee or that pack of gum you bought on the way back from lunch.

Make sure that each expenditure is categorized (see Chapter 5) so that you can get a breakdown of how you spend your money. Then print out a report (see Chapter 11) for that period. The difference between your after-tax income and your expenditures is what you have left for savings. If this figure equals your desired level of savings, great. For most people, however, it is probably nowhere near the percentage of after-tax income you need to set aside for savings.

Now, analyze your expenditures. Decide what is absolutely essential and what you can either do without altogether or do less expensively. You may find that some items that you thought were small really add up over a month. Spending $10 per work day on lunch adds up to more than $200 a month. Spending money on a health club membership that is used twice a month may not be sensible. Having closets full of stylish clothes may be nice, but then is it necessary to buy that new suit you recently saw? On the other hand, perhaps your lunches out are very important to you. That's fine. Only you can analyze your expenditures and decide where you can save money.

The Beauty of Compound Interest

Saving money early in life can be very helpful because of something called compound interest. Compound interest means that if you invest your money at a given interest rate and let the money accumulate, you receive interest not only on the original principal that you invested, but also on the interest that you earn. Investing $100 at 10 percent interest will yield $110 at the end of the first year. At the end of the second year, you will have $121 because you earned interest over the past year on $110. Over time this can really add up.

For example, if you invest $1,000 at 7 percent interest compounded annually, you will have $1,402 at the end of five years. At the end of 10 years, you will have $1,967. If you were getting 10 percent interest, your $1,000 would be worth $1,610 after five years, $2,594 after 10 years and $10,835 after 25 years. This is more than a 10 fold increase. If you were to start with $1,000 and add $1,000 each year for 25 years, it would be worth $109,181.

Don't take my word for this. Use Quicken's Investment Savings Planner (pull down the Plan menu, select Financial Planners and then Savings) and enter in your own scenario. Be sure to uncheck Ending Balance in Today's $ to see your actual accumulation.

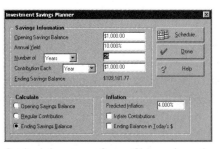

Quicken's Investment Savings Planner shows the power of compound interest.

The length of time an investment collects interest is also very important. Here's a dramatic example: Assume there are twin sisters with very different savings plans. One sister puts aside $100 a month starting on her 20th birthday at 10 percent annual interest, compounded monthly. On her 27th birthday, she stops adding money to her account and just lets the balance accumulate interest. On her 27th birthday, the second twin starts saving $100 a month at the same interest rate as her sister—and continues to save that much until retirement. At age 65, which sister has the greater fortune? The first sister has $532,000 and her twin, who contributed into her retirement for 38 years, has $516,000.

Even if you don't have a twin sister, you can use Quicken's Savings Calculator to create a similar model for your situation. You can also use Quicken's Retirement Planner to calculate the result of annual contributions to a tax-deferred savings plan. Either way, it will quickly become obvious that the earlier you start and the more you save, the better off you are.

Don't be despondent if you're long past 20 years old. We can't turn the clock back, but you can start saving now.

There are a number of ways to force yourself to save. Decide how much you should save each month and write out a check to your investment account each month when you write out your rent or mortgage check. Better yet, if you use online banking (see Chapter 15), program Quicken to make automatic fixed payments to your investment account. Or you can have your banker or broker arrange to have contributions deducted automatically from your checking account.

In essence, pay your future first before you buy the groceries or a new pair of shoes. Another option is to have your employer deduct the amount each paycheck through a payroll savings plan.

People use other schemes to help them save. They may not increase their expenditures when they get a raise, but rather save the increased

NO DUMMY, STEVE TUCKS SOMETHING
AWAY FOR A RAINY DAY.

money. Then, when they get their next raise, they increase their expenditures to last year's income level. This way, they are always saving the current year's raise. Others do some part-time work to earn extra money and save half of whatever they gross. Whatever works to help you save is a great approach.

When you are saving for retirement and plan to let the investment grow until you are about 60 years old, you should take advantage of any of the tax-deferred retirement programs available. One such plan is an Individual Retirement Account (IRA). If you are employed and not covered by a pension plan, an IRA will allow you to deduct your IRA contribution of up to $2,000 per year. If you are in a company plan, you can still deduct part or all of your IRA contribution, depending on your income level.

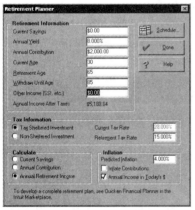

Quicken's Retirement Planner shows the impact of a $2,000 annual IRA contribution over 30 years.

Another tax-deferred retirement plan available to employees at some companies is the 401(k). Some employers will fund part of your 401K plan (sometimes matching dollar for dollar). This fringe benefit of matching contributions amounts to free money, and you should, by all means, take advantage of it.

For the self-employed or those who work for an unincorporated business that does not offer its own pension plan, there is the Keogh plan. A Keogh will allow you to defer up to 20 percent of your income up to $30,000 annually. Another more flexible alternative for many employees and self-employed people is the Simplified Employee Pension Plan (SEPP).

Tax deferral simply puts off the payment of taxes. Despite the fact that you are eventually going to have to pay taxes on this money, there are two advantages to using a tax-deferred retirement plan. First, it is assumed that you will be at a lower income when you are retired and, so, in a lower tax bracket. Secondly, the principal, interest, dividends, and capital gains all compound tax free. This gives the power of compound interest even greater strength. Quicken's Retirement Planner can give you a very good idea of the effect of these savings. It even adjusts for inflation and the variation between your current tax bracket and your likely bracket at retirement.

Introduction to Investments

22

WHAT STARTED
AS AN ADDITION
TURNED INTO A
MULTIPLICATION.

Basic Principles

Everywhere you look, whether
it's television, magazines, newspapers, or
billboards, there are ads describing the highest interest rates in
town, the best-performing mutual funds, a sure-fire real estate
development, or predictions of an impending economic crash and
appeals for you to buy gold. All this advice can seem confusing.
Although many financial planners and brokers would like you to
think it is, please keep this in mind: personal financial planning is
not complicated. There are some *basic principles about investing,
and all investing is simply a variation of the basics.*

Before formulating an investment strategy, there are three major things for you to consider.

1. Make your investment strategy fit your financial needs and your goals.

Your age, family situation, current and future earning capacity, net worth, and temperament are all major factors to consider in developing an investment strategy. If you are a single 28-year-old doctor with no college loans, you should invest very differently than a 59-year-old widow who recently reentered the labor force and works as a clerk at Wal-Mart. Your temperament is important in determining the amount of risk you can feel comfortable with, no matter what your circumstances.

Review your investment strategy periodically, especially if some major change occurs in your life. You may get married, divorced, have more children, buy a house, or inherit some money. Any major life change will probably require an adjustment in your strategy.

2. Review your insurance policies.

Be sure you have adequate insurance including health, disability, and life. You will also want to have three months of income in a savings account or money market fund before you begin to invest in other financial instruments.

3. Set out your financial goals and objectives.

Be realistic. *Goals* are longer term, broader, and more open-ended than objectives. Probably one of your goals is financial security, however you may define that concept. Another example of a financial goal is owning your own business and being your own boss.

Your financial *objectives* are more narrowly defined than your goals and more time-based. Possible objectives include owning your own home by age 35, saving 15 percent of your after-tax income for the next 25 years, paying off your college loans by age 30, or taking a vacation abroad every three years.

After you have developed financial objectives that support your financial goals, then you must embark on your investment strategy to accomplish these objectives.

Developing a Strategy

It is amazing how much easier it is to sleep at night once you have written out your financial objectives and developed your strategy to meet them. As long as you can stay on your investment course, you can see that by the time the children are ready for college or when you plan to retire, the resources will be there.

TIM FOLLOWS AN APPROPRIATIONS BILL THROUGH HIS FINANCE COMMITTEE.

Whether you know it or not, you already have an investment strategy. This is because not having a strategy is actually having one by default. Having all of your money in your mattress or a passbook account is an investment strategy. It is not a particularly wise strategy, nor one that will help you realize your financial goals, but it is a strategy nonetheless.

The Trade-Off Between Risk and Return

There are basic principals of investing that should be understood as you develop your investment plan. The main principal is the trade-off between risk and return. The greater the risk, the higher the return should be; conversely, the safer the investment, the lower the return. If, for example, you invest in Treasury Bonds, which are backed by the federal government (low risk), you should expect a lower rate of return than if you buy stock in a start-up business (high risk).

Stocks are riskier than bonds because if a business goes into bankruptcy, the bondholders get paid off before any money goes to the stockholders.

Diversification is important. The "all of your eggs in one basket" approach is obviously risky, so prudent investors spread out their investments. You can diversify at whatever level of risk you choose. Some cautious investors buy stocks or mutual funds, some corporate bonds, some real estate, and maybe a bit of something very conservative, such as short-term treasury bills. Others diversify by investing in a variety of stocks. Some of these stocks may be solid blue-chip stocks and others may be for more speculative growth companies, but all of the money is in stocks.

Young risk-takers may buy several different growth stocks. They are diversified but at a higher level of risk. However you decide to diversify your investment is your decision, but every financial advisor recommends that you diversify in some way.

Another decision is whether to preserve your principal, or risk losing some of it in hope of greater gain. For example, a person who is saving to go to college next year would not want to invest in growth stocks that might drop in value if the market turns down just when tuition money is needed. Rather, it would be better to invest in a certificate of deposit at a local bank or a money market fund where interest can be collected on the principal. That way, the principal is never in jeopardy.

On the other hand, if you are willing to put your principal at risk, you can possibly earn a much greater rate of return in stocks, mutual funds, or real estate.

If you are going to need your money relatively soon (as in the case of the high school senior), you will want a "liquid" investment that can be converted to cash easily. Stocks, bonds, and money market funds are quite liquid while real estate and small business ventures may be difficult to sell.

As we mentioned earlier, it's a good idea to keep about three months of income in a very liquid investment. After that, depending on your expected needs, you can invest in less-liquid and, hopefully, higher-yielding investments.

How Active Do You Want To Be?

A final consideration in your investment strategy is how actively involved you want to be in the investment. The more actively you are involved, the higher rate of return you should receive. For example, if you buy real estate in your community and manage it, you must spend many hours involved in this investment. On the other hand, you could put your money in a money market fund or a mutual fund and check on it once a year or so.

Most investments fall in one of two categories: either you lend your money and earn interest, or you buy something. If you lend your money, your principal is preserved, and your return (the interest you earn) is often a fixed amount. Putting your money in a savings account, a certificate of deposit, a money market fund, a treasury security, or a corporate bond are some of the more common ways people lend money. To the degree that the after-tax interest rate you receive is greater than the rate of inflation, your investment is growing.

A riskier approach is to buy something that you hope will increase in value so when you sell it you reap a capital gain. These types of ownership investments can also generate a periodic payment to you in dividends, rent, or royalties. Examples include stocks, mutual funds, small business partnerships, commodities, and real estate.

As the American investor has gotten more sophisticated over the past two decades, dozens of new ways to invest have come onto the market. They virtually all fall into one of two categories: interest-earning or ownership investments. The next two chapters will describe these types of investments in more detail.

Interest-earning Investments

23

DOWIST MONK

Interest-earning investments pay interest periodically and pay back the amount invested either on demand or at maturity. Such investments include savings accounts, money market accounts, certificates of deposit, money market funds, and all the varieties of bonds, both private and governmental. These interest-earning investments are safe, conservative ways to invest money, but you will probably not reach your long-term financial goals with only these types of investments.

These investments, however, do have a place in your investment strategy. They offer a way to diversify or to temporarily hold some of your assets while you are waiting to invest in something else. For example, at some time, you may feel that the stock market is overvalued, and you expect it to adjust downward in the near future. In that case, you might want to hold some of your money in a money market fund and wait for the market to drop.

Although interest-earning accounts are often criticized because the potential return is not as exciting as what you can get with stocks or other more aggressive (and riskier) investments, they can pay off in the long run. As an experiment, try playing with Quicken's Savings Planner (from the Plan menu—see Chapter 17 for details) to see the impact of various saving strategies. As the planner will show, it's possible to see dramatic long-term gains thanks to the power of compound interest.

Savings Accounts

You should always have some money that is very liquid and available for immediate use. The least attractive interest-yielding investment is the simple passbook savings account at your local bank. Though the savings account is highly liquid and risk-free (accounts are insured up to $100,000 by the federal government), the interest rate is very low. Rather than have this reserve money in a regular savings account, it is often wiser to divide this money between an interest-bearing checking account at your local bank and a higher-interest money market mutual fund.

An interest-bearing checking account allows you to write checks to cover your daily expenses. Like a savings account, it pays a nominal interest rate and is also federally insured. Regular savings accounts and this type of checking account actually cause your savings to *decrease* each year because the after-tax interest is invariably less than inflation. For this reason, it is wise to keep the minimum balance in your interest-bearing checking account and transfer the rest of the money that you feel you need for emergencies into a higher-yielding money market mutual fund. The money market mutual fund may yield an after-tax interest above the rate of inflation, so you would not be losing money.

When you open your account, shop around. Though typically the interest rates on accounts are nearly the same, the service charges can be very different. Banks require different minimum balances and the service fees and fees per check processed when the balance falls below a required minimum vary as well. Some banks offer free interest-bearing checking accounts if you maintain a mortgage loan or have other funds on deposit at that bank.

A little fancier type of bank account for larger deposits is the money market deposit account, which pays a variable interest rate. In times of high interest rates, your money market account will pay a much more attractive rate than a regular bank savings account or an interest-bearing checking account. Many banks' money market accounts—not to be confused with a money market mutual fund—have some restrictions on withdrawals. For example, only three withdrawals via check might be allowed each month.

See Chapter 8 for information about using Quicken to set up and mange savings and money market accounts.

Money Market Mutual Funds

Besides money for daily transactions, you need other liquid assets for financial emergencies. You need to be able to access this money without risking any of the principal. If you have all these savings in either stocks or bonds, you could get your money almost immediately. But you might lose some of the principal if you had to sell them when the market was down. For that very reason, most people are willing to accept the lower yields of a money market mutual fund because they know their principal is protected even if they must withdraw the money immediately.

Money market mutual funds were created in 1972 in response to the rising sophistication of smaller investors. Small investors saw that large investors could get much higher interest rates on their investments because they could buy commercial paper (IOUs from large corporations), large-denomination certificates of deposit from banks, or large-denomination government securities. Money market mutual funds simply take the savings of small investors and pool the money to buy the kind of higher-yielding money market investments that previously only large investors could afford. Unlike mutual stock funds, money market mutual funds do not invest in stocks.

The main advantages of a money market mutual fund are higher yields than small investors could get individually, total liquidity (investors can withdraw by check), low administrative fees, and lower risk through diversification. Even though money market mutual funds are not federally insured, they are relatively safe because they invest in variety of conservative investments. If you dislike risk, but still want the advantages of a money market mutual fund, you can invest in a money market mutual fund that invests in only government securities.

Certificates of Deposit

A certificate of deposit is a bank deposit left in the bank for a certain time in exchange for a higher interest rate. The larger the amount deposited and the longer the maturity, the higher the interest rate. Maturities range from one month to ten years. The CD's rate should be based on compound interest, not simple interest. The longer the maturity of the CD, the bigger the difference this will make.

Interest rates vary from bank to bank, so call around and compare the yields. The penalties for early withdrawal also vary. If you think there is a possibility that you may have to withdraw early, factor the penalty in when comparing interest rates.

Bonds

Bonds can offer a higher yield than a CD, but they are a more complicated investment than a CD, and can be riskier. A bond is simply an IOU from a corporation or from the federal, state, or local governments. Bonds are ideal for people who want a higher interest rate with relatively low risk, especially if they are willing to hold the bonds for the long term. Bonds offer a fixed interest income over the life of the bonds, but the value of the bond changes as the interest rate fluctuates with the economy.

Bonds are issued when an institution needs to raise a substantial amount of money. For example, a corporation may decide that it needs to build another plant to accommodate the expanding sales of its product, so it must borrow several million dollars. If it seeks money from a bank, it is called a loan; if it borrows from the general public, it is called a "bond offering."

The corporation issues bonds with a coupon rate of, for example, 8 percent for a term of 25 years. With a $1,000 bond, the bond holder will receive $80 a year for the next 25 years and then get the principal (the original face value of the bond) back at the end of the 25 years.

If the company doesn't go bankrupt or "call in" the bond, and the bond-holder chooses to hold the bond for the next 25 years, it is a fairly straight-forward investment. Interest rates can rise and fall, but as long as the bond is held, the bond holder will receive $80 each year.

If the bond holder decides to sell the bond before its maturity date, there could be a capital gain or loss. Most long-term bonds change hands many times before maturity. The value of an existing bond moves in the opposite direction of the interest rate. When interest rates go up, the value of the bond goes down and *vice versa*.

In our previous example, the $1,000 corporate bond with a coupon rate of 8 percent and $80 in annual interest paid those amounts because that was the prevailing interest rate for a bond of that quality when it was issued. Let's assume for a moment that interest rates double. That would mean that a $1,000 bond issued today of the same quality as our older 8 percent bond will have to pay a coupon rate of 16 percent, or an annual interest of $160.

Assuming you own the older bond and you need to sell it today, how much is it worth? It isn't worth $1,000 because a $1,000 bond today has a coupon rate of 16 percent and would pay $160 per year in inter-est—twice what your older bond's paying. Your bond is only paying $80 in interest annually, so your bond is worth only about $500. This is because at 16 percent interest, $500 would generate an annual interest payment of $80. Consequently, if you sold this 8 percent bond today, you would receive $500 and you would suffer a $500 capital loss.

Conversely, if interest rates had fallen to 4 percent, your bond that is yielding $80 in interest would be worth approximately $2,000. This is because 4 percent of $2,000 is $80. Again, you only experience this capital gain or loss if you sell your bond before its date of maturity. Should you hold this bond for the 25 years, you will receive an $80 interest payment annually no matter what the current interest rate, and at the end of the 25 year period, you will get your $1,000 back.

Another thing to consider when buying a bond is the "call in" provi-sion. Most corporate bonds can be "called in" or redeemed at their face value at anytime during the life of the bond. There are, however, some bonds that have certain "call in" restrictions. Again, let's use our previ-ous example. When the interest rate dropped to 4 percent, you were earning $80 annually from a bond with a face value of $1,000. The corporation would almost invariably call in that bond, pay you the face value of $1,000, and reissue that $1,000 bond at a 4 percent coupon rate or a $40 annual interest payment. You now have your original $1,000 back, but the best you can now earn is 4 percent interest.

When buying a bond it's good to find one that is non-callable. If that's not possible, at least be sure that it has partial call protection for five or ten years. Without some protection against a "call," the corporation will always win. If interest rates go up, they win because they will be paying you a below-market rate. If interest rates go down, they call in the bond for face value and reissue it at the lower rate. Government bonds are less likely to have "call in" provisions than private corporate bonds.

Bonds should be bought when interest rates are at their peak. Then, these high rates can be locked in with 20- or 30-year bonds. You will not only get a high annual return while you hold the bonds, but you stand to get a handsome capital gain if you sell the bonds when the interest rates drop.

The interest rate on a bond not only reflects the current interest rates in the world economy but also the level of risk of the institution issuing the bonds. Unlike selecting a stock (where it is important that the company's earnings grow rapidly), with a bond the major concern is for the company to avoid bankruptcy during the life of the bond.

The financial soundness of an institution issuing a bond can be determined by checking the two major bond-rating services, Moody's and Standard and Poor's. The highest rated bonds are triple A bonds followed by double A bonds, all the way down to C-rated bonds. It's wise to buy only high grade bonds initially, either triple A or double A bonds.

C-rated bonds—sometimes called junk bonds—provide higher returns but carry much higher risks. If you are seeking the higher returns that junk bonds provide, buy a junk bond *fund*. These funds are diversified so a single bankruptcy wouldn't wipe out your entire investment. But if you are willing to live with the risk associated with junk bonds, you are better off investing in stocks that could conceivably earn 50 percent or 100 percent on your money over a few years—if you choose your stocks well.

Treasury Securities

When you read about the federal government running a $200 billion deficit, you may wonder where the money comes from to cover this shortfall. Like a private company, the federal government covers its shortfalls by borrowing money. The federal government issues treasury securities, which include treasury bills, treasury notes, and treasury bonds.

The primary differences between treasury bills, treasury notes, and treasury bonds are their lengths of maturity and their minimum denominations. Treasury bills come in three-, six- and twelve-month maturities and their minimum denomination is $10,000. Treasury notes come in maturities between one and ten years, and the minimum denomination depends on the length of maturity. Notes have minimum denominations of $5,000 if the maturity is less than four years and $1,000 minimums for notes longer than four years. Treasury bonds have maturities between 10 and 30 years and minimum purchases of $1,000.

Treasury securities have some real advantages for the average investor who wants to balance his or her portfolio. Treasuries are perhaps the safest investment in the world. By dealing directly with a Federal Reserve Bank or one of its branches, these securities can be purchased without having to pay a commission. And it can be done by mail. Unlike corporate bonds, most treasury securities cannot be "called" when the interest rates fall, and treasuries are exempt from state and local taxes.

Municipal Bonds

Municipal bonds are issued by state and local governments and governmental agencies such as school districts, sewage treatment authorities, stadiums, and even for private corporate construction of new plants. The attractive feature of municipal bonds is that the interest earned is exempt from federal taxes. In addition, if you live in the state where the bonds are issued, the interest is usually exempt from state and local taxes.

There are three main types of municipal bonds:

1. General obligation bonds, which are backed by the full faith and credit of the local unit of government and repaid out of tax revenues;

2. Revenue bonds, which are issued to finance public works projects that generate revenues, such as a county baseball stadium. The revenues from the project are used to repay the bond holders; and

3. Industrial revenue bonds, which are for private business construction. Industrial revenue bonds are issued by a local unit of government on behalf of a private company. The government then lends the money to that business for its construction project. For example, a local government may want to help a company that wants to build a new plant that will employ 50 people. Because the local government issues the bonds, they are tax-exempt, which lowers the interest rate that the company has to pay. The bonds are paid back from the company's income.

Years ago, it was mostly the rich in their very high tax brackets who really benefited from tax-exempt municipal bonds. Now, however, with the federal tax brackets compressed, municipal bonds are probably worth considering if you are in the 28 percent tax bracket, especially if you live in a high-tax state.

If you earn over $22,750 of taxable income and you are single, you are in the 28 percent marginal tax bracket. Depending on the state in which you live, you may pay an additional six or seven percent in state taxes on the last dollars you earn.

Let's assume that with both your state and federal taxes, you are in a 34 percent marginal tax bracket. This means that you pay $34 in taxes on the last $100 that you earn. Let's further assume that you earn 6 percent interest on a municipal bond that is exempt from both federal and state taxes. That 6 percent interest earned on a double tax-exempt bond is equivalent to 9.09 percent interest earned on a taxable investment, such as a bond or certificate of deposit. The interest rates on municipal bonds depend on the current interest rates in the taxable bond market, the credit risk of the issuer, and the current tax laws.

Quicken Tip: *To see how tax-exempt bonds might affect you, use Quicken's Tax Planner (from the Plan Menu) to determine your marginal tax rate and multiply that rate by the amount of interest earned. Or you can use that same planner to enter the interest and see the difference on the Tax Planner's bottom line. See Chapter 18 for details on using the Quicken Tax Planner.*

Municipal bonds carry some risk. You can lose money if you need to sell the bonds before maturity because, like other bonds, municipals are interest-sensitive. If interest rates rise, the value of the bonds decline. Also, the transaction costs can be high for selling a small number of bonds, and, since municipal bonds usually sell for $5,000 per unit, a "small number of bonds" can be worth a significant amount of money.

In addition, the state or local government that issues the bonds can go into default. It doesn't happen often, but it does happen. Because of this risk, municipal bonds, like corporate bonds, are rated by Moody's and Standard and Poor's. Besides buying only double or triple A-rated bonds, there are two ways to protect yourself from default if you want to be in municipal bonds. You can buy insured municipal bonds, which provide protection in case of default, or you can invest in a diversified municipal bond *fund*.

Municipal bond funds come in many varieties, including single-state funds, which provide double tax exemptions for the buyer living in the state where the bonds are issued. The funds are professionally managed and have a management fee of usually less than one percent annually. You can buy "no load" bond funds. This means that you pay no commission when you buy shares in the fund, providing that you buy them directly from the fund through the mail. You'll find ads for bond funds in the business section of the major newspapers. Buying your fund through a broker could mean paying a commission as high as 8.5 percent.

The one major disadvantage of a bond fund is that it never matures. This is a disadvantage because if the interest rates rise and stay high, the value of bonds will fall and remain low. Selling your bonds will then result in a capital loss. Conversely, an individual bond that is held to maturity will give you back the face value of the bond, no matter how high the interest rate has gone.

There are many other interest-earning investments including mortgage-backed securities and foreign bonds. If you want to buy into these types of investments, it is probably wise to look for professionally managed funds in these areas. As we said at the beginning of this chapter, a balanced portfolio should probably have some interest-earning investments. But to earn greater returns on your money, you should consider owning assets rather than simply lending money, an option discussed in the next chapter.

Invest to Own

24

PHIL, WE'VE JUST INHERITED $10,000. KNOW ANYTHING ABOUT INVESTMENTS?

WELL, WE COULD DO SOMETHING BORING, LIKE BONDS...OR I'VE GOT THIS GREAT IDEA FOR CAT-FLAVORED TENNIS BALLS.

To earn a much greater return on your money, you need to go beyond simply lending your money to some institution to earn interest. Ownership investments, where you buy part of a company or some real estate, can be much riskier. But without such risk you may never earn the investment returns necessary to fulfill your long-term financial goals.

Stocks

The most common type of ownership investment is the purchase of common stock listed on one of the major exchanges. When you buy a share of stock, you become part owner of the company. It is a very small part, but it is ownership. As part owner, you make money when the company does well. Obviously, the risk comes in when the company does not do well.

If the company in which you are now part owner begins to lose money, your part becomes less valuable. Hopefully, the company will turn around and the stock will go back up in value. If the company continues to decline and eventually goes into bankruptcy, you get paid last. The creditors are paid off first, including the bond holders. If there is any money left, the preferred stock holders get paid and, finally, the common stock holders. You can, however, always sell your stock in a matter of seconds at the going market price if you begin to sense trouble with the company.

Companies issue stock when they need money to expand and grow. Once that stock has been issued and the company gets its initial money, the stocks are then traded between individuals on what is called a secondary market. A secondary market is one in which already issued shares are sold. The most famous secondary stock market in the world is the New York Stock Exchange (NYSE). Most of the shares sold on the NYSE were issued decades ago. If the price of Ford shares, for example, goes up, Ford does not benefit unless it decides to issue more stock. Usually a company is reluctant to issue more stock because it further dilutes the ownership.

You hear about the stock market on the news every day as the Dow Jones Industrials Average goes up or down. The Dow Jones Industrials is a complicated weighted average of 30 major stocks that provides, in one number, a way to measure the action of the NYSE. Another index is the Standard & Poor's (S&P) 500, which is a weighted average of 500 stocks traded on the NYSE, the American Stock Exchange, and the over-the-counter market. The Dow Jones Industrials track the blue-chip stocks, which may not always move in the same direction as the broader market. The broader market is better measured by the S&P 500.

The stock market moves up and down, but in the long term, it moves up more. Stocks are perhaps the best investments in a balanced portfolio. Stocks do well because a stock is part-ownership in a company with real assets, which rise along with inflation. They also do well because U.S. companies have been very profitable. According to statistics compiled by Ibbotson Associates of Chicago, a $1 investment made at the end of 1925 (four years before the market crash and the "Great Depression") would have grown by the end of 1991 to $11 in treasury bills, or $22 in long-term government bonds, or $675 in common stock.

There are two ways to make money with common stocks: dividends and capital gains. When a company makes a profit, at the end of the year it can either give some of the profit to the owners of the company (the shareholders), or it can reinvest this money back in the company so that it can grow faster. The profits that a company gives out are called *dividends*. If the company reinvests the profits, the company becomes more valuable. Then, when you sell your stock you earn a *capital gain*.

Stocks fluctuate in price by the minute. Some of this fluctuation is due to the circumstances of the particular company. Some of it has to do with the overall market or economy. If a company has a bad quarter and its earnings are down, this would cause the price of the stock to fall. Even if the quarterly earnings rose, the stock could still fall in price if the earnings did not rise as high as the Wall Street analysts predicted. This is because the market had already factored in the predicted earnings, which the company failed to meet. So, even though the earnings were up, the stock price would probably fall. If the company is fundamentally sound and there's a sound explanation why the predicted earnings were not met, this may be a good time to buy the stock.

The price of a stock can also rise or fall because of things beyond the control of the company. If the general industry sector to which the company belongs falls out of favor, it can negatively affect stock prices. For example, in 1994, when health care reform appeared imminent, prices of stocks in the pharmaceutical industry dropped. Even the stock of pharmaceutical companies that were very profitable dropped in price. Also, changes in the overall economy affect individual stock prices. A precipitous rise in the interest rates could cause the market to get nervous and stock prices to fall.

Types of Stock

Despite the fact that the prices of stocks rise and fall for a variety of reasons, the stock of a profitable company will increase in price in the long run. The rate of increase in the price of the stock will depend on the type of stock. Stocks can be divided into several categories: income stocks, growth stocks, blue-chip stocks, and cyclical stocks.

An income stock is usually a stock in a mature industry that will provide a steady income from dividends and will probably not grow very fast. A utility stock is a good example of this. A growth stock, on the other hand, will pay little or no dividend. A growth stock company will reinvest its profits in research and expansion, which will cause capital appreciation. A blue chip is a large high-quality company with a solid history of growth, profit, and consistent dividend payments. Its dividends are less than those of income stocks and its growth slower than that of a growth stock.

Cyclicals are companies whose earnings are very sensitive to the movement of the business cycle. If the interest rates rise and the economy slows, a cyclical industry will slow dramatically. Housing is a good example of a cyclical industry.

Researching a Stock

What should you invest in? Once again, this depends on your situation. If you are young and can take some risks, you will probably lean heavily toward growth stocks. If you are retired, you will probably want the consistent dividends that come from the safer income stocks. After you decide on the type of stocks you want, you will need to choose some individual stocks within your chosen category. Keep in mind that choosing stocks is not an exact science. However, a little research can improve your odds of making money.

The three best places to find information about a particular stock are: the annual report of the company, which is available free from the company; the Standard and Poor's report on individual stocks; and the Value Line Investment Survey, which should be available from your broker or the library. Ask your broker to help you with some research. Once you understand some basic concepts, you will find this to be pretty simple stuff.

You can also get a lot of stock information from the commercial online services such as CompuServe, Prodigy, and America Online. CompuServe's FundWatch and Investment Analysis features and Prodigy's Strategic Investor give you in-depth information on companies and funds. America Online also provides valuable information, as well as a convenient portfolio management service that helps you keep track of the value of your stocks, bonds, and mutual funds.

Quicken Tip: Each of the major online services allows you to download data that can be imported into Quicken. Also, as we explain in Chapter 14, you can use Quicken's Quote feature to obtain information about your securities.

When you research a stock, look beyond the individual stock and also research the industry. Question how the company you're interested in compares with other companies in the industry. Does the industry have a future? Look at the financial statements of the company for the last five years. Has the company had a steady growth in sales? Have the earnings per share been growing consistently? If it is paying a dividend, has the dividend been growing or at least remaining steady? Is the Price/Earnings ratio (the price of the stock divided by the earnings) in the 10 to 15 range for a regular stock and up to the 20 to 25 range for a growth stock? How does the book value of the stock (assets minus liabilities, divided by the number of shares) compare to the price of the stock? Finally, be sure that the company is not carrying too much debt compared to the industry average. Again, you can find much of this information online.

Buying a Stock

Once you have picked your stocks, you need to go through a broker to buy them. Your broker will tell you what the current price is for a stock. You can either buy at the market price, or choose a lower price and hope that the price of the stock dips down temporarily so that you can buy it at the price you've chosen. Of course, you expect it to rise again.

The purchase price of a stock is called the "ask" or "offer." The selling price of a stock that you own is called the "bid." The difference between these two is called the "spread." The spread can be as low as an eighth of a point (12.5 cents) or as large as a full point. Obviously, the ask price will be higher than the bid. Ignoring the commission that you pay the broker, if you bought a stock at the ask price of $25 and sold it immediately at the bid price of $24.50. you would lose $.50 per share, even though the stock did not change price.

A good way to make some additional profit is to take advantage of the dividend reinvestment programs that over 1,000 corporations provide. Rather than pay you a cash dividend, the company takes your dividend and buys more of its stock with the money. There is usually no commission to pay for this transaction, and some companies give a three to five percent discount on the additional shares.

Once you own some stocks, you need to develop a strategy of when to sell. Buying a stock at the "right" price is much easier than deciding when to sell. If a stock goes up in price, most people begin to get a little greedy, hoping that it will rise even more. Then the market turns down or the company comes out with some disappointing quarterly earnings and the stock price falls, wiping out all of your profits.

Investors have devised some criteria for when to sell a stock, though it is a very subjective decision. If your stock price reaches a certain goal, for example, an increase of 50 percent, then sell it and be happy with your healthy profit. If the Price/Earnings ratio jumps by 30 percent, the stock is probably overvalued and it would be wise to take your profits and run. Another thing to do is to ask yourself, if you had the money in hand necessary to buy the stock at the current price, would you buy the stock. If the answer is "no," then sell your stock and use the money to buy another stock.

If the price of your stock goes down after you bought it, what should you do? You can hold on to the stock and wait for it to recover in price. Depending on what caused the fall in price, it may be a reasonable strategy. If the stock fell because the Wall Street analysts expected a 27 percent growth in earnings and the earnings were up only 19 percent, the stock price might rebound in a few months and holding on may be a smart move.

If the stock price fell because the company announced some serious problems with their marketing or their product, then you may wait years for the stock to recover, if it ever does. In this case, you will probably want to sell the stock, cut your losses, and hope that you do better on the next stock. Investors need to get over being afraid to sell at a loss. Every successful investor has sold stocks at a loss. Marty Zweig, an investment advisor seen on PBS's "Wall Street Week" says, "You can be right on your stocks only 40 percent of the time and still do fine if you cut your losses short."

One approach some investors use is to put a "stop loss" order in when they buy their stock. A stop loss is simply an open-ended sell order at 15 or 20 percent below your purchase price, or the current price if your stock has risen. This way the most you can lose on a stock is the 15 or 20 percent limit on your loss that you set. The only problem with this strategy is that the market may take a quick dip and recover. In that period your stock may have fallen the 15 or 20 percent and be sold at a loss.

If all of this sounds interesting and fun, you may be on the road to becoming a serious stock market junkie. If, on the other hand, this seems a little overwhelming or too time consuming, you can find a broker you trust and simply let him or her advise you. Or you can buy a mutual fund.

Mutual Funds

A stock mutual fund is simply a pool of investors' money that is used to buy a professionally managed, diversified portfolio of stocks. An investor buys shares in a mutual fund and each share represents a small portion of the total portfolio of stocks.

Mutual funds are ideal for the small investor because they provide a diversified portfolio with a very small investment. By law, a mutual fund can not have more than five percent of its assets in any one company nor own more than 10 percent of the outstanding shares of any one company.

Mutual funds are professionally managed. This makes them ideal for the investor who has little time or interest in monitoring the stock market. They will also reinvest your dividends and capital gains if you desire. This is a convenient and painless way to accumulate more wealth.

The main negative of a mutual fund is that there is some risk simply because it is a portfolio of stocks. But the risk relative to owning a number of individual stocks is less because the mutual fund is more diversified and it is carefully managed.

Because mutual funds are diversified, their performance tends to approximate the norm, which is similar to the S&P 500. If you own only a few stocks, you will probably do much better or much worse than the average. Over the long run, stock mutual funds have averaged an annual return of about 12 percent.

There are open- and closed-end mutual funds. An open-end mutual fund has an unlimited number of shares. As more people invest in the fund, the percentage ownership of each share decreases but total value of the fund increases. The price of an open-end fund is the net asset value, which is the value of the portfolio of stocks divided by the number of shares. The concern with open-end funds is that they can become so large that they become more difficult to manage effectively.

SO CARSON'S HOME FROM COLLEGE NOT FIVE MINUTES AND SAYS, "DAD, THE WORLD IS TOTALLY SCREWED," AND I SAY, "SURE, BUT THAT'S OPENED UP SOME GREAT INVESTMENT OPPORTUNITIES."

THAT'S WHEN HE TOOK OFF?

NO, HE DID LAUNDRY FIRST...

©JOHN GRIMES

With a closed-end fund, there is a limit on the amount of shares sold and, therefore, a fixed amount of initial capital to invest. After a closed-end fund is started, its shares are then publicly traded on a secondary market similar to any publicly traded corporation. If the fund is doing well because of a good management team, people will want to buy into the fund and thereby drive the price of the shares above their net asset value.

If you decide to buy a mutual fund, you will find literally hundreds of funds to choose from. There are growth funds; aggressive growth funds; income funds; sector funds that specialize in one area of the economy such as health care; international funds for various countries or regions of the world; and socially responsible funds for people interested in ethical investing.

As with other investments, you should first decide how much risk you are willing to take. Some of the international funds, for example, can be very risky. This is because not only is there a concern about the individual stocks in the portfolio, but also the general economic conditions of the foreign economy which, in turn, affects the currency exchange rates.

In late 1994 when the Mexican Peso fell 40 percent against the dollar, the dollar value of Mexican mutual funds fell precipitously, even though the individual Mexican companies might have been doing very well. On the other hand, some international funds have had years of extraordinary growth with people doubling their money in a relatively short period of time. With the risk can come the rewards.

Some people subscribe to a philosophy of socially responsible investing. The definition of socially responsible investing may differ among individuals but the general theme is either to avoid investing in companies that contribute negatively to the world or to seek out corporations that make a positive contribution.

Socially responsible funds vary but, in general, they avoid stocks in such industries as tobacco, nuclear energy, or defense. They support companies that clean up the environment, produce alternative energy sources, or sell healthy consumer products. Some of the socially responsible mutual funds have done quite well, demonstrating that you can "do good" at the same time that you do well. For information on socially responsible investing, call the Social Investment Forum at 617-451-3369.

Before investing in *any* mutual fund, it is wise to call or write for the fund's prospectus and its latest financial report. You can usually find the address or phone number of the funds in the business sections of any major newspaper. In such material you will learn about the fund's investment philosophy and financial objectives and its history of earnings for the past five or even ten years.

You should also find out what commissions or fees the fund charges. Many mutual funds charge what is called a "load." A load is an up-front sales commission deducted from the initial investment. The load can be as high as 8.5 percent, and it usually goes to the broker or financial planner who sells the fund. All mutual funds charge an administrative fee, which should be approximately one percent annually.

In contrast, no-load funds are bought directly from the mutual fund company and no commission is charged. Are load funds better performers? The data show that no-load funds have performed as well as load funds and saved investors a lot of money. Also, beware of other expenses such as back-end loads, which charge a percentage fee when the shares are sold. These back-end loads often decrease each year that one stays in the fund until they ultimately phase out completely.

Some people buy several mutual funds as a means of diversifying. They may put some of their money in an aggressive growth fund, some in a sector fund, some in an international fund, and some in a more conservative income fund.

It is a good idea to buy into a family of funds, a company that manages a variety of mutual funds. Be sure to find one that allows you to transfer your money from one fund to another with a simple phone call and no service charge.

Dollar Cost Averaging

Assume that you invest $200 each month in your favorite mutual fund. The price of the mutual fund goes up and down but you invest the same amount each month. You don't hesitate when you think the market is too high, and you don't panic when you think the market is collapsing. You simply stay the course.

Assume that your favorite mutual fund's shares are selling for $10 per share. Also, to make the point, let's assume the most volatile market in U.S. history. In month two, the market climbs and the value of a share of your mutual fund rises to $15, only to have the market collapse over the next month, and a share of your fund plummets to $5. Then, in month four, it settles back to $10 a share.

At the end of four months, you invested $800 and the average price of the stock was $10.

Month	Investment	Market Price	# Shares Purchased
1	$200	$10	20
2	$200	$15	13.3
3	$200	$5	40
4	$200	$10	20
Total:	$800		
	Average Price:	$10	
		Total Shares:	93.3
Average Cost: $8.57/share			

Dollar Cost Averaging

But, rather than owning 80 shares, you own 93.3 shares, which you purchased at an average price of $8.57 per share. This approach eliminates "when should I buy?" anxiety.

Mutual funds are a good instrument for the small investor who is trying to set aside a fixed amount each month to invest in the stock market. This approach of investing a fixed dollar amount each month, regardless of the price, is called "dollar-cost averaging." Since a fixed dollar amount is invested each month, fewer shares of the mutual fund are bought when the market is up and a greater number of shares are bought when the market is down. As a result of this logic, the average price paid is lower than the average market price.

Quicken Tip: Quicken allows you to track mutual funds along with other types of securities. As with stocks, you can keep track of your total number of shares, the price of the fund, as well as the total value of your holdings. Quicken allows you to maintain a history of prices, which can be printed out or displayed in graph form.

Real Estate

Real estate has been a traditional means for average working people who are willing to manage and repair their property to attain financial independence. It is also the source of some of the world's greatest fortunes. Real estate, like other attractive investments, carries some risk. The risk increases, but so do the rewards, when moving from owning small residential properties in one's own community to owning office buildings and commercial centers.

Real estate produces a steady and growing stream of income if it is rented. Also, it appreciates in value, at least in the long run. Real estate in a desirable neighborhood is a limited commodity, which gives it value. It is also a tangible asset that appreciates with inflation. A building that seemed like an outrageously priced property with unreasonably high rents ten years ago may be selling for 50 percent more today.

The risks associated with real estate are that the units may not rent, or that market conditions may change and the value of the property may decline along with rental rates. Also, your interest rate could rise dramatically with an adjustable mortgage, or the property might suddenly require some very major repairs. With any of these problems, you will often do fine in the long run—if you have the money to feed the property in the meantime. But since real estate is not a liquid asset, serious problems might arise if you need to cash out quickly.

The safest type of real estate investment, beside owning the house that you live in, is to buy single-family homes or duplexes in your community. If you are planning to move within your community, you may simply keep your current house and rent it. You certainly know the condition of the property, the character of the community, and you already have financing for the property. This strategy saves you time and money, and gives you an opportunity to learn what it is like to manage property.

If you are not planning to move soon, you might simply buy a one- to four-unit residential building in your community. Keep in mind that if you live in the building, it is easier to get financing on more favorable terms. Providing that you buy wisely and manage your own property, your risk should be relatively low, unless you live in a declining community or one that just experienced very rapid appreciation.

When buying real estate as an investment, several things are important to consider. Location is on the top of the list, followed by the condition of the property, the current rents, and the selling price. Can the current rents produce a positive or near-positive cash flow after the principal, interest, taxes, insurance, repairs, and maintenance have been subtracted? As rents increase over the years, your cash flow will improve.

How does a real estate investment compare to competing investments? What is the rate of return on your real estate investment today and in the future? The rate of return is your cash flow plus your principal payment, divided by your down payment and various closing costs. To be fair to real estate investments, you need to make some projections about what the rent and the expenses will be over the next number of years and what the rate of appreciation on the property will be. The attractiveness of a real estate investment improves over time. Also, when you eventually pay off the mortgage, your cash flow jumps dramatically. As a result, real estate can be an excellent investment for retirement.

Managing real estate is a time-consuming activity but so is studying the stock market. When you compare investments, factor in the value of your time and energy.

Office buildings and commercial space can be very profitable if purchased carefully and kept fully occupied. They can also be very risky. Unlike residential property, which can usually be rented by lowering the rent 10 percent, office and commercial space can remain empty for years, even if the rent has been lowered.

The small inexperienced real estate investor can get involved with owning office buildings, shopping centers, and industrial property through limited partnerships and real estate investment trusts (REIT). Both limited partnerships and REITs pool the funds of investors and buy large real estate projects. They have certain advantages, such as enabling the small investor to be involved with major real estate projects with a lower risk, but they usually have a lower return than the real estate you manage yourself. The limited partnership is not particularly liquid while the shares of a REIT can be sold quite easily.

Quicken Tip: To track real estate with Quicken, click on the New button from within the Account List and set up an Asset account. You can track the cost and amortization of any mortgage payments by selecting Loans from the Activities Menu.

Credit—The Cost of Borrowing Money

25

Borrowing money is not something you should do lightly. There are times when borrowing money is a wise and necessary thing to do. Purchasing a home, buying an investment property, or paying for your education can be excellent reasons to borrow money. These expenditures can be considered investments. Other borrowing may get you into financial trouble. For example, it's not a good idea to run up your credit card balances to buy new furniture when your current income barely covers your expenses.

Before you borrow money, ask yourself if you really need to buy the item and if you will be able to pay back the money. It makes sense to borrow for big items, like a house or car, if you have enough income to cover the debt payments. If you can't comfortably cover the debt service (the principal and interest) with your current income, don't borrow the money. You don't want to end up in a situation where your purchases are being repossessed, your house foreclosed, or you end up in bankruptcy. Neither do you want to have creditors calling you nor your credit rating ruined.

One rule of thumb is that you should not have more than about 15 to 20 percent of your take-home income going to pay for consumer loans. This does not include your mortgage payments. If there is only one wage earner in the household and there are dependents, the percentage should be less.

Assuming that you can afford to buy those new kitchen appliances, you'll need to decide whether to use your savings for the purchase or to get an installment loan. Assuming that you have enough savings to pay for the appliances and still have enough money for emergencies, you should then compare interest rates. If the interest on the loan is greater than the interest you are receiving on your savings, you would be wise to pay cash. You would also save yourself all the paperwork and any loan origination costs that may come with the loan.

If you do borrow money, try to keep the terms of the loan short. This will minimize the amount of interest you pay, however it will result in higher monthly payments. If you're nervous that the monthly payments may be too high, you can always go for a longer-term loan, but be sure that there's no pre-payment penalty if you pay off the loan early. That way, your monthly payment will be manageable, and if things are working out well for you, you can accelerate your payments.

Don't forget to compare interest rates when you are paying off your loans. Pay off your high-interest loans first. Credit card interest rates, for example, could easily be more than 20 percent and so, should always be paid first.

Types of Loans

Loans come in many variations and forms. There are secured and unsecured loans, installment loans, and lines of credit. There also are a variety of home loans, such as fixed or adjustable rate mortgages. And, of course, there are hundreds of credit cards from which to choose.

A secured loan is backed or collateralized by some asset of value. If a person gets a loan on a car or a house, the car or house is used to secure the loan. The lender determines the value of the house or car and lends a percentage of the value. If the borrower fails to make the payments, the lender will seize the property and resell it, hoping to recover the balance of the loan.

An unsecured loan has no collateral. The borrower is pledging his or her "full faith and credit" as a guarantee to repay the loan. The lender must evaluate the borrower as a credit risk. To evaluate the borrower, the financial institution will examine such factors as the borrower's past relationship with the institution, the amount of money now owed relative to income, employment history, and the reason for the loan. Since there is no collateral for this loan, the interest rate will be higher than for a secured loan. The only backing the lender has is the signature of the borrower, which is the reason these loans are often called signature loans.

An installment loan is the most common type of loan. Money is borrowed and paid back through monthly installments of principal and interest. The loan may be secured or unsecured. An example of a secured installment loan is a four-year auto loan paid off with 48 equal monthly installments.

Quicken Tip: *With an installment loan, which includes most home mortgages, you pay in equal monthly payments but the amount of money that goes to interest and principal changes over time. At first, you're paying mostly interest but as the loan matures, the mix changes. Quicken's Loan Planner (which you get by selecting Financial Planners from the Plan Menu) allows you to enter the amount of the loan and other information and will tell you the monthly payments. If you press the "Schedule" button, it will display an amortization schedule showing how much of each payment is principal and interest, as well as the remaining balance.*

A *line of credit* is obtained when a lender approves a specific loan amount and sets it aside. The borrower can then draw down the line of credit when the money is needed. Interest is paid only on the amount borrowed and only for the time the money is used. A line of credit can be borrowed and repaid as often as it is needed, as long as the borrower stays under the approved limit. Secured lines of credit usually carry a higher loan limit and a lower interest rate than unsecured lines.

Mortgages

Years ago, home loans just came with the standard 30-year, fixed-rate mortgage. Now there is also a range of adjustable rate mortgages. Since a home loan is a major commitment, shop around for suitable terms. A fixed-rate mortgage provides certainty and is very desirable when interest rates are low and can be locked in for 15 or 30 years. A 15-year mortgage will have a quarter or half percentage point lower interest rate than a 30-year mortgage.

Although adjustable rate mortgages (ARMs) carry some uncertainty, they are easier to obtain. ARMs usually start with a lower interest rate than a fixed rate mortgage, but they can be adjusted upward each year. When shopping for an ARM, consider several factors: the initial interest rate; how often the rate can change; how much the rate can change each period; what index, if any, the interest rate is tied to; and what the ceiling is, if any, on the interest rate. Also, with either the fixed or adjustable-rate mortgages, any loan-origination fees or prepayment penalties should be considered. As you shop around for an adjustable loan, ask about the pros and cons of the various "indexes" available in your area.

Credit Cards

Credit cards are very convenient, and, for people who travel, they are almost a necessity. As a source of credit, on the other hand, they are about the most expensive loans available. Not all MasterCards or Visas are the same. Each financial institution that issues credit cards has its own annual fees, interest rates, credit limits, and restrictions imposed by the laws in the state where it is based. There is absolutely no disadvantage in using a Visa or MasterCard from a state 2,000 miles away, so shop around for the card that is best for you.

If you use a credit card with no annual fee, pay off the entire balance each month. If you make your large purchases at the beginning of the billing cycle, you can get about 50 days of free credit. If, on the other hand, you consistently run up high balances with your credit cards and don't pay off the balances promptly, you are paying for a high-interest loan. If this is your style, at least find a card with a relatively low interest rate. Bankcard Holders of America (703-389-5445) is a nonprofit public interest group that will send you its "Fair Deal" list of low-interest or no-fee bank cards for $4.

Some credit card companies charge you interest from the day you make each purchase, if you have any outstanding balance that month. Many people are unaware of this "hidden" interest charge. Of course, it's not really hidden since credit card companies have to disclose their terms. Trouble is, a lot of people don't read the fine print. Read it.

Some credit cards offer frequent flyer miles (usually one mile per dollar spent) for using the card. This does lead to free travel but be sure to consider the annual fee, the percentage rate, and other factors. You can also get a credit card that makes a small contribution per dollar charged to a charity, environmental group, alumni association, or other non-profit group of your choice. Unfortunately, the credit card company, not you, gets the tax deduction

Avoid using the cash advance feature available with most credit cards. The annual interest rate on these loans is about 20 percent, and often there is an additional loan fee of about two percent. Another gimmick to avoid is the premium card. Most credit card companies offer premium cards or gold cards. In some cases, these have a higher annual fee. They offer some additional benefits, which may or may not be of any use to you. One advantage of most Visa and MasterCard Gold cards is that they cover collision insurance on rental cars. Some also extend the warranty or provide theft or loss insurance on products bought with the card. The exclusions on such coverage varies from card to card.

Like other things in life, credit card fees are often negotiable. If you get a bill for a $40 or $50 annual fee, call the company, tell them that some competitors offer a card without fees, ask if they'll waive the fee to keep your business. They often will.

Quicken Tip: Quicken offers its own credit card. The big advantage here is that statements can be delivered via modem or on a floppy disk and are recorded automatically in your Quicken credit card register. If you're not that good about entering data and need to keep a record of your expenses (for tax or other purposes), this is a great way to capture that information. The Quicken card doesn't offer all the amenities (like frequent flyer miles) of some credit cards, so it might not be for you.

Another type of plastic card is the debit card. The debit card looks like a credit card, but it draws money directly out of your checking account the minute you use it. There is no credit provided. With a debit card, you need to keep close track of your expenditures so you don't overdraw your account.

Getting a Loan

Before going to a bank, savings & loan, or credit union for a loan, consider that you may own some assets that could provide you with a convenient loan at an interest rate lower than most banks. If you have any stocks or bonds, you can put them in what is called a "margin account" at any brokerage house and borrow against them. You can borrow up to 50 percent on the market value of the stocks and 80 percent of the market value of the bonds. The interest rate is a little above the rate the banks charge the brokerage houses. The interest rate on the margin loan changes whenever the banks change their prime interest rates.

A margin account is not only easy to attain and offers a lower-than-average interest rate, but the interest paid on a margin account is tax-deductible to the extent that it offsets any investment income for the year. This includes interest, dividends, and capital gains. There is, however, a serious downside. If your stocks and bonds fall significantly in value so they do not adequately collateralize your loan, you will get a "margin call." With a margin call, you must either pay down some of your loan or increase the collateral. This means that you must bring in more stocks and bonds. One way to provide some protection from a margin call is to borrow less than the limit of your margin loan.

Another source of lower-interest credit is to borrow against your life insurance policy. You can borrow up to the cash value of your policy. For policies written before 1980, the rate of interest is six percent or less. For policies written after 1980, it is somewhat higher. Before you borrow against your life insurance policy, check with your insurance broker to see what effect, if any, a loan has on the terms of the policy.

If neither of these avenues is open to you for credit, you'll have to go to a bank, savings and loan, or credit union. Getting a loan from a financial institution may not be as difficult as you might think. The financial institution is being asked to risk its depositors' money when considering making a loan. Your job is to convince the loan officer that the risk to them is relatively low. Banks love to lend money to people who really don't need it.

The Three C's of Credit

In determining risk, lenders rely on the three C's of credit: *character*, *capacity*, and *capital*:

Character is your personal qualities that give the lender some indication as to whether you will repay the loan. Some of the things considered in character are documented evidence, such as your history of paying off other loans (student loans, charge card balances, etc.) your employment history, whether you bounced any checks recently, or whether you ever filed for bankruptcy.

Capacity is your financial ability to repay the loan. Are you earning enough money each month to comfortably cover the payments? This includes analyzing your current employment situation and your future job prospects.

Capital is the amount of assets that you have, such as a car, a house, jewelry, or antiques that you can use to collateralize the loan.

Lenders also rely on a credit report prepared by one of the four or five national private, for-profit companies called credit bureaus. These credit bureaus collect credit information from various businesses and computerize this information as credit files on individuals and then sell this information to businesses. If you ever had a loan of any form, including a charge card from your local department store or an installment loan on a television set, you are on file with the credit bureaus. They have files on an estimated 170 million Americans.

The credit report that they sell to businesses provides a history of your credit. This history includes what you owe, to whom you owe it, and whether you repay your debts in a timely manner. Credit bureaus do not determine your credit-worthiness or approve or deny loans. They merely pass on the information that was provided to them.

Credit bureaus can receive inaccurate information from their sources or they can err in their processing of accurate information, causing you to appear as a bad credit risk. This misinformation in your credit report can prevent you from getting a loan. Because these private credit bureaus can inadvertently destroy a person's credit, the federal government had to step in to protect the rights of the average citizen trying to get a loan.

Before passage of the Fair Credit Reporting Act in 1970, people had no legal rights to see their credit reports, let alone try to correct any errors. Now you are entitled to learn the name and address of any credit bureau whose report caused you to be denied a loan. You have a right to obtain a copy of your credit report free of charge if you have recently been turned down for credit. A fee of $10 or $20 is charged if you just want to review your credit report; however, TRW, a major credit reporting company, will provide you with a free annual credit report by calling 800-422-4879. You also have a right to get a list of all the people who have requested your credit report in the last six months.

USED TO BE HOT IN THE CURRENCY BIZ. AND YOU?

If you find inaccurate information in your credit report, you have the right to demand that the disputed information be investigated and removed from your file if it cannot be verified or if it is found to be inaccurate. If the credit bureau made a mistake, they must correct the error and then, at their own cost, provide the corrected information to all the people who received the misinformation. If they conclude that the disputed information is accurate, you have the right to include your explanation in the file. Finally, except for a few minor exceptions, all information, including detrimental information, must be removed from your file after seven years. Bankruptcy information can remain in your file for 10 years.

Index

municipal, 356–358
risk and, 354, 355
tax-exempt, 356–358
See also investments; mutual funds;
    securities; stocks
Budget report, 173
categories, 179
See also reports
budgets, 5, 292–299
Budget, 293
categories, 294, 295
creation methods, 293
data display, 295
dates, 294
default, 293
editing, 295–296
entering, 295–296
reports, 198–199
    creating, 298
    monthly, 299
saving, 296
setting up, 293–295
supercategories and, 84–85, 294–295
transfers and, 295
variance graph, 299
See also planning
Budget Variance graphs, 189
creating, 189
defined, 189
illustrated, 189
See also graphs
Business and Finance window (Prodigy),
    245–246
business categories, 307
business income, 312–313
Business Reports, 172
Buy Shares window, 219

C
Calculator dialog box, 57, 94
Calculators
Refinance, 302–303
Savings, 302, 342
Calendar dialog box, 51, 59
Calendar Options window, 150–151
Accounts tab, 150
QuickFill tab, 150–151
See also Financial Calendar
Canada, 15, 18, 21, 23
capital gains
deferring, 337
defined, 361

Capital Gains report, 171
creating, 316
defined, 316
exporting, 317
illustrated, 317
for Tax Planner, 319
tax schedules and, 307
See also capital gains; reports
cash
spending evaluation, 205
tracking, 6, 204–208
transactions, 121–122
who should track, 205–206
Cash accounts, 40
additional information about, 207
colors, 208
creating, 121–122
description for, 206
investment, 211–212, 218–219
    cash reserve, 218
    depositing in, 219
    purpose of, 218
    transferring in, 219
name of, 206
register, 121, 207–208
setting up, 206–207
starting point, 206
uses for, 121
See also accounts; cash
Cash Flow report, 170, 172
categories, 28
account names as, 77
adding new, 307–309
budget, 294, 295
business, 307
colon (:) and, 78, 87
credit card, 199
defined, 75
deleting, 80–81
deleting line, 56
demoting, 80
description of, 80
editing, 79–80
entering
    on checks, 94
    in register, 54
grouping, 84
home, 305–306
inserting lines, 56
merging, 81
name of, 80
Quicken, 76